Tools for Researching Vocabulary

SECOND LANGUAGE ACQUISITION

Series Editors: **Professor David Singleton**, *University of Pannonia, Hungary* and Fellow Emeritus, *Trinity College, Dublin, Ireland* and **Dr Simone E. Pfenninger**, *University of Salzburg, Austria*

This series brings together titles dealing with a variety of aspects of language acquisition and processing in situations where a language or languages other than the native language is involved. Second language is thus interpreted in its broadest possible sense. The volumes included in the series all offer in their different ways, on the one hand, exposition and discussion of empirical findings and, on the other, some degree of theoretical reflection. In this latter connection, no particular theoretical stance is privileged in the series; nor is any relevant perspective – sociolinguistic, psycholinguistic, neurolinguistic, etc. – deemed out of place. The intended readership of the series includes final-year undergraduates working on second language acquisition projects, postgraduate students involved in second language acquisition research, and researchers, teachers and policy makers in general whose interests include a second language acquisition component.

Full details of all the books in this series and of all our other publications can be found on http://www.multilingual-matters.com, or by writing to Multilingual Matters, St Nicholas House, 31–34 High Street, Bristol BS1 2AW, UK.

SECOND LANGUAGE ACQUISITION: 105

Tools for Researching Vocabulary

Paul Meara and Imma Miralpeix

MULTILINGUAL MATTERS
Bristol • Buffalo • Toronto

Library of Congress Cataloging in Publication Data
Names: Meara, P.M. (Paul M.) author. | Miralpeix, Imma, author.
Title: Tools for Researching Vocabulary/Paul Meara and Imma Miralpeix.
Description: Bristol; Buffalo: Multilingual Matters, [2016] | Series: Second Language Acquisition: 105 | Includes bibliographical references and index.
Identifiers: LCCN 2016022809 | ISBN 9781783096466 (hbk : alk. paper) | ISBN 9781783096459 (pbk : alk. paper) | ISBN 9781783096497 (kindle)
Subjects: LCSH: Language and languages—Ability testing. | Vocabulary—Ability testing. | Vocabulary—Databases. | Vocabulary—Research. | Second language acquisition—Research. | Education, Bilingual—Research.
Classification: LCC P53.9.M328 2014 | DDC 401/.4—dc23 LC record available at https://lccn.loc.gov/2016022809

British Library Cataloguing in Publication Data
A catalogue entry for this book is available from the British Library.

ISBN-13: 978-1-78309-646-6 (hbk)
ISBN-13: 978-1-78309-645-9 (pbk)

Multilingual Matters
UK: St Nicholas House, 31–34 High Street, Bristol BS1 2AW, UK.
USA: UTP, 2250 Military Road, Tonawanda, NY 14150, USA.
Canada: UTP, 5201 Dufferin Street, North York, Ontario M3H 5T8, Canada.

Website: www.multilingual-matters.com
Twitter: Multi_Ling_Mat
Facebook: https://www.facebook.com/multilingualmatters
Blog: www.channelviewpublications.wordpress.com

Copyright © 2017 Paul Meara and Imma Miralpeix.

All rights reserved. No part of this work may be reproduced in any form or by any means without permission in writing from the publisher.

The policy of Multilingual Matters/Channel View Publications is to use papers that are natural, renewable and recyclable products, made from wood grown in sustainable forests. In the manufacturing process of our books, and to further support our policy, preference is given to printers that have FSC and PEFC Chain of Custody certification. The FSC and/or PEFC logos will appear on those books where full certification has been granted to the printer concerned.

Typeset by Nova Techset Private Limited, Bengaluru and Chennai, India.

Contents

Acknowledgements		vii
Introduction		ix

Part 1: Processing Vocabulary Data

1 V_Words v2.0 and V_Lists v1.0   3

Part 2: Measuring Lexical Variation, Sophistication and Originality

2 D_Tools v2.0   21

3 P_Lex v3.00   44

4 Lexical Signatures   66

5 V_Unique v1.0   84

Part 3: Estimating Vocabulary Size

6 V_YesNo v1.0   113

7 V_Size v2.01   134

8 V_Capture v1.0   156

Part 4: Measuring Lexical Access

9 Q_Lex v4.0   185

Part 5: Assessing Aptitude for L2 Vocabulary Learning

10 LLAMA_B v2.0   215
    A brief evaluation of the LLAMA_B Test   218
    Original contribution from Vivienne Rogers

Part 6: Modelling Vocabulary Growth

11	Mezzofanti v1.0	233
	Envoi	255
	Author Index	260
	Subject Index	263

Acknowledgements

The articles in Chapters 1, 3, 4 and 8 first appeared in the following journals: Chapter 1: *The Modern Language Journal* 10 (7), 427–430; Chapter 3: *Prospect* 16 (3), 5–24; Chapter 4: *ITL Review of Applied Linguistics* 135–136, 85–96; and Chapter 8: *Reading in a Foreign Language* 22 (1), 222–236.

The book chapters in Chapters 2, 6, 9 and 11 first appeared in the following books: Chapter 2: C. Muñoz (ed.) (2006) *Age and the Rate of Foreign Language Learning* (pp. 89–106). Clevedon: Multilingual Matters; Chapter 6: P. Grunwell (ed.) (1988) *Applied Linguistics in Society* (pp. 80–87). London: CILT; Chapter 9: V.J. Cook (ed.) (1986) *Experimental Approaches to Second Language Learning* (pp. 101–110). Oxford: Pergamon Press; Chapter 11: M. Gill, A. Johnson, L. Koski, R. Sell and B. Wårvik (eds) (2001) *Language, Learning, Literature: Studies Presented to Håkan Ringbom* (pp. 151–167). Åbo: Åbo Akademi.

Introduction

This book is aimed at beginning researchers who want to work in the area of L2 vocabulary acquisition. A number of introductory books of this kind have appeared over the last few years, notably Schmitt (2010) and Nation and Webb (2011), but this book is very different from these volumes. It is not an introductory textbook, and it does not summarise large amounts of vocabulary research. Instead, it presents you with a set of computer programs that will allow you to do interesting research of your own.

In our experience, beginning research students are often left to their own devices when it comes to designing their projects. Some universities provide compulsory research training courses, but these courses are often not very relevant to the kind of work students in applied linguistics may want to do. Sometimes they provide a general introduction to research approaches (quantitative versus qualitative research, survey methods, ethical issues, and so on) and they very often contain large quantities of inedible statistics. What they do not do is to provide you with practical tools that you can use immediately. As a result, a lot of students end up trying to develop meaningful research ideas, *and* the tools they need to test these ideas at the same time. This is generally not a realistic plan for a research project.

This book is intended to provide readers with a set of research tools that can be used more or less out of the box. The tools consist of a set of computer programs that we have developed for students doing final-year undergraduate projects, or Masters' level research projects. Tools of this sort – which are typically *not* provided as part of a research training course – are useful because they allow you to sidestep the difficult problems of designing your own research tools, and let you concentrate instead on the deeper questions that the tools are designed to address.

All the programs in this book are written to run on the internet, and not on stand-alone computers. This means that you will need to have access to the internet to make the programs work. The programs are written in HTML code, but most of the difficult programming is written in PERL and jQuery. HTML is quite limited in what it can display on screen, and it lacks the sophisticated graphics of other programs. Readers who are familiar with our earlier Windows programs might find that the programs in this book are simpler and less 'fancy' to look at. This was a deliberate choice. We wanted to write programs that would work on as many platforms as possible and, more importantly, would not need to be updated every year as computer manufacturers 'upgraded' their operating systems. The programs in this book should run on all the main operating systems (Windows, Linux, MacOS). Readers should be aware, though, that the programs will not always work on tablets, and that the programs work best with the Chrome web browser. Other browsers will usually work, but there are some issues with Internet Explorer that we have not succeeded in resolving.

The book is divided into six main parts and each part contains one or more chapters. The first part presents two programs (**V_Words** and **V_Lists**) which will help you to carry out basic operations with raw data, such as turning texts into different word lists, providing counts of types and tokens and comparing word lists. The second part comprises four chapters that put forward several tools to measure lexical richness in short texts: in Chapter 2, **D_Tools** helps to calculate lexical variation with D, a statistic developed by Malvern et al. (2004) which offers advantages over other variation measures. **P_Lex** in Chapter 3 measures lexical sophistication. **V_LexSig** and **SigSorter** (Chapter 4) and **V_Unique** (Chapter 5) deal with lexical originality. Part 3 contains three programs to quantify vocabulary size: Chapter 6 presents **V_Yes/No**, a test that gives an indication of the number of words known receptively in English by test takers. Programs in Chapters 7 and 8 (**V_Size** and **V_Capture**) aim at providing estimates of productive vocabulary size through different approaches. The last three parts each consist of a single program. Part 4 is devoted to **Q_Lex** (Chapter 9), a tool to measure lexical access. Part 5 (Chapter 10) is concerned with assessing aptitude for learning L2 vocabulary – an important individual difference in foreign language learning. The assessment is carried out by **LLAMA_B**. Finally, the last chapter shows an example of vocabulary modelling research methods. It provides a simple introduction to simulation research, using **Mezzofanti** to model the growth of vocabularies in different environments.

Each of the 11 chapters in this book starts with a general *introduction* which explains the background to the program, how it works and what it does. Next, the chapter presents a set of *instructions* on how to use the program. After this, we have included a *real research study* which addresses the type of questions the programs are designed for, and a set of *reflections* on the work reported. The reflections are personal comments on the work in the background reading paper. Sometimes the paper will be one that uses the actual program discussed in the chapter. In other cases, we have provided an older paper which does not use the program because at the time the paper was published computers had not been invented and most work of this sort was carried out using pencils and paper. It is instructive (and slightly sobering) to discover that people were once awarded PhDs and professorships for carrying out work that you could now do in a few hours thanks to programs like the ones we have developed here. Finally, each chapter contains a section called *'More Research is Needed ...'*. This section consists of several questions which you might be able to explore using the program in the chapter, and a list of thought-provoking papers which illustrate the technique discussed in the chapter, or which are closely related to the topic under discussion.

The book is loosely organised around the three-dimensional approach to vocabulary knowledge that is outlined in Meara (1996): vocabulary size, organisation and accessibility. The programs in Parts 3 and 4 deal with size and accessibility. Readers interested in the organisation and structure of L2 lexicons will find some interesting ideas and some more programs to use in Meara (2009).

The selection of programs in this book focuses on the four necessary and often challenging jobs that any (vocabulary) researcher needs to be aware of when developing a new project: processing, collecting, analysing and generating data. The programs provide some technical support that should make these jobs less onerous. However, the main purpose of this book is to encourage readers to think creatively and critically about L2 vocabulary research. We also hope that the examples provided in this book will convince readers that it is worthwhile investing some time in learning to write computer programs of their own. None of the programs in this book is very complicated – most of them are less than a hundred lines of code – and yet they open up a world of research which is rich and exciting. If you enjoy working with these programs, please tell your friends. If you already write your own programs, and want to share them with other people via the Lognostics website, get in touch with us.

Paul Meara
Imma Miralpeix 2016

References

Malvern, D., Richards, B., Chipere, N. and Durán, P. (2004) *Lexical Diversity and Language Development: Quantification and Assessment.* Basingstoke: Palgrave Macmillan.

Meara, P.M. (1996) The dimensions of lexical competence. In G. Brown, K. Malmkjaer and J. Williams (eds) *Performance and Competence in Second Language Acquisition* (pp. 35–53). Cambridge: Cambridge University Press.

Meara, P.M. (2009) *Connected Words: Word Associations and Second Language Vocabulary Acquisition.* Amsterdam: John Benjamins.

Nation, I.S.P. and Webb, S. (2011) *Researching and Analysing Vocabulary.* Boston, MA: Heinle Cengage Learning.

Schmitt, N. (2010) *Researching Vocabulary: A Vocabulary Research Manual.* Basingstoke: Palgrave Macmillan.

Part 1
Processing Vocabulary Data

1   V_Words v2.0 and V_Lists v1.0

Introduction

This chapter describes two simple programs that are useful for carrying out basic operations on vocabulary data. The programs are not especially innovative: to some extent they duplicate the programs that already exist, some of which are briefly described at the end of the chapter. However, using our programs (V_Words and V_Lists) will help you to become familiar with the conventions used in the other programs in this book.

Part 1. V_Words v2.0

V_Words is a small utility program that turns short texts into word lists. It produces a basic count of all types and tokens in the text, in addition to alphabetical and frequency lists of the word types that the text contains.

Using V_Words

You will find the V_Words program on the Lognostics Tools website, available at: http://www.lognostics.co.uk/tools/V_Words/V_Words.htm.

(1) The V_Words workspace will open for you.
(2) V_Words may require some data preparation so that the text can accurately be turned into lists. There are also some features that you should be aware of before you use the program:
  - V_Words is a small program, and it is not designed to be used with very large texts. Your text should be in simple text format and it should not be longer than 8500 words. If your text is longer than this, then you should split it into smaller sections.
  - V_Words takes as a word (token) any written unit with a space on either side. Contractions (e.g. *he's, you'd*) will be treated as one word unless you replace them by the full forms (*he is, you would* …).

- We recommend that you add hyphens whenever you want to take different contiguous tokens as just one word (e.g. open compounds: *school-bus*, phrasal verbs: *get-off* ...).
- The program is NOT case sensitive and therefore uppercase or lowercase letters will not interfere with the counts.

(3) Load the text that you want to work with into the V_Words workspace. You can do this by typing your text directly, or by copying and pasting a pre-prepared text into the workspace. The V_Words workspace looks like Figure 1.1.
(4) Edit your text as necessary.
(5) V_Words will ignore any punctuation in your text. If you want V_Words to ignore any other symbols, then you can add them to the punctuation list underneath the workspace.
(6) Click the **Submit** button when your text is ready for analysis.
(7) V_Words generates a report that looks like Figure 1.2. The report contains three columns:
    - Column 1 on the left is a simple list of all the words (tokens) in the text. They are presented in the same order as they appear in the text.
    - Column 2 is an alphabetically organised type count for the text.
    - Column 3 is a frequency ordered type count for the text.
(8) You can save the reports by copying and pasting the relevant columns to a new document.
(9) Click the **Reset** button to start over with another text.

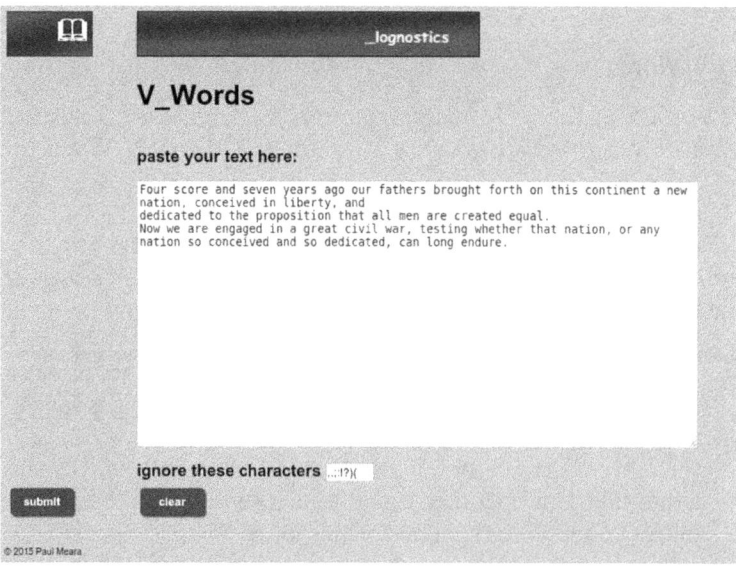

Figure 1.1 V_Words workspace

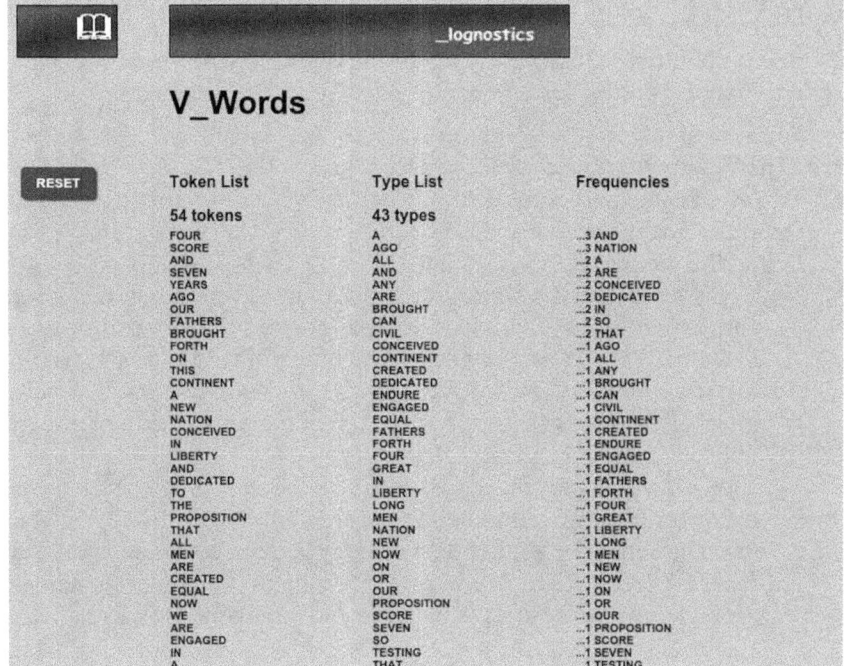

Figure 1.2 V_Words report page

Even if your research does not involve collecting large word sets, you will find that it is worthwhile experimenting with the V_Words program before you go any further, as many of the features in this program appear in other programs in later chapters. In particular, you need to make sure that you know how to copy and paste a text to be analysed into the V_Words working space, and how to copy and save the results of an analysis back into another document. If you do not know how to do these basic operations, then you need to ask someone to show you before you go any further.

Part 2. V_Lists v1.0

V_Lists allows you to carry out some basic operations on word lists. Specifically, V_Lists takes two word lists as input and reports the words which occur in only one of the lists, the words which occur in both of the lists and a cumulative list that contains words that appear in either of the original lists. This output can be used to perform different types of analyses.

6 Part 1: Processing Vocabulary Data

Using V_Lists

You will find the V_Lists program on the Lognostics Tools website, available at: http://www.lognostics.co.uk/tools/V_Lists/V_Lists.htm

(1) The V_Lists workspace will open for you.
(2) V_Lists may require some data preparation in order to produce accurate reports. There are also some features you should be aware of before using the program:
    – V_Lists requires two word lists as input. The lists should be in simple text format. Each list will consist of a set of words, one word to a line. The easiest way to prepare a list of this sort is to use **V_Words**, the program described in the previous section. The total number of words in the lists to be compared should not exceed 4000.
    – The V_Lists data input page looks like Figure 1.3. It contains two data slots. You can input data to the program directly by typing your word lists into the V_Lists data page, or you can copy and paste data from other sources if your lists are too long to type. Check your lists carefully to make sure that they do not contain inconsistent spellings.

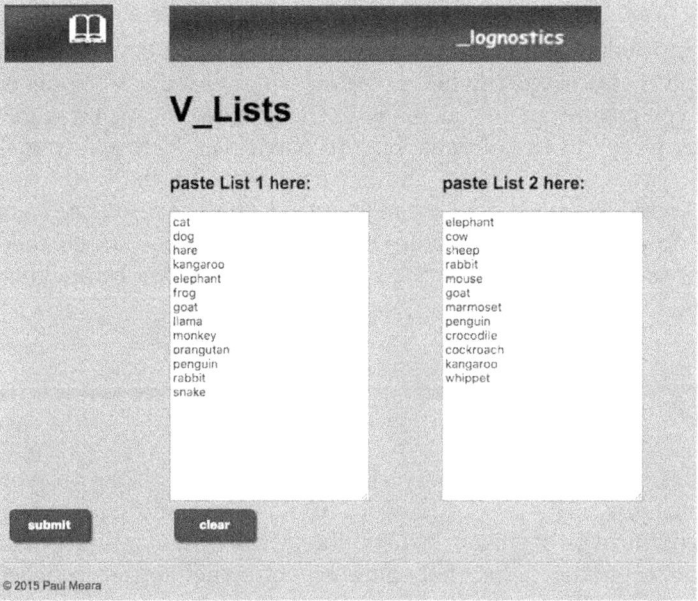

Figure 1.3 V_Lists data input page

- Any punctuation marks may need to be removed from your list items. You will also need to make sure that you have not accidentally left blank spaces at the end of lines. The easiest way to do this is to use the **search and replace** function in the program you used to prepare the lists.
- V_Lists treats as a word any unit/s written on the same line. For this reason, make sure that what you want to count as one word is always written on the same line and that spelling is consistent in both input lists (e.g. *well-being, wellbeing* and *well being* would each be counted as different words). It is also recommended that contractions are replaced by full forms (e.g. *he's* by *he is*) and that each word is written on a separate line.
- V_Lists is NOT case sensitive. This means that *HAPPY, Happy* and *happy* will all be treated as a single word type.

(3) Edit your lists as necessary.
(4) Click the **Submit** button.
(5) V_Lists generates a report that looks like Figure 1.4. The report contains four columns:
- Column 1 lists the word types that appear in list 1 but not in list 2.
- Column 2 lists the word types that appear in list 2 but not in list 1.
- Column 3 lists the word types that occur in both list 1 and in list 2.
- Column 4 is a cumulative word list that contains the word types occurring either in list 1 or in list 2.

(6) You can save the reports by copying and pasting the relevant columns into a new document.
(7) Click the **Reset** button to start another analysis.

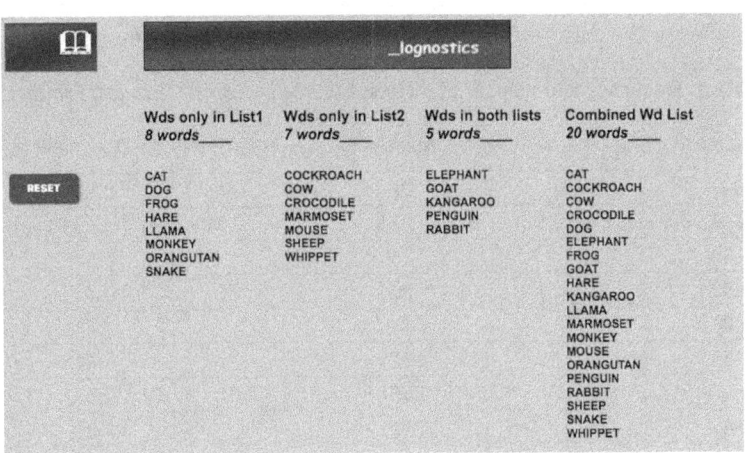

Figure 1.4 V_Lists report page

Background Reading

> **Morgan, C. (1926) Vocabulary analysis of a second-year Spanish text.** *Modern Language Journal* **10** (7), 427–430.
>
> During the past two years the interest taken by our modern language teachers in the question of vocabulary has been steadily increasing. There have been efforts to select a standard vocabulary, attempts to estimate the number of words which we may reasonably expect our pupils to know at the end of a given time, and helpful suggestions on the best way to present and drill the new words. But with all this, if you ask a regular classroom teacher, even one of the wide-awake ones who read *The Modern Language Journal* regularly, about the difficulty of a given text with regard to vocabulary, the answer which you receive will be very vague indeed.
>
> Some time ago I determined to take one text, suitable for second-year work, and analyse the vocabulary thoroughly. The results were so interesting to me and to the friends to whom I showed them that I am offering them to other language teachers in the hope that they may shed a little light on a question of which we all realise the importance.
>
> The text chosen was Azorín's *Pequeño Filósofo* (ed. Louis Imbert, D.C. Heath & Co., 1923). In this text 2737 different words are used (exclusive of proper nouns). The frequency with which these words occur varies from 1870 to 1. Table 1 shows the number and percentage of words which occur more than 100 times, between 50 and 99 times, etc. It is especially worthy of notice that 82% of all the words occur only four times or less.
>
> Since the difficulty of any vocabulary depends not only on the number of words used, but also on the relationship between it and the vocabulary already mastered, I compared this vocabulary with the list published by Miss Elsie I. Jamieson in *The Modern Language Journal* for
>
> **Table 1** Frequency and number of different words in Azorín's *Pequeño Filósofo*
>
> | Frequency | Number | % of total words |
> | --- | --- | --- |
> | 100+ | 22 | 0.80 |
> | 50–99 | 22 | 0.80 |
> | 40–49 | 15 | 0.54 |
> | 30–39 | 20 | 0.73 |
> | 20–29 | 40 | 1.46 |
> | 10–19 | 121 | 4.42 |
> | 5–9 | 256 | 9.35 |
> | 1–4 | 2241 | 81.87 |
> | Total | 2737 | |

March 1924 and with the list prepared by the New York Society for the Experimental Study of Education, published as a supplement to *El Eco*, 15 December 1922. I shall refer to the former as List J, the latter as List E.

List J contains 1098 words. All pronouns, articles and numbers have been omitted. It was compiled by comparing the vocabularies of 10 Spanish grammars. In order to compare our vocabulary with List J it was necessary to credit on the latter list the pronouns, articles, etc. – 53 words in all. List E contains 1746 words. To this a very few words were also added to make the lists comparable.

Table 2 shows the number and percentage of the words occurring in *El Pequeño Filósofo* which appear on List J and on List E and the sum of the frequencies of the words occurring in each list with the percentage of the total frequencies for the whole book.

We see then that as far as this book is concerned it makes no difference whether the student has learned List J or List E. He has mastered only a small percentage of the words, 28% in one case, 31% in the other, but from the percentage of the total frequencies, 79% in both cases, we see that both lists have undoubtedly included the most important words, i.e. the words most frequently used. Table 3 makes this even clearer. From this table we see that all words occurring 30 times or more in the text appear on both lists. As the frequency of use in the text decreases, the percentage of the words occurring in Lists J and E also decreases.

The similarity of the results secured from Lists J and E suggested to me that a grammar chosen at random might show similar percentages. I then compared all of the words occurring five times or more with the vocabulary of the Espinosa and Allen *Elementary Spanish Grammar*. The results given in the column headed *E&A* of the Table 3 are practically the same. Other grammars would probably give similar results. We may conclude then that as far as this text is concerned, it makes no difference whether the student has mastered List J, List E, or the vocabulary of the

Table 2 Number of words appearing in Azorin's *Pequeño Filósofo* appearing on Lists J and E

	No. of words	%	Σf	% F
El Pequeño Filósofo	2737		19,647	
List J	714		10,833	
	53		4,754	
	767	28.02	15,590	79.35
List E	831		14,489	
	16		0.991	
	847	30.9	15,480	78.79

Table 3 Frequency of words in Azorin's *Pequeño Filósofo* appearing on Lists J and E and in E&A Grammar

		J		E		E&A	
F	No. of words	No.	%	No.	%	No.	%
100+	22	22	100	22	100	22	100
50–99	22	22	100	22	100	22	100
40–49	15	15	100	15	100	15	100
30–39	20	20	100	20	100	20	100
20–29	40	35	87.5	37	92.5	36	90
10–19	121	98	80.9	105	86.7	101	83.5
5–9	256	144	56.3	167	65.2	159	62.1
Totals	496	356	71.8	388	78.2	375	75.6

Espinosa and Allen grammar. About 79% of the words on a page are familiar to him. Or, if we wish to consider the problem from the point of view of the number of new words per page, we find:

No. of words	2737
List E	847
No. of new words	1890
No. of pages	78
No. of new words per page	24

Then, even assuming that the pupil remembers all of the vocabulary previously acquired, and that after once meeting a word in the text under discussion he will not need to look it up again, he will find on average 24 unfamiliar words per page. Every teacher will recognise that these assumptions are not valid. This would tend to increase the number of unfamiliar words per page, but I believe that the number of words similar to English or to Spanish words already known would balance these, so the figure given might be trusted in measuring the difficulty of an assignment.

I do not suggest that it is possible or even desirable for a teacher to analyse as completely as this the vocabulary of every textbook that he uses, but I believe that even a superficial examination will show most teachers that they are underestimating the difficulty of vocabulary, especially when the change is made, usually in the second year, from constructed or adapted material to real Spanish or French as the case may be.

Reflections on Morgan (1926)

We chose this article for inclusion in this chapter because it is typical of an important strand of vocabulary research that appeared in the 1920s.

Surprisingly, much of this work seems to have been forgotten in later years, and had to be reinvented in the 1990s. One of the reasons for this must have been that research of this kind is very labour intensive without computers. Morgan's paper involved carrying out type counts and token counts on a longish text, and then comparing these counts to counts derived from another set of texts. All of this work would have been carried out by hand. It is sobering to realise how very much easier work of this sort becomes once you have access to a suitable set of computer programs that will do the donkey work for you. Replicating Morgan's study would be very easy today. The most time-consuming part of the work would be to generate a computer-readable version of the original texts, but with modern optical character readers even this would not be a big job. The rest of the work could be completed in a few hours at most.

In this article Morgan analyses the vocabulary of a book that students of Spanish as a foreign language had to read at high school. The book, which is entitled *Las Confesiones de un Pequeño Filósofo* (*Confessions of a Little Philosopher*), was written in 1904 by Azorín, a well-known Spanish writer. It is composed of very short chapters and in its pages the author describes his infancy in his hometown from a child's point of view.

The analysis Morgan performs consists of determining the number of tokens, types and their frequency of occurrence in the book. This work could easily have been carried out by a program like V_Words. She also compared types occurring in the text with the types occurring in Spanish word lists and grammars of that time (a *grammar* here means a textbook designed to teach Spanish to speakers of English – this paper was written long before modern communicative approaches to language teaching were developed). These more complex analyses involving word lists comparisons could have easily been performed using V_Lists. Among the results she reports, there are three that deserve close attention, especially because they have some resonance with more modern research on vocabulary acquisition.

The first finding that Morgan considers worthy of notice is the high percentage of words in the book (82% of the word types) that occur just four times or less. She considers that this is a very low value for a text containing about 20,000 word tokens. This observation is one that would probably not surprise modern researchers. Anyone who has done any work using corpora will be familiar with an idea developed in George Zipf (1935), which later became known as Zipf's Law. The law implies that in any large text, the number of times a word appears in the text is inversely proportional to its rank in the frequency table. That is, the most common word occurs approximately twice as often as the second most common word, three times as often as the third most common word, four times as often as the fourth most common word, and so on. One consequence of this relationship is that a few highly frequent words will generally make up a very large proportion of any normal text. Another consequence is that any normal text will contain a very large number of word types that occur only once. These generalisations are very reliable for long texts, but not so reliable for short texts, although, as Morgan shows, in broad terms they still apply to short texts too. Zipf's work has seen something of a revival in recent years, notably in work by Edwards and Collins, who used Zipf's Law to model the outputs made by L2 learners (Edwards & Collins, 2011, 2013). We have also made use of Zipf's work in some of the programs that appear later in this book, particularly in the V_Size program presented in Chapter 7.

A second finding in Morgan's paper that needs to be considered is the fact that the Spanish grammars analysed include the words most frequently used in the book by Azorín (79% of the vocabulary is shared). This suggests that the textbooks of the time accurately included the most useful words that learners needed when reading real materials (i.e. the most frequent words in real written texts). This finding would not necessarily coincide with more recent research on the lexis in textbooks for language learners. For example, an analysis of the vocabulary in textbooks for beginner learners of German in the UK (1990s–2006) suggests that they include very specific vocabulary in a limited number of semantic fields, neglecting words that are essential for independent language use (Häcker, 2008). Similarly, Davidson et al. (2008) claim that standard frequency counts do not provide a good account of the words that are likely to appear in textbooks for learners of Dutch. Other studies examining EFL coursebooks report findings along the same lines: Jiménez Catalán and Mancebo (2008) analyse four popular textbooks in Spain, two in primary and two in secondary education, and show that even those from the same educational stages contain different amounts of words and a high proportion of vocabulary which is not shared, highlighting a lack of systematic criteria in vocabulary selection. In another study with EFL books, O'Loughlin (2012) explores in detail three levels of a coursebook series and concludes that intermediate-level EFL learners using these textbooks will have encountered only about 1500 English words, which will not allow learners to function at an appropriate level.

The third finding to comment on is Morgan's estimate of the amount of vocabulary unknown to the students that appears on each page of the reading text (about 24 words). Her view is that this is an unreasonably high vocabulary load for learners at this level, and that the syllabus is probably underestimating the difficulty of the vocabulary that students will be confronted with when reading the book. More recent research would agree with this view: Morgan's analysis suggests that the number of words in the text amounts to 19,647 tokens across 78 pages, which is about 250 words per page. If the number of unknown words per page amounts to 24, this would in turn mean that students would be familiar with about 90% of the words on a page, but one word in every 10 would be a new, unfamiliar one. Recent studies on vocabulary and reading (e.g. Nation, 2001) argue that 90% text coverage is not sufficient for text comprehension, and that 95% text coverage (i.e. one unknown word in every 20 words) might allow for intensive reading. However, for extensive reading to be effective and enjoyable, coverage of about 98% is needed – i.e. only one unknown word in every 50 running words. Morgan also points out that the large number of similar words in English and Spanish (cognate words) might favour comprehension and facilitate reading. However, recent research suggests that learners – especially beginner and intermediate learners – do not always recognise cognates when they meet them in texts (Dressler et al., 2011; Hall, 2002; Tonzar et al., 2009).

As we have seen, Morgan's paper is concerned with analysing the written inputs (in books) that students are exposed to. However, it would also be possible to use V_Words and V_Lists to analyse aural inputs and outputs generated by language learners. Regarding aural input, there is a line of research investigating the effects of listening to radio broadcasts in the target language on learners' interlanguage, a topic initially explored in Meara (1993) with a detailed lexical analysis of a large number of individual BBC broadcasts. Similarly, aural input in language or CLIL classes can be analysed by making initial use of the same methods and tools (see, for instance, Meara et al., 1997, studying classrooms as lexical environments). Regarding the analysis of outputs, one of the main uses for a simple program like V_Words in modern research would be to analyse word association data (cf., for example, Fitzpatrick, 2007; Meara, 1978). If you have a large study, say 500 subjects generating a single response to a set of 100 stimulus words, then you will have 50,000 data points, which is a huge amount of data to sort and evaluate by hand. However, if you sorted the data into 100 sets of 500 responses – one set for each of the stimulus words – then V_Words would be able to analyse the data in a very short space of time, listing the responses by frequency. Likewise, if you asked a large group of participants to give you 10 words that might be useful in a given context, then a program like V_Words could easily sort out the resulting responses by frequency. This kind of data is common in research on 'lexical availability'. Research of this type was commonly used to build basic vocabularies for foreign language teaching in the 1960s (e.g. Gougenheim et al., 1964) and it is now seeing something of a revival – see, for instance, Morris (2010/2011) for Welsh, and Jiménez Catalán's (2014) collection of papers dealing with lexical availability research in Spanish. This approach also seems to be a useful technique for developing special purposes vocabulary. V_Lists is also particularly helpful if you want to compare the words used by two groups of learners on a single task (e.g. Jiménez Catalán & Ojeda, 2005), or if you want to compare a set of texts generated by a single student over a long period of time (cf. Bell, 2009).

If you want to perform analyses that are more sophisticated than the simple analyses that V_Words and V_Lists can handle, then you will find on the internet a number of other programs that are worth looking at. Frequency (Heatley et al., 2002), Voyant Tools (Sinclair et al., 2012), AntConc v3.4.3 (Anthony, 2014) or Wordsmith Tools v7 (Scott, 2016) can extract basic characteristics from texts and analyse them in multiple ways (e.g. making frequency lists of the words they contain). Regarding word lists comparisons, programs like Range for texts v3 by Tom Cobb allows the uploading of different texts or word lists in order to find word frequencies in the combined collection, the range of each word across texts, etc. Also Range (Heatley et al., 2002) compares texts with three frequency lists, but in this case it shows how much coverage of a text each list provides (i.e. it gives the 'lexical frequency profile' of a text).

More Research is Needed ...

On word counts

A lot of the programs presented later in this book make use of this basic process of turning texts into word lists, and it is useful to understand the limitations of the procedures. You can get a feel for these issues by thinking about the following examples.

(1) How many words are there in these sentences and why might this matter?
 (a) *The dog saw the house.*
 (b) *Le chien a vu la maison.*
(2) How many different words are there in this list:
 bank manager, merchant bank, river bank, you can bank on me, Bank of England, cloud bank, Peter Bank
(3) How many words are there in this sentence:
 He said: 'er, well, I dunno, like.'
(4) How many words are there in this sentence:
 The CEO thought that DfI's SWAT assessment was OK.
(5) Compare these five-word sentences; what features would a word count analysis miss:
 (a) *The man saw the woman.*
 (b) *The gentleman observed the lady.*
 (c) *The Bishop ogled the actress.*
(6) How many different words would you expect to find in a text 100 words long?
(7) What makes a text difficult to read?
(8) What features of proper names make them difficult for learners to understand?
(9) How many words is it reasonable to expect an adult L2 learner to learn in a week?
(10) What is odd about these four texts:
 (a) *The man tried to open the door. The door was heavy, and the man struggled to open the door. Was the door stuck? Or was the man too tired to open the door? The man did not know.*

(b) *toilet paper, polish, washing up liquid, toothpaste, soap, kitchen towels, and a dish cloth.*
(c) *Love, love me do You know I love you I'll always be true So please, love me do Whoa, love me do*
(d) *'...!', he said.*

There are actually a lot of unresolved issues where word counts are concerned. Some research discussed later in this book analyses texts in terms of their type–token ratio – that is, the number of different word types a text contains compared to the number of word tokens it contains. The questions above should have shown you that counting words is not straightforward, and this means that computing type–token ratios is not straightforward either. Some research uses word families or lemmas rather than words as its basic unit of counting.

On frequency counts

Most vocabulary research makes use of the idea of word frequency. Sometimes this means the number of times a word (or a word type or a word family) appears in a text, but sometimes it refers to the frequency of a word in a very large corpus. This raises some interesting questions about whether 'low-frequency' words are harder to learn than higher frequency words, and where the cut-off point between high- and low-frequency words lies. Some researchers have argued that learners need to experience words a minimum number of times before they 'learn' them. This idea is usually tested by giving learners texts to read which contain words repeated, once, twice, three times, four times, etc. Try writing a short text which has 10 words repeated a different number of times. What characteristics does the text have?

Some ideas that could easily be worked up into small-scale research projects are the following

- How do different texts/teaching materials compare regarding their vocabulary load?
- How can the oral input in real SL classes be described? What amount of vocabulary is usually recycled in different sessions? How is that reflected (if it is) in the students' output?
- How can watching undubbed TV series enhance vocabulary acquisition at different proficiency levels? How many new words do we find in successive episodes of a series?
- Most of the research on coverage concerns written texts. Is it possible to develop a coverage measure for listening texts as well? How might the results differ from what we find for written texts?
- Which new vocabulary items do students acquire as a result of periods of instruction when performing the same task? What can this tell us about vocabulary growth?

References

Bell, H. (2009) The messy little details: A longitudinal case study of the emerging lexicon. In T. Fitzpatrick and A. Barfield (eds) *Lexical Processing in Second Language Learners* (pp. 111–127). Bristol: Multilingual Matters.

Davidson, D.J., Indefrey, P. and Gullberg, M. (2008) Words that second language learners are likely to hear, read and use. *Bilingualism: Language and Cognition* 11 (1), 133–146.

Dressler, C., Carlo, M.S., Snow, C.E., August, D. and White, C.E. (2011) Spanish speaking students' use of cognate knowledge to infer the meaning of English words. *Bilingualism: Language and Cognition* 14 (2), 243–255.

Edwards, R. and Collins, L. (2011) Lexical frequency profiles and Zipf's Law. *Language Learning* 61 (1), 1–30.

Edwards, R. and Collins, L. (2013) Modelling L2 vocabulary learning. In S. Jarvis and M. Daller (eds) *Vocabulary Knowledge: Human Ratings and Automated Measures* (pp. 157–184). Amsterdam: John Benjamins.

Fitzpatrick, T. (2007) Word associations: Unpacking the assumptions. *International Journal of Applied Linguistics* 17 (3), 319–331.

Gougenheim, G., Michéa, R., Rivenc, P. and Sauvageot, A. (1964) L'élaboration du français fondamental (Ier degré). Paris: Didier.

Häcker, M. (2008) Eleven pets and 20 ways to express one's opinion: The vocabulary learners of German acquire at English secondary schools. *Language Learning Journal* 36 (2), 215–226.

Hall, C.J. (2002) The automatic cognate form assumption. *International Review of Applied Linguistics in Language Teaching* 40 (2), 69–87.

Jiménez Catalán, R.M. (ed.) (2014) *Lexical Availability in English and Spanish*. Berlin: Springer.

Jiménez Catalán, R.M. and Mancebo, R. (2008) Vocabulary input in EFL textbooks. *Revista Española de Lingüística Aplicada* 21, 147–165.

Jiménez Catalán, R.M. and Ojeda, J. (2005) The English vocabulary of girls and boys: Similarities or differences? Evidence from a corpus-based study. In L. Litosseliti, H. Sauton, K. Harrington and J. Sunderland (eds) *Theoretical and Methodological Approaches to Gender and Language Study* (pp. 103–118). London: Macmillan.

Meara, P.M. (1978) Learners' word associations in French. *Interlanguage Studies Bulletin* 3 (2), 192–211.

Meara, P.M. (1993) Tintin and the World Service: A look at lexical environments. Hornby Trust Lecture, IATEFL Conference, Swansea.

Meara, P.M., Lightbown, P.M. and Halter, R. (1997) Classrooms as lexical environments. *Language Teaching Research* 1 (1), 28–47.

Morris, S. (2010/2011) Geirfa Graidd i'r Gymraeg: Creating an A1 and A2 core vocabulary for adult learners of Welsh – a Celtic template? *Journal of Celtic Language Learning* 15, 111–127.

Nation, I.S.P. (2001) *Learning Vocabulary in Another Language*. Cambridge: Cambridge University Press.

O'Loughlin, R. (2012) Tuning in to vocabulary frequency in coursebooks. *RELC Journal* 43 (2), 255–269.

Tonzar, C., Lotto, L. and Job, R. (2009) L2 vocabulary acquisition in children: Effects of learning method and cognate status. *Language Learning* 59 (3), 623–646.

Zipf, G.K. (1935) *The Psycho-Biology of Language: An Introduction to Dynamic Philology*. Boston, MA: Houghton Mifflin.

Alternative programs performing similar functions to V_Words or V_Lists:

Anthony, L. (2014) AntConc v3.4.3 [computer program]. Tokyo: Waseda University. See http://www.laurenceanthony.net/.

Cobb, T. Range for texts v3 [computer program]. See http://www.lextutor.ca/cgi-bin/range/texts/index.pl

Heatley, A., Nation, I.S.P. and Coxhead, A. (2002) RANGE and FREQUENCY programs. http://www.victoria.ac.nz/lals/about/staff/paul-nation

Scott, M. (2016) WordSmith Tools v7. Stroud: Lexical Analysis Software.

Sinclair, S., Rockwell, G. and the Voyant Tools Team (2012) Voyant Tools [web application]. See http://voyant-tools.org

Suggestions for further reading

Bull, W.E. (1950) Spanish word counts: Theory and practice. *Modern Language Journal* 34 (1), 18–26.

Carroll, S.E. (1992) On cognates. *Second Language Research* 8 (2), 93–119.

Harlech-Jones, B. (1983) ESL proficiency and a word frequency count. *English Language Teaching Journal* 37 (1), 62–70.

Horst, M. (2010) How well does teacher talk support incidental vocabulary acquisition? *Reading in a Foreign Language* 22 (1), 161–180.

Hwang, K. and Nation, I.S.P. (1989) Reducing vocabulary load and encouraging vocabulary learning through reading newspapers. *Reading in a Foreign Language* 6 (1), 323–335.

Johnson, C.L. (1927) Vocabulary difficulty and textbook selection. *Modern Language Journal* 11 (5), 290–297.

Richards, J.C. (1974) Word lists – problems and prospects. *RELC Journal* 5 (2), 69–84.

Taylor, J.R. (ed.) (2015) *The Oxford Handbook of the Word*. Oxford: Oxford University Press.

Webb, S. and Rodgers, M. (2009) The vocabulary demands of television programs. *Language Learning* 59 (2), 335–366.

Part 2

Measuring Lexical Variation, Sophistication and Originality

2 D_Tools v2.0

Introduction

D_Tools is a program that computes a statistic reflecting the lexical richness of a text. It is based on work by Malvern and Richards (e.g. Malvern *et al.*, 2004). The statistic that the program computes (called D) is essentially the same measure that is computed by Malvern and Richards' vocd program, but whereas vocd requires that data are formatted according to the conventions used by the CHILDES system (MacWhinney, 2000), D_Tools allows the user to work directly with raw text. Given that the conventions used by CHILDES require some considerable learning effort, the version presented here has some practical advantages for ordinary researchers.

What is D?

Malvern and Richards' *vocd-D* is a complex statistic. It is basically a type/token measure, and as such belongs to a large family of statistics which use the ratio of word types to word tokens (TTR) in a text as a way of analysing the text's lexical richness. These measures have been widely used in lexicostatistics, particularly in the area of stylistics and authorship studies (e.g. Smith & Kelly, 2002) and in the area of clinical and developmental linguistics (e.g. Fairbanks, 1944; Miller, 1981). By the 1980s, as vocabulary was becoming a focus for research in L2, they were beginning to be used in studies of second language acquisition (SLA). The most notable of these studies was perhaps the ESF project on language acquisition by adult immigrants in Europe, particularly Broeder *et al.* (1988), which meticulously logged changes in the outputs of naturalistic L2 learners, and used a number of TTR-based indices as a way of measuring these changes.

Some researchers had noted that TTRs and the statistics that are based on them are not as straightforward as they appear at first glance (e.g. Richards, 1987). Specifically, all other things being equal, TTRs will tend to fall as the number of words in a text increases. Obviously, the longer a text is, the more likely it is to contain a word token which has already occurred in the text. This happens for two reasons. First, most text contains high-frequency grammatical words like *the, a, is,* etc. It is almost impossible to produce texts in which these words occur only once, and this means that the number of word tokens in a text normally increases faster than the number of word types. Inevitably, then, this means that the TTR falls as the text gets longer. Secondly, if we think in terms of a single author producing a very long text and introducing new words into this text, we will eventually reach a point where the author's entire stock of new words has been exhausted. At that point, any additional words will necessarily be repetitions: the number of word tokens in the text gets bigger, but the number of word types has reached a limit, and cannot increase in value. Inevitably, then, the TTR will fall as the text continues to grow. This problem with TTRs has led a number of scholars to develop alternative measures of lexical richness in which the influence of text length is mitigated. There is also considerable argument in the literature about how successful these attempts have been (e.g. Vermeer, 2000). Malvern and Richard's work is generally agreed to be a good solution to this problem. Their vocd measure has been widely adopted by researchers working in child language acquisition, and is fast becoming a standard measure for research in SLA as well (cf. the collection of papers in Daller *et al.*, 2007).

Malvern and Richards' approach to lexical richness is considerably more complex than the simpler methods that have been used to address this question. Whereas most researchers have been content to ignore the interaction between TTRs and text length, Malvern and Richards' approach tackles this problem head on. They accept that texts of different lengths will produce different TTR values, and argue that a text is best described not by a single TTR value, but by a set of TTRs, each describing text samples of different sizes. These values can be presented as a curve, which typically falls from left to right. Malvern and Richards then argue that this curve can be summarised by a single parameter, D.

The process by which D is computed can be summarised as follows: the first step is to get your text. Next, Malvern and Richards generate 100 samples of 35 words from this text by randomly selecting words from it. For each sample, the TTR is calculated and the mean TTR for all of the 100 35-word samples is computed. Next, Malvern and Richards generate 100 samples of 36 words, and compute a mean segmental TTR for each of these 100 samples. This process is repeated with 100 samples of 37 words, 100 samples of 38 words, 100 samples of 39 words, and so on up to 100 samples of 50 words. The result is a set of 16 mean segmental TTR values.

The value of D for the text is computed by matching these values to a series of curves generated by the formula:

$$TTR = D/N * ((1 + 2 * N/D)^{1/2} - 1)$$

The value of D that produces the best-fitting curve is taken to be the value which best describes the lexical richness of the text.

Using D_Tools

You will find the D_Tools program on the Lognostics Tools website, available at: http://www.lognostics.co.uk/tools/D_Tools/D_Tools.htm.

(1) Before you can use D_Tools to analyse your text, you may need to do some preparatory work on your text.

Make sure that your text contains at least 50 words. Otherwise, the program will give you an indication that the text is too short to analyse.

Delete from your text any odd symbols or other extraneous matter that you do not want the program to include in the analysis.

You may need to make some decisions about how certain words are to be handled by the program. Errors are a particular problem: if you leave them in place, or correct them, then your data may be unreliable; if you simply delete errors, then you will be increasing the number of high-frequency function words in the text. The solution here seems to be to work with texts that are relatively error free. A second problem concerns proper names. You can treat a name like *Abraham Lincoln* as two words, or you can use an underscore to turn them into a single lexical item, like this: *Abraham_Lincoln*. In this case, the name will count as only one word for the purposes of analysis. We tend to prefer this solution: it probably does not matter much as long as you are consistent and keep a record of how you treated items of this sort, which you can include in any formal reports. Hyphenated words like *bookworm* will be counted as two words by D_Tools, as will words which include apostrophes, such as *don't*. If you do not want this to happen, then edit these items to *bookworm* and *dont* (or *do not* if you use the full forms in contractions).

(2) Load the text that you want to work with into the D_Tools workspace. You can do this by typing your text directly, or by copying and pasting a pre-prepared text into the workspace. The D_Tools workspace is shown in Figure 2.1.

(3) Give a name to your text and add any extra punctuation marks into the punctuation list underneath the workspace. D_Tools will strip out any punctuation marks when it analyses a text.

(4) Click the **Submit** button when you are ready to proceed.

(5) D_Tools samples the text, and computes a series of TTRs for samples of different lengths. The program then compares the data it collects to Malvern and Richards' model, and reports the best-fitting match it can find.

(6) D_Tools generates a report that looks like Figure 2.2 (the text being analysed is the first paragraph of this chapter). The report compares

24 Part 2: Measuring Lexical Variation, Sophistication and Originality

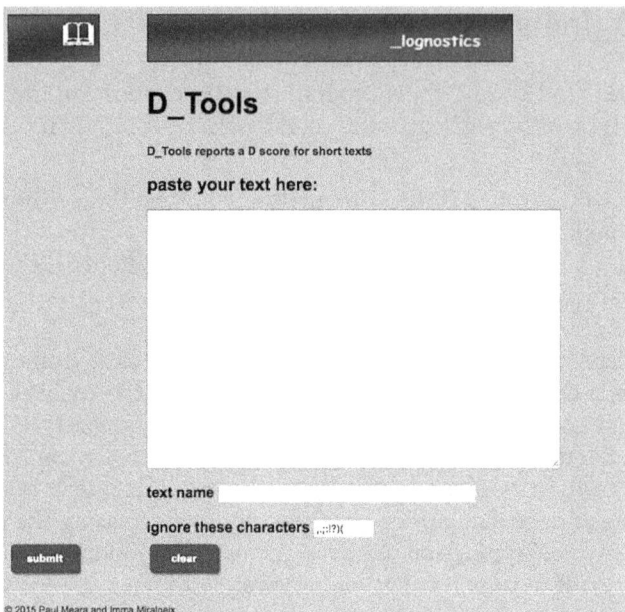

Figure 2.1 D_Tools workspace

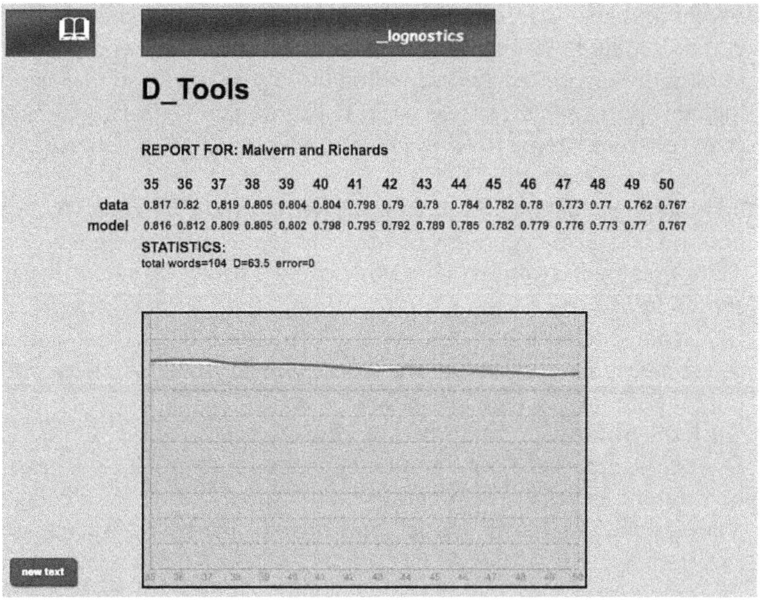

Figure 2.2 D_Tools report

the mean segmental TTR values for samples of 35–50 words and the values generated by the best-fitting value of D in Malvern and Richards' theoretical model. The mean TTRs can vary from 0 to 1. Higher TTR values generate a higher D score. The report lists the total number of words processed, the best-fitting value of D, and an error figure which tells you how closely the data fit the model. The smaller this error figure is, the closer is the match between your data and the theoretical curves that the program works with. Generally speaking, the error figure should be close to zero if the program is making sense of your data. If your error figure is larger than 0.1, then the theoretical curve found by the program is not a good match for your data. This sometimes happens if the text being analysed has unusual stylistic properties.

D_Tools also generates a graph which shows the data curve and the best-fitting model curve. In the report screen of the program, the former appears in blue and the latter in yellow (dark line and clear line in the screenshot, Figure 2.2). These curves should normally coincide closely with each other.

D can theoretically vary between 0 and 120, but values above 90 usually indicate that there are some unusual features in the text (see Malvern *et al.*, 2004: 182). Low values of D indicate that the source text contains a lot of repetition, and is not lexically rich. High values of D indicate that the source text is lexically rich, and tends not to repeat the same words over and over again. Note that the most common source of repetition comes from the use of high-frequency function words, so D is strongly affected by sentence structure. In theory, you can compute D for any text which contains at least 50 words. In practice, you get better data if your source text is longer than you do if your source text is short.

(7) Click on the **New text** button if you want to analyse another text.
(8) As mentioned above, D_Tools reports for each text a set of 16 values. These are the mean segmental TTR values for texts of 35, 36, 37, 38 ... 50 words and each mean is based on 100 text samples. The samples are made by selecting the requisite number of words at random from the text with replacement. Therefore, because the analysis used by D_Tools uses random selection of words, you can sometimes get slightly different values of D if you analyse the same text twice. This is entirely normal, and not an indication that the program is malfunctioning.

For the same reason, the scores produced by D_Tools will also differ slightly from the values generated by the official D program vocd that you will find on the CHILDES site. Again, this is not an indication that either program is malfunctioning. Correlations between vocd scores and the scores generated by D_Tools are usually very high, e.g. Miralpeix (2008) reports correlations in the order of 0.97.

Background Reading

> **Miralpeix, I. (2006) Age and vocabulary acquisition in English as a foreign language. In C. Muñoz (ed.)** *Age and the Rate of Foreign Language Learning* **(pp. 89–106). Clevedon: Multilingual Matters. Abridged version.**
>
> ### Introduction
>
> The present study is concerned with age effects on vocabulary acquisition. It has been conducted within the framework of the Barcelona Age Factor (BAF) project. One of the aims of the BAF project is to find out if an earlier introduction to English, in a Catalan/Spanish bilingual context, has any positive effects (linguistic, attitudinal ...) in the long run. This study analyses the productive vocabulary of two groups of students towards the end of secondary education. They all have received the same amount of formal exposure to English, but they have started instruction at two different ages. We want to know if those who started learning English earlier will have better productive vocabularies than those who started later. Both oral and written data have been analysed: oral free vocabulary was assessed from an interview, a storytelling task and a role play; written free vocabulary was assessed from a composition. Written controlled vocabulary was tested in a cloze.
>
> ### Measures to assess lexical richness
>
> Different measures have been used to assess learners' lexical knowledge: vocabulary scales, c-tests and clozes are among the most frequent. Lexical richness has also often been measured by TTR, that is, the number of different words as a ratio of the total number of running words in a text. This measure is supposed to show how likely it is for a learner to repeat the same words. However, one of the main problems that this measure presents is its sensitivity to text length (Daller *et al.*, 2003; Faerch *et al.*, 1984; Richards, 1987; Vermeer, 2000, 2004), basically because the rate at which new word types appear in a text decreases as the text size increases. There have been some attempts to overcome this problem, for instance the use of adapted measures like the Guiraud Index, the Mean Segmental TTR or the Bilogarithmic TTR, which are just small variations of the TTR and therefore not feasible solutions in most cases. Another possibility has been to fix the length of all the samples to be analysed so as to keep length constant, but this also implies that data are lost when cutting the texts.
>
> Apart from the TTR, lexical density (LD) has often been used to assess lexical richness. LD is the proportion of content words as opposed to function words (Ure, 1971), but it does not seem to be a good measure

at low levels either, due to the fact that some students use telegraphic style; thus they do not make use of many function words. This would yield higher LD values while it would actually reflect the inability to construct a coherent text (Hyltenstam, 1988).

Recently a new measure, D, has been proposed by Malvern and Richards (1997, 2002) and Malvern et al. (2004). D is an index that measures lexical diversity through a process of curve fitting, which is the general problem of finding equations of approximating curves that fit given sets of data. It is claimed to be more informative than TTR because, as opposed to the single value of the TTR, it represents how TTR varies over a range of token sizes for each speaker or writer. This measure also has two other advantages. First, because it is not a function of the number of words in the sample, it uses all the data available in the text, so it is not necessary to standardise text length. Secondly, it is claimed to work with short texts (50 tokens are needed), which is especially relevant when working with low-level learners and oral data, since these learners do not normally produce much.

Jarvis (2002) compares the D formula with other indices of lexical diversity that can also be used in a curve-fitting approach. He concludes that D is accurate for analysing whole texts (with both content and function words), as opposed for instance to Uber Index (U), which seems to be more reliable when carrying out the analysis with just the content words from each text. However, Jarvis points out that more evidence is needed to check whether the efficacy of D extends to other types of written and oral texts (he used written narratives in his study) produced by a greater variety of learners and native speakers (NSs).

It is difficult to say if D will actually become a standard measure for lexical richness but, up to now, and according to the studies carried out by Malvern and Richards, it seems to be one of the most reliable. Our study is also an attempt to provide the so-often requested evidence for or against the adequacy of this measure for vocabulary acquisition research, compared to other more traditional measures. Moreover, it would be of great interest to use D in age-related studies in particular, given the variety of measures that have been used in previous studies, which makes it difficult to generalise and compare the results obtained in different contexts.

Method

Subjects

The subjects of this study were two groups of Catalan/Spanish bilinguals who were learning English as an L3 in state-funded schools in Barcelona. The first group, Early Starters, (ES, $N = 57$) started learning

Table 1 Participants

	N	Onset age	Age at testing	Hours of instruction
ES	57	8	16.3	726 hours (8–9 school years)
LS	41	11	17.9	726 hours (7 school years)

English at the age of eight and were tested when their average age was 16.3. The second group, Late Starters, (LS, $N = 41$) began learning English at the age of 11 and were tested at the age of 17.9. The amount of exposure was the same for both groups: 726 hours (see Table 1), although distributed differently: seven school years for LS and eight to nine years for ES. For the purpose of this study, we chose the students with curricular exposure only. Those with stays abroad, attending language schools and repeaters were not included in the sample.

Instruments

Background questionnaire

A questionnaire written in Catalan was used to elicit information about when students started receiving English classes and for how long instruction had taken place, to make sure that the hours of exposure were kept equal for both groups. It also elicited information about extracurricular exposure, if any, and extensive biographical and linguistic information about the learners.

Oral tests
Free productive vocabulary

Learners were asked to perform three tasks: (1) a semi-guided interview, where they were asked about their daily lives, hobbies, etc. by a researcher; (2) a storytelling, where they had to tell a story given to them in six pictures with no text; and (3) a role play, where two students (a father/mother and a son/daughter) talked about organising a party (see Table 2).

Table 2 Tests

Background questionnaire

Oral tests	Free	Semi-guided interview Storytelling Role play
Written tests	Free	Composition
	Controlled	Cloze

Written tests
Free productive vocabulary

Students wrote a composition about themselves; the maximum time allowed for them to write was 15 minutes.

Controlled productive vocabulary

A cloze test was used to assess learners' written controlled productive vocabulary. Reliability of the cloze test was assessed by computing Cronbach's Alpha for a group of ES ($N = 51$) and a group of LS ($N = 51$). The results, 0.8860 and 0.7832, respectively, show that the test has internal consistency. It was also shown to have a good discrimination and difficulty rate in subjects with different proficiency levels in the BAF project.

Procedure

As regards oral data, it became necessary to make a selection of the items that were going to be included in the analyses. Oral data were transcribed and revised at least twice by a different researcher and all the transcripts were checked and adapted in order to ensure that the learners' amount of types and tokens produced was neither overestimated nor underestimated: following Broeder *et al.* (1988) and Richards and Malvern (2000), immediate self-repetitions, false starts, laughter and fillers were not included in the final analyses. Both in the oral and written data, non-completed words which normally occur in the shortened form (*disco-discotheque, vet-veterinary, cos-because*) were turned into their completed forms, mistakes (*childrens, nouse*) were corrected, lexical inventions (*impersonality, cistel*) and all words in L1 or languages different from English were excluded, and words with more than one spelling (*programme-program*) were consistently changed into one.

Number of types, tokens and word families were obtained using *VocabProfile* (Nation, 1995) and for the computation of D a new instrument was created: *D_Tools* (Meara & Miralpeix, 2004), following Malvern and Richards. All the measures were calculated with and without standardising text length in all of the tasks. The reason for keeping length constant in one of the analyses is to control for a possible length effect in the results. Length was set at 50 tokens for the standardised tasks because it was the minimum number of tokens needed to calculate D and most of the tasks in our study were at least 50 tokens long. For the storytelling, role play and composition, the first 50 tokens were chosen; for the interview we left out the first 20% of learners' production and counted the next 50 tokens, as the openings of the interviews were very similar in all cases (name, grade, age …).

t-Tests for independent samples were performed to see if there were any significant differences between ES and LS. Alpha was set at 0.01 as the analyses involved multiple comparisons. Pearson correlations were carried out between D and the other measures (TTR, types and tokens). We performed these correlations with a twofold purpose: to check how this new measure was related to other measures of lexical richness, and to see if D correlated with the number of tokens in each task and was therefore affected by text length.

Results

Tables 3–6 show the results for each group (ES and LS) in all of the tasks. The first five columns in the tables correspond to the means of the measures computed for each group without standardising length. The last three columns present the results when length is set at 50 tokens. Table 7 summarises the measures and tasks where the differences between the two groups are found, as well as the significance of these differences.

Results from the interview show that LS significantly outperform ES with regard to the number of tokens, types and word families when length is not standardised. There is also a significant difference in TTRs between the two groups in favour of ES (see Tables 3 and 7 and Figure 1).

In the storytelling task, we find significant differences between ES and LS in all measures except when TTR is calculated without standardising length (see Tables 4 and 7 and Figure 2).

Table 3 Interview

	Non-standardised					Standardised		
	Tokens	Types	WF	TTR	D	Types	WF	TTR
ES (*N* = 57)	145.54	70.79	56.42	0.5340	40.36	31.96	26.80	0.6392
LS (*N* = 41)	207.85	91.83	72.46	0.4653	44.53	32.88	28.05	0.6566

Table 4 Storytelling

	Non-standardised					Standardised		
	Tokens	Types	WF	TTR	D	Types	WF	TTR
ES (*N* = 57)	89.79	38.54	35.23	0.4570	18.90	26.81	24.72	0.5362
LS (*N* = 41)	110.78	49.46	43.90	0.4606	23.86	29.23	26.35	0.5845

Table 5 Role play

	Non-standardised					Standardised		
	Tokens	Types	WF	TTR	D	Types	WF	TTR
ES (N = 54)	65.06	35.61	31.06	0.6111	33.78	31.27	27.64	0.6255
LS (N = 41)	70.56	40.00	35.88	0.6214	38.85	32.89	29.96	0.6579

Table 6 Composition

	Non-standardised					Standardised		
	Tokens	Types	WF	TTR	D	Types	WF	TTR
ES (N = 56)	93.50	53.48	41.30	0.5979	40.80	33.20	25.56	0.6640
LS (N = 35)	96.54	54.34	45.69	0.5902	43.97	34.86	29.04	0.6971

Table 7 Significant differences in the t-tests, when $p < 0.01$

	Tokens	Types	WF	TTR	D	Types	WF	TTR
Int	0.000[a]	0.000[a]	0.000[a]	0.000[b]	–	–	–	–
Story	0.007[a]	0.000[a]	0.000[a]	–	0.000[a]	0.002[a]	0.037[a]	0.002[a]
Role	–	–	–	–	–	–	0.022[a]	–
Comp	–	–	–	–	–	0.031[a]	0.000[a]	0.031[a]

Notes: [a]LS > ES; [b]ES > LS.

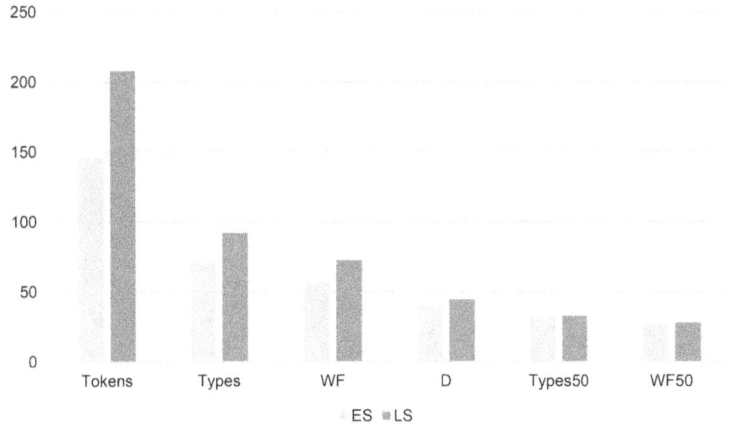

Figure 1 Interview

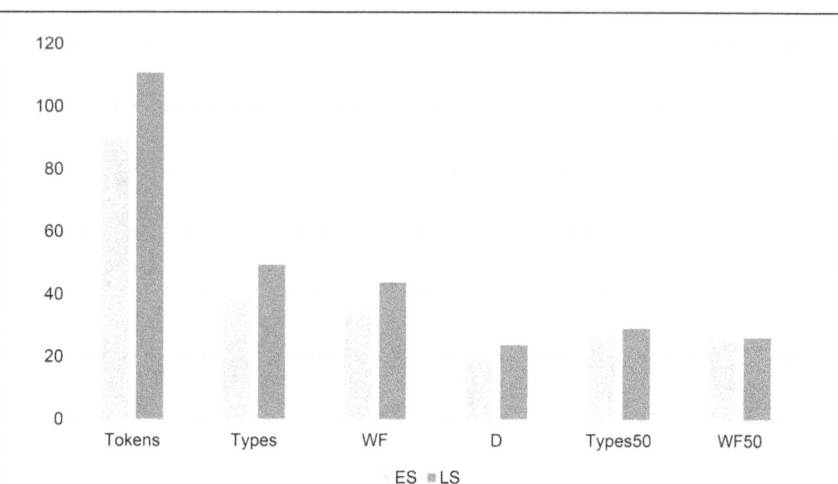

Figure 2 Storytelling

In the role play, ES and LS perform very similarly, there are no significant differences except for word families when length is kept equal, in which LS significantly outperform ES (see Tables 5, 7 and Figure 3).

Significant differences between ES and LS are found in the composition only when length is standardised in the amount of types, word families and TTR (see Tables 6, 7 and Figure 4).

In the English cloze, which was taken as a measure of controlled productive vocabulary, LS significantly outperformed ES: ES ($M = 58.53$, S.D. = 27.59); LS [$M = 82.52$, S.D. = 10.46; $t(70) = 5.814$, $p = 0.001$].

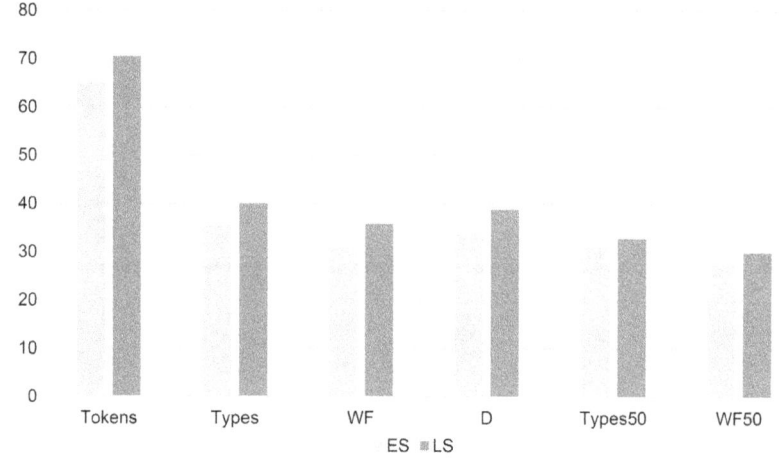

Figure 3 Role play

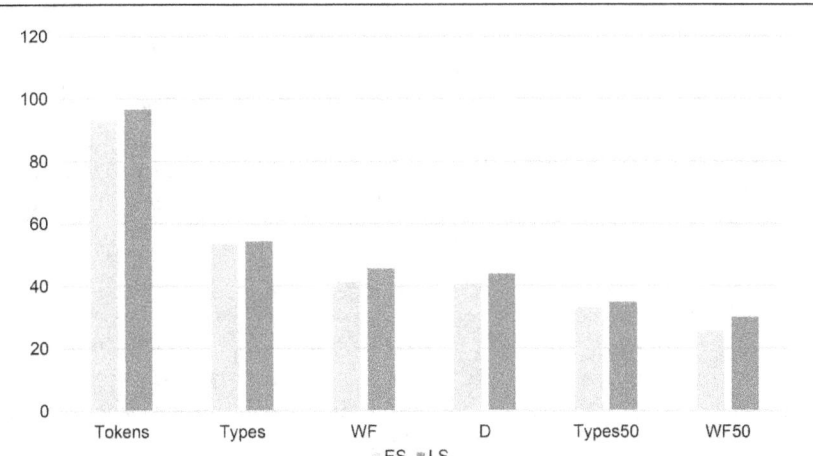

Figure 4 Composition

The correlations between D and the other measures in each task have a similar pattern. They are shown in Table 8. Positive moderate–strong correlations are found between D and the number of types (and word families), especially when length is standardised, e.g. in the storytelling [$r = 0.881$, $n = 98$, $p < 0.001$]. There are also positive (moderate–strong) correlations between D and TTR, most of the time when length is kept constant, e.g. in the composition [$r = 0.708$, $n = 91$, $p < 0.001$]. Very small correlations are found between D and the number of types and word families in the interview when length is not standardised. There is no correlation either between D and the number of tokens produced in any of the tasks, except from a very small one in the storytelling.

Therefore, significant differences between the two groups are always in favour of the LS (both in free and controlled productive vocabulary), except for the TTR of the interview and composition, which is higher for ES when length is not fixed. While standardising length does not

Table 8 Correlations between *D* and the other measures in each of the tasks

	Non-standardised				Standardised		
	Tokens	Types	WF	TTR	Types	WF	TTR
Dint ($N = 98$)	0.034	0.257*	0.252*	0.379**	0.537**	0.450**	0.537**
Dnarr ($N = 98$)	0.223*	0.642**	0.625**	0.620**	0.881**	0.821**	0.881**
Drole ($N = 95$)	−0.032	0.365**	0.394**	0.608**	0.808**	0.733**	0.808**
Dcomp ($N = 91$)	0.134	0.383**	0.301**	0.565**	0.708**	0.347**	0.708**

*$p < .05$; **$p < 0.001$.

imply big differences in the significance of the results in the storytelling and the role play, results vary in the interview and composition depending on whether we kept length equal in all texts. In addition, although D significantly correlates with other measures of lexical richness: number of types, word families (even with TTR), this is not so with the number of tokens, and only in the storytelling is a very weak correlation between number of tokens and D found.

Discussion

In this study we set out to explore if, towards the end of secondary education, students who had been learning English from the age of eight in a formal context outperformed the students who had started it at 11, as regards oral and written productive vocabulary. It was also our purpose to analyse how the D measure was related to other vocabulary measures and to check if it was useful to describe the vocabularies of our learners, who are not at an advanced level and produce short texts.

Results show that, as regards free productive vocabulary, after 726 hours of formal exposure, learners who started learning English earlier did not outperform those who started three years later. We have many instances in which the differences do not reach significance, although LS productive vocabulary is shown to be a bit more diverse. LS tend to obtain higher results in some of the tasks (for example, LS outperform ES in the storytelling). However, there is another task where the two groups performed similarly (the role play), and two other tasks where the advantage of the older group is just shown in some of the measures (i.e. the interview and the composition). The differences in favour of the LS are obvious in controlled productive vocabulary, as they obtain significantly better results in the cloze test. Therefore, these findings are consistent with previous research in other formal contexts (Burstall *et al.*, 1974; Oller & Nagato, 1974; Singleton, 1999), which do not provide evidence in favour of the ES either.

Our results are also in line with other long-term studies carried out in the Basque Country. In a similar context to ours – where Basque/Spanish bilinguals learn English as an L3 – after six years of EFL instruction, LS (starting at 11 and being 16 when they were tested) significantly outperformed ES (starting at eight and being 13 when they were tested). Vocabulary was assessed in an oral storytelling task, a cloze and a composition. In this last written task, Jacobs *et al.*'s (1981) profile was used in the ratings (see Cenoz, 2002). The older the students were, after a similar amount of English language instruction, the greater the lexical complexity found in their compositions (Lasagabaster & Doiz, 2003).

It can also be seen in our data that the interview and the composition show length effects. In the interview, differences are found between the groups in the amount of tokens, types and word families when length is not set at 50 tokens, but there are no differences when length is kept equal. This might be due to the nature of the task: the interviewer introduces new topics, which may act as a trigger for more lexical variety in these oral data, something which cannot be shown when length is set at 50 tokens. With the help of the interviewer who asks and provides topics to talk about, it is easier for students to talk more, which does not happen in a task where the interviewer is not present or does not have such an active role, such as in the storytelling. Therefore, LS have more lexical variety that can only be shown in longer texts.

Unlike what happens in the interview, differences between the groups in the composition are only found when length is standardised. Given equal length to the texts of both groups, LS significantly outperform ES. Hence we see here the importance of standardising length in these two tasks so as not to obtain misleading results with traditional measures.

The results from the storytelling and role plays are not so dependent on length as the ones obtained from the interview and the composition, as most of the measures do not give different results when length is not kept constant. Of all the oral tasks, the storytelling may be the most adequate to assess productive vocabulary knowledge. First, the results do not vary according to length. Secondly, it elicits more words from the students than the role play. Probably, the reason why the two groups performed in such a similar way in the role play is that it is a dual task and they have to take into account the limitations not only of their own lexical resources but also those of their partners. Therefore, more proficient learners might adapt to the demands of a low-proficient partner (use of a less varied vocabulary, asking or answering using very short utterances ...). As they are not performing the task alone and they do not have any planning time, like in the composition or the storytelling, it is also more difficult for them to think just after their partner's turn of what they are going to say, which might also be the reason why it is the task where they produce fewest tokens.

As regards TTRs, there is variation in the results when length is not kept constant. Sensitivity to text length is clearly seen in the interviews, where LS have more types and tokens than ES (and where we find the biggest difference between the group means in these measures). However, it is ES who have a higher TTR. This finding is in line with what has been repeatedly shown in the literature, that is, the dependency of TTR on the number of tokens (Lenko-Szymanska, 2002; Richards, 1987; Vermeer, 2000). Nevertheless, we notice a resemblance between the results given by the TTR with length standardised and D-values. This might seem to contradict Richards and Malvern's (2000) results, as they find no correlation between D and TTR. Our correlations between D and TTR without keeping length constant are moderate, but they get stronger if we correlate D and the TTRs computed after standardising length. This fact makes us wonder about the necessity of D and of a curve-fitting approach if the results given by TTRs and Ds are correlated. Actually, D itself might be also considered a variation of the TTR because at some point we do take into account the relationship between types and tokens, but it is theoretically more valid and, in addition, much more appropriate for practical purposes as we do not need to standardise text length and discard part of the data. Apart from this, the positive correlations between D and the number of types confirms its potential as a measure of lexical variation (maybe more useful at these elementary stages than LD). The lack of correlation between D and amount of tokens shows that this measure is not affected by text length as TTR is.

These results, however, cannot be taken in isolation, but interpreted together with other findings in the BAF project. The fact that ES are not superior to LS in productive vocabulary has been gauged in this study only by some lexical measures. A more complete view of their competence emerges if we take into account that ES ask for assistance in the oral tests more often than LS do (see Grañena, 2006), which may also be seen as an indicator of their poorer lexical competence (i.e. asking for help in vocabulary they do not know). In the written data, Navés *et al.* (2003) also show that LS do normally produce more and that significant differences in favour of the ES are very rarely found (see also Torras *et al.*, 2006). An advantage of LS over ES in lexical knowledge (especially written) seems to be present since the first stages of learning the foreign language. In the compositions, for instance, the lexical gains of LS after 200 hours of school instruction are superior to those of ES after the same number of hours of exposure (Miralpeix, 2002). In the storytelling task, Muñoz (2000) finds significant differences between the v/n ratio of ES and LS, who were already performing better than their peers. Moreover, by Time 2 (after 416 hours of instruction), LS do not resort to the L1 as often as ES do (Muñoz, 2003), which would mean that LS have more vocabulary available in the L2. Taken together, these results would be an indication that, given similar opportunities, efficiency in second language learning increases with age as regards productive vocabulary knowledge as well.

Conclusion

In summary, we have seen that, regarding productive vocabulary, ES did not obtain better results than LS in spite of their earlier exposure to the foreign language. Differences in other lexical abilities (receptive vocabulary, speed of retrieval ...) may be shown by further research. From a pragmatic perspective, more information could be obtained that might also offer an account of lexical performance, i.e. speed at answering, silences or, as suggested in Lorenzo-Dus and Meara (2005), the time spent on the topics selected for conversation in the oral tasks.

In this study, we have used intrinsic measures; that is, the assessment has been carried out in terms of the words that appear in the text itself. This has given us a gross indication of learners' levels, which can be further explored by using extrinsic measures of vocabulary (Daller *et al.*, 2003; Laufer & Nation, 1995; Meara & Bell, 2001; Vermeer, 2004); i.e. classifying items according to criteria external to the text itself would help us to study the vocabularies of these two groups of learners (Miralpeix, in preparation).

As productive vocabulary knowledge is not always easy to assess, especially when we deal with oral production from low-level students, we find it worth exploring new ways to analyse the data. D is a measure that has not been widely used, but the fact that it can become a standard index which can work in a variety of contexts and languages suggests that it can be a more adequate measure of lexical diversity than TTR. Thus, curve-fitting approaches can solve some of the problems that traditional lexical richness measures have been shown to have. We are also well aware of the limitations of a curve-fitting approach (Jarvis, 2003), but it can be regarded as a good start to explore how lexical diversity might be approached in the future.

Acknowledgements

This study was supported by grants 2001FI-0062 from Generalitat de Catalunya to the author and BFF2001-3384 from the Ministry of Education in Spain to the BAF Project. Thanks are also due to Professor Paul Meara and the Centre for Applied Language Studies at University of Wales Swansea. Responsibility for the final version, however, rests with the author.

References

Broeder, P., Extra, G., van Hout, R., Strömqvist, S. and Voionmaa, K. (eds) (1988) *Processes in the Developing Lexicon. Final Report to the European Science Foundation* (Vol. 3). Strasbourg, Tilburg and Göteborg: European Science Foundation.

Burstall, C., Jamieson, M., Cohen, S. and Hargreaves, M. (1974) *Primary French in the Balance*. Windsor: NFER Publishing.

Cenoz, J. (2002) Age differences in foreign language learning. *ITL Review of Applied Linguistics* 135–136, 125–142.

Daller, H., van Hout, R. and Treffers-Daller, J. (2003) Lexical richness in the spontaneous speech of bilinguals. *Applied Linguistics* 24 (2), 197–222.

Faerch, C., Haastrup, K. and Phillipson, R. (1984) Vocabulary. In C. Faerch, K. Haastrup and R. Phillipson (eds) *Learner Language and Language Learning* (pp. 77–102). Clevedon: Multilingual Matters.

Grañena, G. (2006) Age, proficiency level and interactional skills: Evidence from breakdown in production. In C. Muñoz (ed.) *Age and the Rate of Foreign Language Learning* (pp. 183–207). Clevedon: Multilingual Matters.

Hyltenstam, K. (1988) Lexical characteristics of near-native second-language learners of Swedish. *Journal of Multilingual and Multicultural Development* 9 (1–2), 67–84.

Jacobs, H.L., Zinkgraf, S.A., Wormuth, D.R., Hartfiel, V.F. and Hughey, J.B. (1981) *Testing ESL Composition*. Newbury: Rowley.

Jarvis, S. (2002) Short texts, best-fitting curves and new measures of lexical diversity. *Language Testing* 19 (1), 57–84.

Jarvis, S. (2003) Measuring lexical diversity through 'exhaustive sampling'. Personal communication, Second Language Research Forum, Tucson, AZ.

Lasagabaster, D. and Doiz, A. (2003) Maturational constraints on foreign-language written production. In M.P. García Mayo and M.L. García Lecumberri (eds) *Age and the Acquisition of English as a Foreign Language* (pp. 136–160). Clevedon: Multilingual Matters.

Laufer, B. and Nation, I.S.P. (1995) Vocabulary size and use: Lexical richness in L2 written production. *Applied Linguistics* 16 (3), 307–323.

Lenko-Szymanska, A. (2002) How to trace the growth in learners' active vocabulary? A corpus-based study. In B. Kettermann and G. Marko (eds) *Teaching and Learning by Doing Corpus Analysis. Proceedings of the Fouth International Conference on Teaching and Language Corpora, Graz, 19–24 July 2000* (pp. 217–230). Amsterdam: Rodopi.

Lorenzo-Dus, N. and Meara, P.M. (2005) Examiner support strategies and test-taker vocabulary. *IRAL* 43 (3), 239–258.

Malvern, D. and Richards, B. (1997) A new measure of lexical diversity. In A. Ryan and A. Wray (eds) *Evolving Models of Language* (pp. 58–71). Clevedon: Multilingual Matters.

Malvern, D. and Richards, B. (2002) Investigating accommodation in language proficiency interviews using a new measure of lexical diversity. *Language Testing* 19 (1), 85–104.

Malvern, D., Richards, B., Chipere, N., and Durán, P. (2004) *Lexical Diversity and Language Development: Quantification and Assessment*. Basingstoke: Palgrave Macmillan.

Meara, P. M. and Bell, H. (2001) P_Lex: A simple and effective way of describing the lexical characteristics of short L2 texts. *Prospect* 16 (3), 5–19.

Meara, P. M. and Miralpeix, I. (2004) D_Tools (version 1.0). Swansea: Lognostics.

Miralpeix, I. (2002) Lexis in free written production of learners of English as an L3 with different starting ages: A computational analysis. Unpublished manuscript. Barcelona: Universitat de Barcelona.

Miralpeix, I. (in preparation) The influence of age on vocabulary acquisition in English as a foreign language. Doctoral dissertation, University of Barcelona.

Muñoz, C. (2000) The effects of age on rate of acquisition in a foreign language. In P. Gallardo and E. Llurda (eds) *Proceedings of the XXII International Conference of AEDEAN* (pp. 567–571). Lleida: Universitat de Lleida.

Muñoz, C. (2003) Variation in oral skills development and age of onset. In M.P. García Mayo and M.L. García Lecumberri (eds) *Age and the Acquisition of English as a Foreign Language* (pp. 161–181). Clevedon: Multilingual Matters.

Nation, I.S.P. (1995) *VocabProfile*. Wellington, NZ: Victoria University of Wellington.
Navés, T., Torras, M.R. and Celaya, M.L. (2003) Long-term effects of an earlier start. An analysis of EFL written production. In S.H. Foster-Cohen and S. Pekarek (eds) *Eurosla Yearbook* 3 (pp. 103–129). Amsterdam: John Benjamins.
Oller, J. and Nagato, N. (1974) The long term effects of FLES: An experiment. *Modern Language Journal* 58, 15–19.
Richards, B. (1987) Type/token ratios: What do they really tell us? *Journal of Child Language* 14, 201–209.
Richards, B. and Malvern, D. (2000) Measuring vocabulary diversity in teenage learners of French. Paper presented at the British Educational Research Association Conference, Cardiff University, 7–10 September 2000. Cardiff: Education-line Electronic Database.
Singleton, D. (1999) *Exploring the Second Language Mental Lexicon*. Cambridge: Cambridge University Press.
Torras, M.R., Navés, T., Celaya, M.L. and Pérez-Vidal, C. (2006) Age and IL development in writing. In C. Muñoz (ed.) *Age and the Rate of Foreign Language Learning* (pp. 156–182). Clevedon: Multilingual Matters.
Ure, J. (1971) Lexical density and register differentiation. In G.E. Perren and J.L.M. Trim (eds) *Applications of Linguistics. Selected Papers of the Second International Congress of Applied Linguistics, Cambridge, 1969* (pp. 443–452). Cambridge: Cambridge University Press.
Vermeer, A. (2000) Coming to grips with lexical richness. *Language Testing* 17 (1), 65–83.
Vermeer, A. (2004) The relation between lexical richness and vocabulary size in Dutch L1 and L2 children. In P. Bogaards and B. Laufer (eds) *Vocabulary in a Second Language* (pp. 173–189). Amsterdam: John Benjamins.

Reflections on Miralpeix (2006)

Following the publication of Malvern *et al.*'s (2004) book, Miralpeix (2006) was one of the first studies that used D as a measure of lexical diversity with EFL learners. As the objective of the paper was examining the lexical performance of two groups of learners mainly with measures of lexical diversity, comparisons were established between the results obtained for D and those achieved with more traditional indices.

One of the points the article highlights is the high correlation found between D and TTR (the latter computed with the same fixed number of tokens for all learners). However, it is suggested that D is theoretically more valid given the formula it uses, and that it is more appropriate for practical purposes. As a way to illustrate how D can be more useful in this respect, we gave the same story used in the article to two NS teachers, two upper-intermediate EFL learners and a NS child. After recording their retellings, different measures of lexical diversity were calculated, namely TTR (types/tokens), TTR with standardised length (72 tokens in this case, as in the shortest text), Guiraud index (types/√tokens) and D.

Table 2.1 Measures obtained from the oral storytelling of NSs and learners

	Tokens	Types	TTR	Standard TTR (72 tokens)	Guiraud	D
NS teacher	373	156	0.42	0.71	8.08	39.24
NS teacher	269	115	0.43	0.72	7.01	43.75
L2 learner	124	58	0.47	0.60	5.21	30.32
L2 learner	114	55	0.48	0.54	5.15	25.80
NS child	72	38	0.53	0.53	4.48	20.89

As Table 2.1 shows, TTR values actually show the opposite of what we would expect (with NS adults exhibiting the lowest values). Standard TTRs and Guiraud would then give a better approximation to what we think is really happening (with NS teachers having the highest values and the NS child the lowest, although the child's score is closer to the upper-intermediate learners). D values would rank the five participants in a similar way to the two last measures. However, the fact that the ranges of TTR and Guiraud are narrower than that of D makes the scores harder to interpret: all TTRs go from 0 to 1, so it is difficult to make sense of a difference between 0.53 and 0.72. In contrast, D can go from 0 to 90 in highly academic texts and up to 50–60 in learners' output; therefore we may be more confident of a difference between 20.89 and 43.75. The same can be observed in the group means as they are presented in the article under discussion (Tables 3–6, pp. 30–31).

Furthermore, the evaluation of results in the paper might have been more straightforward had several indications or milestones for D been available (i.e. indices of what NS and learners can obtain at different levels for certain tasks in English). Some corpora of children's writing and of interviews with teenage learners of French have been analysed with this measure and explanatory figures have been provided by Malvern and Richards (e.g. Malvern et al., 2004: 182). However, further research is needed with (a) other languages, (b) L1 speakers and L2 learners, and (c) different registers and genres, before we can make more sense of what this measure reveals in terms of linguistic development and achievement.

It is also worth noting that, in spite of the fact that the Ds of LS tend to be higher than those of ES, D does not always discriminate between groups even when other measures do (e.g. in the interview or the composition). These results are in line with those obtained by Read when analysing learners' oral productions in the IELTS speaking tests. Read's candidates were divided into four bands or levels and more proficient learners tended to use a wider range of vocabulary than those that were less proficient; however, D itself could not 'reliably distinguish candidates by band score' (Read, 2005: 13). This could be related to the homogeneity of the groups – although the differences in proficiency in Read's data are broad. It may also be due to the fact that D, like TTR, is influenced by word repetition rather than by the sort of words that the speaker chooses, and this could not suffice to distinguish between different proficiency groups.

Consequently, several researchers have claimed that attention should also be paid to other features that can make one text/speech lexically richer than others. That is why there have been attempts at modifying type/token based measures accordingly, e.g. by adding to these measures some frequency information (i.e. how frequent words are in external lists or well-known corpora). Daller et al. (2007) made a distinction between advanced (less frequent) and non-advanced (more frequent) types to compute 'advanced Guiraud'. Also Vermeer (2004) used frequency information in his 'measure of lexical richness' (MLR) to better analyse input from books and children's production in Dutch.

Other ways of complementing the results from type/token based measures would be, for example, a 'qualitative analysis of vocabulary use in a more general sense' (Read, 2005: 15). This can be considered a way to better capture 'lexical richness'. That is, 'lexical richness' is understood as a construct of which 'lexical diversity' would be just a component (Read, 2000: 200–201). Other components could be, among others, sophistication (low-frequency words appropriate to the topic) or density (the percentage of content to function words). McCarthy and Jarvis (2007) have also proposed a construct including several properties that could be useful to analyse texts: apart from the two that D takes into account, namely variegation (the number of types in a text corpus) and mass (the size of the sample in which diversity is being considered), other features could be balance (how evenly balanced the number of tokens is for each type), dispersion (clustering of types) or rarity (use of infrequent words). This construct, which they call 'lexical diversity', would be conceptually similar to what Read called 'richness', in spite of the fact that these two terms are often used interchangeably in the literature (Jarvis, 2013).

Also Meara (2014: 421) argues that we should look at other approaches to assessing lexical richness. He proposes 'one that makes a preliminary guess about the lexical resources available to an interlocutor and then adjusted this initial assessment in the light of individual words the speaker uses', which, he suggests, could be studied using Bayesian statistical approaches. Jarvis (2013), who advocates a multidimensional model of diversity, recommends as well incorporating elements of perception in its assessment. This could have been done in the study by Miralpeix (2006) to further examine the vocabulary elicited from the two groups of learners. Most probably, these measurements would have helped describe the lexical knowledge of the students more accurately.

All in all, in spite of the fact that a model of 'lexical richness' may comprise much more than 'lexical diversity' alone, the latter can be informative about both lexical and general linguistic development. D may actually be measuring just part of a construct and there may be room for improving this measure. However, D can be more useful and less controversial for research than other type/token measures. As McCarthy put it in 2005, some years later it is still 'the best yet attempt at a lexical diversity thermometer'.

More Research is Needed ...

This section contains some ideas that could easily be worked up into small-scale research projects.

- Test D against a number of different vocabulary measures and with a wide range of language samples and corpora (in different languages, registers and proficiency levels).
- How is D related to other aspects that have been considered to influence lexical richness such as Lexical Density or sophistication?
- How accurately can D predict target language proficiency or vocabulary size?
- How is lexical diversity, as measured by D, related to individual differences such as age or aptitude?
- Malvern and Richards 'put us on the right track' (Jarvis, 2002: 82) with this measure. However, think about possible ways in which its calculation could be improved (e.g. substituting random sampling by exhaustive sampling?). See McCarthy and Jarvis (2007).

References

Broeder, P., Extra, G., van Hout, R., Strömqvist, S. and Voionmaa, K. (eds) (1988) *Processes in the Developing Lexicon. Final Report to the European Science Foundation* (Vol. 3). Strasbourg, Tilburg and Göteborg: European Science Foundation.
Daller, H., Milton, J. and Treffers-Daller, J. (eds) (2007) *Modelling and Assessing Vocabulary Knowledge*. Cambridge: Cambridge University Press.
Fairbanks, H. (1944) Studies in language behavior: II. The quantitative differentiation of samples of spoken language. *Psychological Monographs* 56, 19–38.
Jarvis, S. (2013) Capturing the diversity in lexical diversity. *Language Learning* 63 (Supp. 1), 87–106.
MacWhinney, B. (2000) *The CHILDES Project: Tools for Analyzing Talk, Vol 1: Transcription Format and Programs* (3rd edn). Mahwah, NJ: Lawrence Erlbaum.
Malvern, D., Richards, B., Chipere, N. and Durán, P. (2004) *Lexical Diversity and Language Development: Quantification and Assessment*. Basingstoke: Palgrave Macmillan.
McCarthy, P.M. (2005) Book review, *Lexical Diversity and Language Development: Quantification and Assessment*. Linguistlist 16, 47.
McCarthy, P.M. and Jarvis, S. (2007) vocd: A theoretical and empirical evaluation. *Language Testing* 24 (4), 459–488.
Meara, P.M. (2014) Book review, *Vocabulary Knowledge: Human Ratings and Automated Measures*. International Journal of Applied Linguistics 24 (3), 418–421.
Miller, J.F. (1981) *Assessing Language Production: Experimental Procedures*. London: Arnold.

Miralpeix, I. (2006) Age and vocabulary acquisition in English as a foreign language. In C. Muñoz (ed.) *Age and the Rate of Foreign Language Learning* (pp. 89–106). Clevedon: Multilingual Matters.
Miralpeix, I. (2008) The influence of age on vocabulary acquisition in EFL. PhD thesis, University of Barcelona.
Read, J. (2000) *Assessing Vocabulary*. Cambridge: Cambridge University Press.
Read, J. (2005) Applying lexical statistics to the IELTS listening test. *Research Notes* 20, 12–16.
Richards, B. (1987) Type/token ratios: What do they really tell us? *Journal of Child Language* 14 (2), 201–209.
Smith, J.A. and Kelly, C. (2002) Stylistic constancy and change across literary corpora: Using measures of lexical richness to date works. *Computers and the Humanities* 36 (4), 411–430.
Vermeer, A. (2000) Coming to grips with lexical richness. *Language Testing* 17 (1), 65–83.
Vermeer, A. (2004) The relation between lexical richness and vocabulary size in Dutch L1 and L2 children. In P. Bogaards and B. Laufer (eds) *Vocabulary in a Second Language* (pp. 173–189). Amsterdam: John Benjamins.

Suggestions for further reading

The main source of background research using D with second language learners is to be found in Malvern *et al.* (2004), listed in the bibliography. Other interesting books and papers dealing with D and/or making extensive use of it include:

Crossley, S.A., Salsbury, T., McNamara, D.S. and Jarvis, S. (2011) Predicting lexical proficiency in language learner texts using computational indices. *Language Testing* 28 (4), 561–580.
Foster, P. and Tavakoli, P. (2010) Native speakers and task performance: Comparing effects on complexity, fluency and lexical diversity. *Language Learning* 59 (4), 866–896.
Jarvis, S. (2002) Short texts, best-fitting curves and new measures of lexical diversity. *Language Testing* 19 (1), 57–84.
Jarvis, S., and Daller, H. (eds) (2013) *Vocabulary Knowledge: Human Ratings and Automated Measures*. Amsterdam: John Benjamins.
Koizumi, R. and In'nami, Y. (2012) Effects of text length on lexical diversity measures: Using short texts with less than 200 tokens. *System* 40 (4), 554–564.
Kormos, J. (2011) Task complexity and linguistic and discourse features of narrative writing performance. *Journal of Second Language Writing* 20 (2), 148–161.
McCarthy, P.M. and Jarvis, S. (2010) MTLD, voc-D and HD-D: A validation study of sophisticated approaches to lexical diversity assessment. *Behaviour Research Methods* 42 (2), 381–392.
Treffers-Daller, J. (2013) Measuring lexical diversity among L2 learners of French: An exploration of the validity of D, MTLD and HD-D as measures of linguistic ability. In S. Jarvis and M. Daller (eds) *Vocabulary Knowledge: Human Ratings and Automated Measures* (pp. 79–104). Amsterdam: John Benjamins.
Yu, G. (2010) Lexical diversity in writing and speaking task performances. *Applied Linguistics* 31 (2), 236–259.

3   P_Lex v3.00

Introduction

P_Lex was designed as a way of assessing the vocabulary used by L2 learners when they produce texts. The program was designed to address two problems with the standard ways of evaluating productive vocabulary use in L2. Malvern and Richards' D measure, which we described in Chapter 2, is good at describing lexical diversity, but it does not tackle lexical sophistication, and we felt that this was an important aspect of development in second language speakers. The second standard measure is Laufer and Nation's *Lexical Frequency Profile* (LFP; Laufer & Nation, 1995). LFP does address the issue of lexical sophistication, but it does so by describing the vocabulary in a text in terms of the frequency of the words the text contains. The Profile is a set of values, rather than a single value, however, and this makes it rather difficult to interpret, or to make comparisons between sets of texts whose profiles vary in detail. Additionally, both LFP and D need relatively long texts as input – 200–300 words is a safe minimum, but texts of this length are not easily generated by low-level learners, and this restricts the type of research that you can carry out with these measures. P_Lex was an attempt to overcome these problems. What we were aiming at was an assessment tool that could work on relatively short texts, and provide a single overall score that was easy to understand and transparent in its computation.

Briefly, P_Lex divides a text up into 10-word segments, and counts the number of 'difficult' or 'unusual' words that appear in each segment. The score it generates is the mean number of difficult words in each segment. P_Lex has the advantage that it can be used with relatively short texts, although the scores it produces become more reliable with longer texts. In theoretical terms, P_Lex is an unlikely approach to measuring lexical sophistication: slicing a text into 10-word segments and disregarding punctuation and paragraph structure does not make sense in linguistic terms, as it disregards a lot of information that is carried by the syntax of the sentences and in the text structure. Nevertheless, P_Lex has turned out to be surprisingly effective in practice. We offer it here as an example of an 'engineering solution' to the problem of assessing the vocabulary used in L2 texts – for practical purposes it seems to work, but more research is needed for us to understand exactly why it works as well as it does.

Using P_Lex

You will find the P_Lex program on the Lognostics Tools website, available at: http://www.lognostics.co.uk/tools/P_Lex/P_Lex.htm.

(1) P_Lex works with short texts in English. The current version has no provision for working with other languages, but we hope to be able to do this in future versions of the program.
(2) P_Lex is mainly intended to process short texts generated by second language learners. As such, it works best with texts that are not longer than 300 words. The program will handle texts that are longer than this, but the displays are designed for shorter texts.
(3) You will need to do some editing work on the texts that you want to process using P_Lex. The main problem that you will have to deal with concerns errors. There are two possibilities here. You can leave the errors intact or you can correct them. Since P_Lex uses an inbuilt dictionary that will not recognise incorrectly spelled words, it is probably best to correct errors of this sort. Other errors should probably be left intact. You might want to mark some words as multi-word units for the purposes of the analysis. For example, in the text shown, you might want to mark *four score and seven* or *civil war* as items of this type. You can do this by inserting an underscore (_) between the words like this: *four_score_and_seven* and *civil_war*. Proper names such as *Abraham Lincoln* can be treated in the same way: *Abraham_Lincoln*.
(4) The P_Lex workspace is shown in Figure 3.1.
(5) Load the text that you want to work with into the P_Lex workspace. You can do this by typing your text directly, or by copying a pre-prepared text into the workspace. You can also edit the text in the workspace if you need to. Add an identifying label for this text in the box underneath the main workspace.
(6) P_Lex will ignore any punctuation marks or other symbols in the text that are included in the list underneath the main workspace. You can change these symbols, or add new ones if you need to.
(7) Click the **Submit** button to analyse your text. P_Lex will generate a preliminary report which includes any words that it does not recognise. This report will look something like Figure 3.2. P_Lex has an in-built dictionary file that includes a number of highly frequent words, and it treats any word that does not appear in this internal dictionary list as 'unknown'. Generally, these words will be low-frequency words.

46 Part 2: Measuring Lexical Variation, Sophistication and Originality

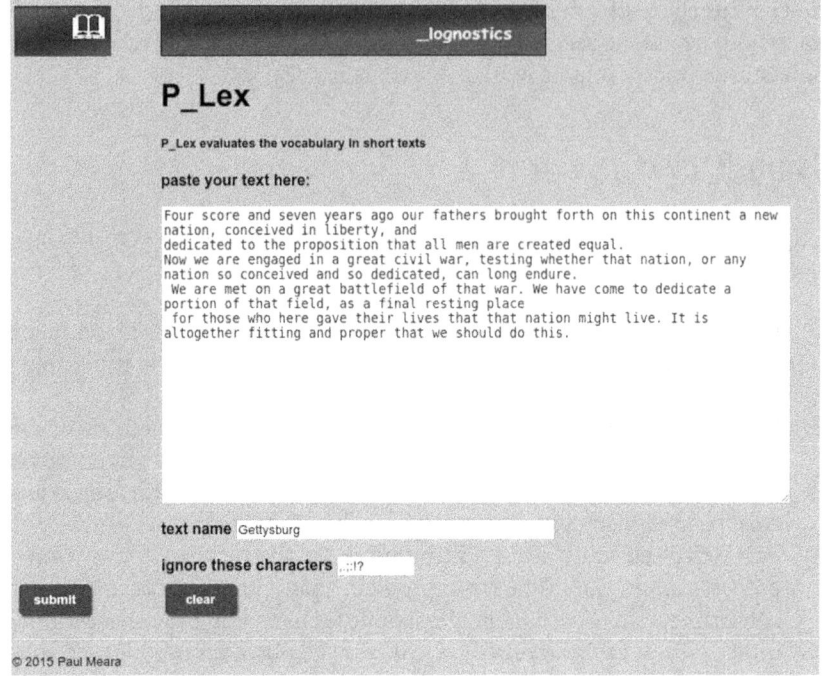

Figure 3.1 P_Lex workspace

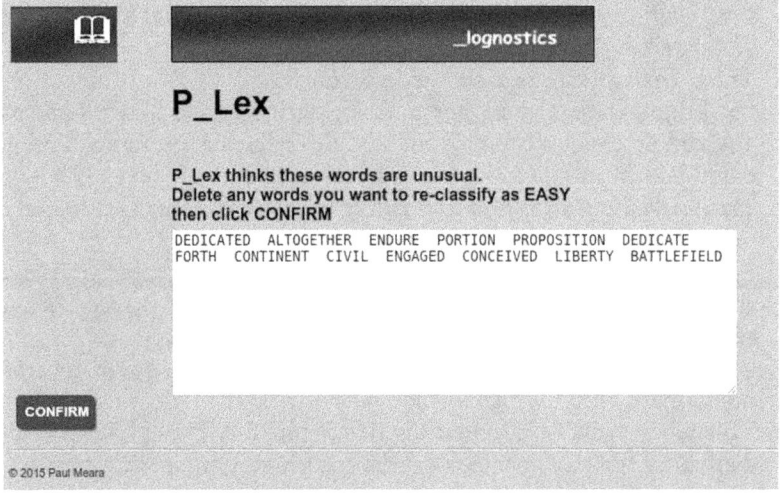

Figure 3.2 P_Lex preliminary report page

However, you may not agree with the classification that P_Lex makes. For example, if you are dealing with a group of Icelandic learners of English who are describing their home town, then the texts they generate are very likely to include *Reykjavik*. P_Lex would report this item as an unusual word, but you would probably want to override this classification. P_Lex will also report mis-spelled or invented words as unknown. Again, you will probably want to override this classification.

You can override P_Lex in two ways when you want to take out words from this 'unusual words' list. The first way is to go back to the original input screen and edit your text in the workspace. You might want to use this method to correct spelling errors, for example. Click **Submit** again when you are satisfied that your editing is complete, and P_Lex will reanalyse your text. The second way is to delete items directly from the unknown words report. P_Lex will add any deleted words to its dictionary file, and treat them as easy words when it computes the statistics for your text.

(8) When you are happy that the words identified by P_Lex are indeed unusual words, and not errors or misclassified items, then click the **Confirm** button to proceed. P_Lex generates a report that looks like Figure 3.3. The report tells you the name of the text it has analysed,

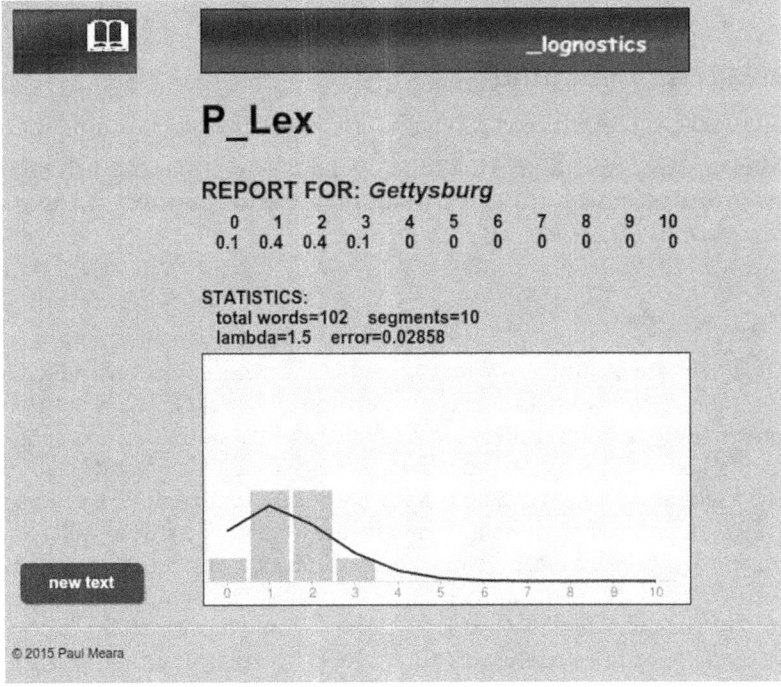

Figure 3.3 P_Lex report page

how many 10-word segments have been processed by the program, and what proportion of the 10-word segments contain N difficult words. It also reports a value (lambda) which summarises the data presented in the table. This is the value that you would normally use to summarise a P_Lex analysis. For the complete explanation on how this value is calculated, please read the appendix to the paper by Meara and Bell that is reproduced in the next section.

The solid line superimposed on the data tells you how well the P_Lex model fits the actual data. In the example above, the data and the model fit moderately well, and the error figure is correspondingly low. However, this result needs to be treated with caution when the text analysed is very short.

(9) Click on the **New text** button if you want to analyse more texts.

The technical bits

The dictionary that P_Lex 3.00 uses to identify unusual words is based on the 1K section of Paul Nation's Range words lists (Nation, 1986). This list has been extended to include the more common derivatives of the basic words in the 1K list (cf. Bauer & Nation, 1993). All words that are not included in this list are treated as 'unusual' words, and reported as such by the program.

Background Reading

Meara, P.M. and Bell, H. (2001) P_Lex: A simple and effective way of describing the lexical characteristics of short L2 texts. *Prospect* **16 (3), 5–19.**

Introduction

There are a number of reasons why it would be useful to have a formal measure of the lexical characteristics of L2 texts. The most obvious of these is that teachers are frequently called upon to make judgements about the types of vocabulary their students use, and to judge the adequacy of this vocabulary. Recent work, for example, by Engber (1995) suggests that these judgements are actually an important component in the way teachers make overall assessments of texts that L2 learners produce. For example, Engber found that a significant proportion of the oral marks awarded to L2 texts could be accounted for by a vocabulary rating. Assessments of this sort also play an important part in the public examinations system, with many examinations requiring examiners to assess explicitly the vocabulary used by candidates. To a very large extent, however, these assessments rely on subjective judgements. Clearly, it would be helpful if we could be more specific about exactly what constitutes 'wide' or 'adequate' vocabulary.

The most common approach to this problem has been to work with measures of lexical richness, or lexical diversity. Indices of this sort have been widely used in studies of lexico-statistics (e.g. Herdan, 1960) and L1 development (e.g. Miller & Klee, 1995), and they have begun to appear with increasing frequency in work on L2 speakers (e.g. Arnaud, 1984; Broeder et al., 1988; Malvern & Richards, 1997). Most of this work uses measures that compare the number of lexical types in a text with the number of lexical tokens in the same text. A number of measures of this sort exist (see Table 1), but there is no clear agreement about which is the best variant to use in the context of L2 learners. Indeed, there is some considerable disagreement about exactly what features of texts these methodologies describe.

The main practical difficulty with measures based on types and tokens is that they are sensitive to the length of the text being assessed (longer texts typically have lower type/token ratios than shorter ones do), and this makes things difficult in real assessment situations, where it is often hard to control the length of the texts you need to assess. Malvern and Richards (1997) have suggested that their measure D is largely insensitive to length, but this measure has not been widely taken up in L2 studies yet, partly because it is computationally more complex than the other measures listed in Table 1.

The measures listed in Table 1 are all examples of what we might call intrinsic measures of lexical variety. In these measures, variety is assessed solely in terms of the words that appear in the text itself. The critical variables here are the number of tokens and the number of types in the text, and no attempt is made to categorise these items according to

Table 1 The principal measures of lexical variation based on types and tokens

Measure	Name of measure
N	Number of tokens in a text
V	Number of types in a text
V1	Number of 'hapax legomena' words occurring only once in a text
V/N	Type/token ratio
V/$\sqrt{N}$	Guiraud's Index
logV/logN	Herdan's Index
V^t	Theoretical vocabulary

criteria that are external to the text itself. This strikes us as an odd way to go about evaluating the lexical resources of L2 speakers. Put in the simplest terms, any analysis that relies on types and tokens will produce identical scores for the examples below:

Example 1: the man saw the woman.
Example 2: the bishop observed the actress.
Example 3: the magistrate sentenced the burglar.

Each example consists of five words, two of which are repeated, giving a total of five tokens and four types. Whichever variant of the type/token ratio we adopt, these data are identical from the point of view of a type/token analysis. Intuitively, however, the three examples are quite different. Example 1 uses vocabulary that is very common, while Examples 2 and 3 use more unusual vocabulary. It would be difficult to say anything very significant about the vocabulary resources of a learner who produced Sentence 1, but Sentences 2 and 3 are unlikely to have been produced by beginners with limited vocabulary resources.

Notice, however, that we are now making a judgement that is not based simply on the evidence available in the text itself. We consider the vocabulary in Example 1 to be simple, because we know about the frequency characteristics of words in the language as a whole. This knowledge allows us to say that 'man' and 'woman' are 'easy words' – words that are frequent in English, and that we would expect most speakers in English to know – whereas 'bishop' and 'actress' or 'magistrate' and 'burglar' are not, and we can use this information to make some fairly strong inferences about the total lexical resources that are available to the writer. This suggests that there might be a case for developing some extrinsic measures of lexical richness for use with L2 learners. These measures would not be limited to the number of types or tokens appearing in an L2 text: they would supplement this information with additional information about the sort of words being used, and the sorts of lexical choices that are being made in a particular text.

An example of a measure of this sort is to be found in Laufer and Nation's (1995) LFP. The operation of the LFP is essentially very simple. LFP takes a raw text as input and returns as output a profile of the text in terms of the frequency distribution of its words. Laufer and Nation suggest that a profile based on four frequency categories is useful – the four categories being based on Nation's earlier work on word lists for L2 learners (Nation, 1984). Category 1 consists of the 1000 most frequent words in English as defined by Nation's lists; Category 2 consists of the second 1000 most frequent words; Category 3 consists of words in the University Word List (Xue & Nation, 1984); Category 4 includes any word not found

Table 2 Part of a LFP analysis

Word list	Tokens/%	Types/%	Families
One	100/76.3	51/73.9	48
Two	10/7.6	6/8.7	4
Three	15/11.5	8/11.6	7
Not in lists	6/4.6	4/5.8	???
Total	**131**	**69**	**59**

Number of BASEWORD1.DAT types 2804   Number of BASEWORD1.DAT families: 958
Number of BASEWORD2.DAT types 2614   Number of BASEWORD2.DAT families: 1028
Number of BASEWORD3.DAT types 2847   Number of BASEWORD3.DAT families: 836

Note: This table shows the data in the format generated by the LFP program.

in the previous three lists. An example of the output from LFP can be seen in Table 2, which contains an LFP analysis of this paragraph.

The figures should be interpreted as follows:

- Line 1 indicates that 100 word tokens can be found in Nation's Level 1 word list. This figure represents 76.3% of the total word token count. Fifty-one word types can be found in Nation's Level 1 list. This figure represents 73.9% of the total type count. When these words are collapsed into their appropriate word families, e.g. by treating 'happy', 'unhappy', 'happiness' as a single word family – then we are left with 48 distinct word families from Nation's Level 1 list.
- Lines 2 and 3 are to be interpreted in a similar way for the Level 2 and Level 3 word lists.
- Line 4 indicates that LFP was not able to process six word tokens (4.6% of the total) because the words are not in Nation's list. (This usually means that the words in question are very low frequency words.) In terms of word types, these four items made up 5.8% of the total type count. LFP is not able to assign these words to word families, since it did not recognise them.
- The last three lines of the output report how many words LFP recognises at each of its three levels. Level 1, for example, contains 2804 word types, which LFP classifies as belonging to 958 different word families.

Laufer and Nation make a number of strong claims for LFP. Specifically, they claim that the ratio of Category 3 and Category 4 words to Category 1 and Category 2 words provides a reliable index of the vocabulary resources available to an L2 writer. They claim that these LFP scores are stable over time, correlate closely with proficiency measures, and are relatively unaffected by task. That is, Laufer and Nation claim that L2 writers have characteristic LFP scores, which are reliably stable over a number of different test conditions:

> The LFP has been shown to be a reliable and valid measure of lexical use in writing. It provided similar stable results for two pieces of writing by the same person, and discriminates between learners at different proficiency levels. It correlates well with an independent measure of vocabulary knowledge. (Laufer & Nation, 1995: 319)

It is not our intention here to quarrel with Laufer and Nation's interpretation of their results – although it might be worth pointing out that our own experience with LFP-type measures suggests that they are much less reliable and much less sensitive than Laufer and Nation claim. In our experience, LFP has poor measurement characteristics, and does not discriminate well between texts, because it relies very heavily on a simple count of the Category 3 and Category 4 words in the text. The number of these words in a 'typical' text is usually very small, and this severely limits the way LFP works. In practice, the percentage of Category 3 and Category 4 words in a text rarely exceeds 10%, so the range of scores produced by LFP is fairly limited, and we think that this lack of variation may be the biggest contributor to Laufer and Nation's stable scores. A particular problem arises with text produced by very low-level learners, when the percentage of Category 3 and Category 4 words is often close to zero.

More importantly, a serious practical problem with LFP is that it requires relatively long texts for stable measures to emerge. Laufer and Nation (1995: 314) claim that in their data 'profiles over 200 words were found to be stable, while those done on less than 200 words were not'. This seems to us to be a very serious practical limitation. Two hundred words is a substantial amount of text, and our experience suggests that it is very difficult to extract texts of this length from learners unless they are relatively advanced, or unusually cooperative. LFP appears, in any case, to be very sensitive to text length, and this makes it difficult to compare LFP scores from different sources. It seems, then, that there might be a case for developing an alternative measure which, like LFP, uses extrinsic characteristics of words to evaluate the vocabulary resources of their authors, but has the additional advantage that it works with short texts and produces scores with good measurement characteristics. A measure of this sort is described in the next section.

P_Lex

P_Lex is based on the idea that it might be possible to make a virtue out of the fact that 'difficult' words occur only infrequently in texts. P_Lex looks at the distribution of difficult words in a text, and returns a simple index that tells us how likely the occurrence of these words is. The underlying assumption here is that people with big vocabularies are more likely to use infrequent words than people with smaller vocabularies are, and that we can use the index we derive from the texts as a pointer to vocabulary size. P_Lex is a first step in this direction.

P_Lex works as follows. Suppose we want to process text T. First, we divide T into a set of 10-word segments, ignoring punctuation. Next, we categorise the words in each segment in terms of their objective frequency. The current version of P_Lex is based on Nation's (1984) word lists. It treats all words occurring in the first 1000 word list as 'easy'. Proper nouns, numbers and geographical derivatives are also categorised as 'easy' words. All other words are categorised as 'hard'. Next, we count the number of infrequent words in each segment, and calculate the number of segments containing zero infrequent words, the number of segments containing one infrequent word, the number of segments containing two infrequent words, and so on. This gives us a P_Lex profile for text T. We can make this a bit more concrete with a real example. Consider the following text:

> *I come from Japan. My home town is Okinawa. Is in the south of Japan, and there is a very big American air-base. My father is engineer at home. I come to Swansea to study engineering, like my father did. But he is teaching engineer and I want to be real scientist. My teacher wants me to work on a new kind of protein found only in seaweed. You have lots of this seaweed in Swansea, so this is a good place for me to come. My journey was very long, and I am very tired now. I have been to Wales before when I was a boy.*

The text contains a total of 108 words, which P_Lex splits into 10 ten-word segments like this:

(1)	*I come from Japan. My home town is Okinawa. Is*	0
(2)	*in the south of Japan, and there is a very*	0
(3)	*big American air-base. My father is engineer at home. I*	2
(4)	*come to Swansea to study engineering, like my father did.*	1
(5)	*But he is teaching engineer and I want to be*	1
(6)	*real scientist. My teacher wants me to work on a*	1
(7)	*new kind of protein found only in seaweed. You have*	2

(8) *lots of this seaweed in Swansea, so this is a*   1
(9) *good place for me to come. My journey was very*   0
(10) *long, and I am very tired now. I have been*   0

The first and second segments contain no hard words. Segment 3 contains two hard words (*air-base* and *engineer*). Segments 4, 5 and 6 contain one hard word each (*engineering, engineer, scientist*). Segment 7 contains two hard words (*protein, seaweed*). Segment 8 contains one hard word (*seaweed*). Segments 9 and 10 contain no hard words. We use these data to construct a P_Lex profile, like the one shown in Table 3. Table 3 simply tells us that four of the segments (40%) contain no hard words, four segments (40%) contain one hard word, and two segments (20%) contain two hard words. No segments contain three or more hard words.

Not surprisingly, it turns out that the distributions we get for this type of analysis are strongly skewed to the left: most texts contain few difficult words, and texts that contain a very high proportion of such words are themselves quite unusual. Distributions that are strongly skewed to the left are often well described by so-called Poisson distributions, (see Appendix), and this turns out to be the case with the data that our analysis produces. Figure 1, for example, shows the data from Table 3 together with the Poisson curve that fits these data very closely.

Table 3 Number of segments in the text that contain *N* difficult words

N	0	1	2	3	4	5	6	7	8	9	10
nmbr.	4	4	2	0	0	0	0	0	0	0	0
prop.	0.4	0.4	0.2	0	0	0	0	0	0	0	0

Notes: nmbr., the raw number of segments containing *N* hard words; prop., the same figures reinterpreted as proportions.

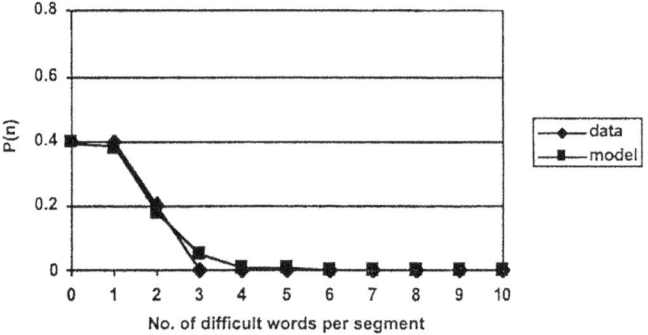

Figure 1 Matching data to a theoretical curve, lambda = 0.92

The mathematics of fitting curves to data is fairly complex, so we have summarised this process in detail in the Appendix. For readers who do not want to get so involved, it is enough to know that there is a procedure which makes it possible to turn data like those in Table 3 into a single figure, conventionally known as **lambda.** Our contention is that these lambda values provide much tidier data than the ratio figures that are produced by LFP. The lambda figures are much easier to work with than the LFP ratios, and are much more intuitive to interpret. The lambda values typically range from 0 to about 4.5, with higher figures corresponding to a higher proportion of infrequent words. Lambda values have good measurement characteristics, and this allows them to be added and averaged straightforwardly. More importantly, however, lambda scores are much less sensitive to text length than the LFP scores are and, critically, the P_Lex methodology gives lambda scores that are reasonably stable with very short texts. These characteristics are illustrated and discussed in the next section.

An Evaluation of P_Lex

This section illustrates the way P_Lex works with a large set of texts produced by L2 learners of English. It addresses the issue of how reliable P_Lex scores are and how well the scores correlate with other measures of productive vocabulary in L2. We also consider how well P_Lex works with texts of different lengths.

Method

A total of 49 subjects took part in this study. All were learners of English as a foreign language, taking part in summer courses at the University of Wales Swansea. These learners came from a variety of L1 backgrounds, and they exhibited a range of proficiency, ranging from lower-intermediate to advanced.

Each subject produced two pieces of written work. For the purposes of comparison, we asked subjects to produce two discursive essays, using the same titles as were used in Laufer and Nation's study (1995: 320 – *'Should a government be allowed to limit the number of children and family can have?'* and *'A person cannot be poor and happy: Discuss.'*). We also set the same conditions as Laufer and Nation did: each essay was to be written in an hour, without dictionaries. We asked subjects to produce about 300 words, although in practice many subjects produced essays that were shorter than this. The two essays were written within a week of each other, and we assume that this time lapse was too short for any real linguistic gains to have taken place in the subjects' vocabulary knowledge. Each student also took the active version of the Vocabulary Levels Text (Laufer & Nation, 1999).

The essays were transcribed into machine-readable format. Minor spelling errors were corrected at this stage. Following this, the essays were processed using the P_Lex methodology described above. The shortest essay included in the analysis consisted of just over 250 words, and we therefore used the first 250 words of each essay in the analysis that follows.

Analysis

Our basic question was whether the P_Lex methodology is reliably stable across administrations, and in order to evaluate this question we calculated the lambda values for each subject's two essays. If the lambda values are reliable, then there should be no difference between the mean lambda values of the two essays, and across the group as a whole there should be a close correlation between the two sets of lambda values. The analysis confirmed that there was not a significant difference between the mean lambda scores, and that the two sets of scores correlated modestly (see Table 4).

This is a reasonably good result. The data confirm that the P_Lex scores on Essay 1 and Essay 2 do not differ significantly, and there is a modest correlation between the P_Lex scores on the two essays. The correlations account for about 43% of the total variance ($r = 0.655$). These figures are all broadly in line with the results reported by Laufer and Nation (1995).

We also examined whether the P_Lex measure was able to distinguish reliably between groups of learners at different levels of proficiency. We used the results of the Levels test to divide the subject base into two subgroups: Group H comprised the top 24 subjects on this measure; Group L comprised the bottom 25 subjects (see Table 5). Independent t-tests indicated that the P_Lex scores of these two groups were reliably different ($t = 4.69$, $p < 0.01$ for Essay 1; $t = 2.79$, $p < 0.01$ for Essay 2).

The overall correlation between P_Lex scores and the Levels test were also good. Essay 1 and the Levels test correlated moderately and

Table 4 Mean lambda scores and correlations: 250-word texts

	Essay 1	Essay 2
Mean	1.466	1.309
S.D.	0.56	0.51

Correlation: *Essay 1* and *Essay 2*: $r = 0.655$; $p < 0.001$

Table 5 Mean P_Lex scores for group H (high scorers) and group L (low scorers)

	Essay 1: 250 words		Essay 2: 250 words	
	Group H	Group L	Group H	Group L
Mean	1.785	1.160	1.503	1.124
S.D.	0.503	0.429	0.500	0.451

significantly ($r = 0.565$, $p < 0.001$), and Essay 2 and the Levels test correlated more modestly, but still significantly ($r = 0.339$, $p = 0.017$). A similar pattern of correlations between two pieces of written work and the Levels test results was also found in Laufer and Nation's (1995) report.

These findings, then, broadly replicate the pattern of findings reported in Laufer and Nation (1995). A further analysis of the data showed that this was not a fluke: an analysis of all the texts using Laufer and Nation's LFP methodology also showed no difference between the means scores on Essay 1 and Essay 2, a moderately good correlation between the LFP scores on Essay 1 and Essay 2 ($r = 0.665$, $p < 0.001$), and much weaker, but still significant, correlations between the LFP scores and the Levels test (for Essay 1, $r = 0.303$, $p < 0.05$; for Essay 2, $r = 0.287$, $p < 0.05$).

Figure 2 shows a more detailed analysis of the P_Lex data for three subjects at different levels of proficiency: Subject A is an advanced learner, Subject B an intermediate-level learner, and Subject C a low-level learner. The figure shows the effects of using different lengths of text in the P_Lex analysis. P_Lex values were calculated for the first 10 words of each text, the first 20 words of each text, the first 30 words of each text,

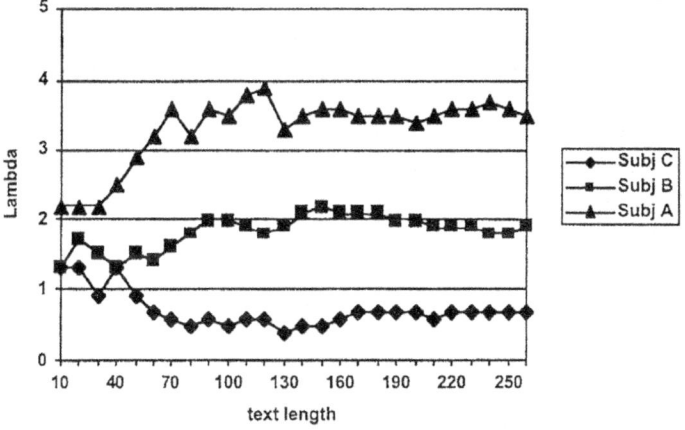

Figure 2 Data for three illustrative cases, $n = 10$–250 words

Table 6 Mean lambda scores and correlations: 150-word texts

	Levels test	Essay 1	Essay 2
Mean	51.02	1.465	1.295
S.D.	7.29	0.65	0.54
Correlation: Essay 1 and Essay 2:	$r = 0.655, p < 0.001$		
Correlation: Essay 1 and Levels test:	$r = 0.555, p < 0.001$		
Correlation: Essay 2 and Levels test:	$r = 0.371, p < 0.001$		

and so on up to a maximum of 240 words. There is some variation in the P_Lex scores as the sample size increases. However, it is clear from Figure 2 that P_Lex is essentially stable from about 120 words, and that texts of this length clearly discriminate between the proficiency levels illustrated. Indeed, we could argue that texts shorter than 120 words can also discriminate, but at this level the P_Lex values appear not to be reliably stable. Interestingly, low-level texts appear to stabilise faster than higher level texts – Subject C stabilises at about 90 words, while Subject A stabilises at about 150 words. This is a convenient outcome for us, as it suggests that the short texts typically extractable from low-level learners may still be long enough for evaluation purposes.

The data in this figure suggest that it might be possible to get reliable P_Lex data from texts that were considerably shorter than the texts analysed in the main experiments. We therefore repeated the analysis described in the previous section, using data from all 49 subjects, but processing only the first 150 words of each text. These data, summarised in Table 6, are essentially identical to the data produced with the 250 words analysis: no difference between the means scores on the two texts; good correlations between the P_Lex scores on the two texts; and a modest correlation between the P_Lex scores and scores on the Levels test. This suggests that P_Lex is effective even with text lengths that are considerably shorter than the minimum figures recommended by Laufer and Nation (1995) with their LFP measure. In fact, a detailed examination of the data indicates that 120 words might be a reasonable lower bound for the analysis we have described.

Discussion

The data reported above suggest that the P_Lex methodology is basically a reliable one, which produces data very similar to the data produced by LFP. However, P_Lex has the advantage that it seems to work with much shorter texts than the recommended minimum text length for LFP, and this makes it a more useful tool for analysing the output of L2 learners, particularly lower level learners.

The question of validity is much more awkward to deal with. There are two basic problems here. The first problem is that there are no other tests of productive vocabulary with which we can compare these data. Our approach here has been to use the so-called Productive Version of the Levels test as a comparison point, but there are a number of reasons for viewing the Levels test as a poor instrument when it comes to measuring productive vocabulary: it gives subjects very little freedom of choice in their responses, which are highly constrained by the context provided in the items. Nor does it allow them to display their vocabulary knowledge freely, as it tests only a very small number of items. In short, the Levels test is constrained in a way that is totally different from P_Lex and, given these fundamental differences between the two tests, we should perhaps not be surprised that the correlations we found between P_Lex and the Levels test were only modest.

The second problem concerns our selection of 'difficult' words. In the work reported here, we have defined 'difficult' in terms of frequency, a practice that is largely unquestioned in this field. The P_Lex version used here used Nation's (1984) word lists as a way of discriminating between 'easy' words and 'hard' words. We arbitrarily assigned words in Nation's 1000 word list to the former category, along with proper nouns, numerals and geographical derivatives, while any other words were assigned to the latter category. We think, however, that there might be a case for exploring alternative ways of characterising vocabulary. Specifically, we think that 'difficult' vocabulary is not entirely to be defined in terms of frequency: words are unusual in particular contexts for particular groups of L1 speakers, and it may not be possible to draw up a list of 'difficult' words that applies to all contexts and all L1 groups. This suggests to us that P_Lex might be most effective if it were combined with a set of standardised tasks – e.g. picture description tasks – where data can also be elicited from native speakers (NSs), and task-specific word lists could be constructed on the basis of these data. For example, it might be the case that NSs asked to describe a particular picture make use of very specific vocabulary, which will be very common in this specific context but unusual in other contexts. Learners describing the same picture might also use 'difficult' words, but these words only really indicate good vocabulary control if they come from the same set of difficult words that the NSs use in this context. Other 'difficult' words would then actually indicate a lack of appropriate vocabulary. A task-specific vocabulary list would be able to distinguish these cases. Some work along these lines is currently in progress in Swansea.

Conclusions

In this paper we have outlined an alternative approach to the question of describing the vocabulary resources contained in a text. Like Laufer and Nation's (1995) LFP, P_Lex compares the lexical content of a text with external norms, essentially with frequency lists. In fact, both LFP and P_Lex use the same frequency lists, taken from Nation (1984). However, P_Lex seems to have a number of advantages over LFP in that it works well with shorter texts, and this makes it particularly suitable for use with low-level learners. P_Lex also has better measurement characteristics than LFP does – it is not a ratio, and it is anchored on zero – and this makes it more amenable to standard statistical treatments than LFP.

Given these advantages, we think that P_Lex might turn out to be the kind of tool that will have a number of interesting and very practical applications. Our own work to date has largely been concerned with using P_Lex as a way of evaluating texts used in examinations. We might expect that difficult examinations would use texts that had higher P_Lex values than easier examinations and on the whole this turns out to be the case. P_Lex can thus be used to provide an objective support for exam-setters' hunches about the appropriateness of a test passage for a particular group of students. Our more recent work has been more concerned with using P_Lex as a way of assessing the vocabulary resources commanded by learners at different levels of proficiency, and we think that in the longer term this methodology might be used to provide objective support for the intuitive and subjective judgements that examiners are required to make in oral assessments of speakers' abilities. At the moment, we are some way from this goal, but we think that the methodology holds more than a little promise.

Notes

The authors would like to acknowledge the support of colleagues at Concordia University Montreal and the support of FCAR in the development of these ideas.

References

Arnaud, P.J.L. (1984) The lexical richness of L2 written productions and the validity of vocabulary tests. In T. Culhane, C. Klein-Braley and D.K. Stevenson (eds) *Practise and Problems in Language Testing* (pp. 14–28). Occasional Papers 29. Colchester: Department of Language and Linguistics, University of Essex.

Broeder, P., Extra, G., van Hout, R., Strömqvist, S. and Voionmaa, K. (1988) *Processes in Developing Lexicon.* Tilburg: KU Brabant.

Engber, C.A. (1995) The relationship of lexical proficiency to the quality of ESL compositions. *Journal of Second Language Writing* 4 (2), 139–155.
Herdan, G. (1960) *Type-Token Mathematics*. The Hague: Mouton.
Laufer, B. and Nation, I.S.P. (1995) Vocabulary size and use: Lexical richness in L2 written production. *Applied Linguistics* 16 (3), 307–322.
Laufer, B. and Nation, I.S.P. (1999) A vocabulary-size test of controlled productive ability. *Language Testing* 16 (1), 33–51.
Malvern, D. and Richards, B. (1997) A new measure of lexical diversity. In A. Ryan and A. Wray (eds) *Evolving Models of Language* (pp. 58–71). Clevedon: Multilingual Matters.
Miller, J.F. and Klee, T. (1995) Computational approaches to the analysis of language impairment. In P. Fletcher and B. MacWhinney (eds) *The Handbook of Child Language* (pp. 545–572). Oxford: Blackwell.
Nation, I.S.P. (1984) *Vocabulary Lists: Words, Affixes and Stems*. Occasional Publications No. 12. Wellington: English Language Institute, Victoria University of Wellington.
Xue, G. and Nation, I.S.P. (1984) A university word list. *Language Learning and Communication* 3 (2), 215–229.

Appendix: How the Lambda Scores are Calculated

P_Lex is based on the assumption that 'hard' words are relatively rare events, and that most of the words that occur in a text are simpler, high-frequency words. This means that we would expect most 10-word segments to contain only one or two hard words, and that segments containing three or four words will be relatively unusual. Distributions with these characteristics are often well described by Poisson distributions. The first recorded use of these distributions was a study of the number of Prussian cavalry officers kicked to death by their horses. Clearly, most days ought to contain no deaths from horse kicks, but it would not be unusual to find one Prussian cavalry officer kicked to death in a single day. However, if we found a day where 10 officers received fatal kicks, then we might want to infer that something unusual happened on that day.

The advantage of fitting Poisson curves to our data is that these curves are conveniently described by a compact formula:

$$P_N = (\lambda^N * e^{-\lambda})/N!$$

The critical value in this formula is the variable λ (lambda), which defines the overall shape of the curve. If we know the value of lambda, then we know what the curve will look like, and this means that we can use lambda as a shorthand for describing data like the sample presented in Table 3. These data are in fact a close approximation to a Poisson curve with a lambda value of 0.92, as we can see from the table below, and we can use a least squares method to calculate that this value is indeed the best-fitting match.

N	0	1	2	3	4	5	6	7	8	9	10
Actual	0.4	0.4	0.2	0	0	0	0	0	0	0	0
$\lambda = 0.92$	0.39	0.36	0.16	0.05	0.01	0.00	0.00	0.00	0.00	0.00	0.00

Inevitably, these curves are not exact fits, so P_Lex reports an Error Figure, which shows how well the data are described by the best-fitting Poisson curve. At 120 words, this error figure is typically less than 5%, which is very low considering how few data points are involved. High error figures usually indicate texts that are abnormal in some way. A text that was generally very simple, for example, but contained a number of segments that contained five or six unusual words – e.g. *capture, recapture and removal statistics for estimation of demographic parameters*, where $N = 7$ – would have a profile that does not match the standard Poisson profile, and would therefore produce a large error score. We would perhaps not want to include a text of this sort in a group analysis, and indeed, the good figures reported in the results section can be considerably improved if we eliminate subjects with error figures over 5%.

At 200 words, the mean error value falls to about 2%. This suggests that, despite its simplifications, the model is basically a good one. The close fit between the theoretical curves and the actual data suggests that, in addition to its role as a measure of vocabulary, P_Lex might be able to function as a simple diagnostic tool, identifying L2 speakers who are showing abnormalities in the way they write in English. For example, it might be possible to use P_Lex to pick out learners who over-rely on Romance cognate words in their writing.

Reflections on Meara and Bell (2001)

P_Lex was one of a set of 20 vocabulary tests (rather unimaginatively called A_Lex, B_Lex, C_Lex, etc. through to S_Lex and T_Lex) that we developed with the help of a grant from the EU's Lingua program. Unlike most of the other programs, which had a short lifespan and were not widely taken up by other researchers, P_Lex has been extensively studied by other researchers, and it seems to have been particularly influential with people working on Tasks and people using the Complexity, Accuracy and Fluency framework (cf. Pang & Skehan, 2014; Qian, 2014; Skehan, 2009a, 2009b). The main advantage of P_Lex in these contexts is that it is much simpler to use than most of the competing ways of assessing lexical outputs, and the measures P_Lex generates can easily be compared with other variables. For example, it has been seen that lambdas can discriminate between NSs' and non-NSs' performance in different tasks and that planning time enables speakers to produce more lexically sophisticated output (Skehan, 2009a, 2009b). Also Miralpeix (2007) found that written tasks tended to give higher lambdas than oral tasks, which are more spontaneous. Qian (2014) showed that post-task transcribing, as a focus-on-form activity at the post-task stage, was beneficial for L2 learning. Results of this study evidenced that the lexical sophistication in the oral performance of students who did the activity was significantly higher than that of the students who did not. However, Skehan (2009a) found non-existent or very low correlations between Ds and lambdas, which suggests that the relationship between lexical diversity and sophistication is not straightforward.

Given that P_Lex is not backed up by a proper theory, the results of these studies need to be treated with some caution. In general, though, studies comparing P_Lex with other proficiency assessments suggest that the methodology is robust: in their study of spoken vocabulary use in a testing context, Read and Nation (2006) observed that high-proficiency candidates used a greater proportion of low-frequency words in their speech than lower proficiency students, and that lambda values confirmed the profile patterns found in the LFPs of the candidates. Also Pang and Skehan (2014) found significant differences in oral performance, as measured by lambdas, between high- and low-proficiency university learners.

It is worth mentioning that the dictionary used in this version of P_Lex is based on the 1K section of Nation's (1986) word lists. This list, which is partly based on West's (1953) *General Service List*, is not very different from other 1K lists such as the BNC list (Leech *et al.*, 2001) or the JACET list (Ishikawa *et al.*, 2003). The list is predominantly determined by the frequency of the words in a standard corpus and, for high-frequency words, there is general agreement over what the most frequent words are. However, there would be a strong case for using a different dictionary if the texts you were analysing were non-standard in some way; for example, if your texts were spoken texts, then it might be more appropriate to use a dictionary that was based on a spoken corpus, rather than one that was built from written texts. There is also a case for not using frequency-based lists at all. For example, we might want to consider all examples of cognate words as easy words, irrespective of their objective frequency in English. This might be an important consideration if we were working with texts generated by L1 speakers of Spanish or other Romance languages. One particularly interesting possibility is to construct specific word lists for particular tasks, and to treat words as unusual or difficult only if they are unusual or difficult for that particular task. This idea is explored in a tangential way in Chapter 4, where we look at the unique vocabulary that learners use in very simple, stripped down tasks.

Version 3.00 of P_Lex does not include a facility for you to add your own dictionary to the program, but future versions of the program may incorporate this feature.

We commented earlier about the lack of a theoretical justification for the way P_Lex works. In some ways, however, P_Lex does much the same job as Laufer's *Beyond 2000* measure (Laufer, 1995). Laufer's paper suggested that texts might be evaluated by counting the number of words they contained that did not appear in Nation's 1K and 2K lists. This proposal considerably simplifies the analysis of LFP data, in that it reduces the profile to a single characteristic, and does this by disregarding the high-frequency words occurring in a text. However, the number of words falling outside the 2K range in texts generated by low-level learners of English is generally quite small – often only a few percent of the total number of word types, and we think this means that the *Beyond 2000* measure may not work well with short texts, or with low-level learners.

More Research is Needed ...

This section contains some ideas that could easily be worked up into small-scale research projects.

- Is there a relationship between lambda scores and the ratings that judges make of texts generated by NSs? If so, is this relationship the same for oral and for written texts?
- Is there a relationship between lambda scores and vocabulary size in L2 learners?
- How much variation is there in the lambda scores generated by a single individual over a short space of time?
- Do lambda scores distinguish reliably between groups at different levels of proficiency?
- Can we use lambda scores to measure increasing levels of proficiency over short time frames?
- Can lambda scores be used to show accommodation between two speakers involved in a conversation?
- Do different genres typically elicit texts with different lambda values?
- Do lambda scores correlate with other measures of lexical richness?

References

Bauer, L. and Nation, I.S.P. (1993) Word families. *International Journal of Lexicography* 6 (4), 253–279.

Ishikawa, S., Uemura, T., Kaneda, M., Shimizu, S., Sugimori, N., Tono, Y., Mochizuki, M. and Murata, M. (2003) *JACET 8000: JACET List of 8000 Basic Words*. Tokyo: Japan Association of College English Teachers.

Laufer, B. (1995) Beyond 2000: A measure of productive lexicon in second language. In L. Eubank and M. Sharwood-Smith (eds) *The Current State of Interlanguage* (pp. 265–272). Amsterdam: John Benjamins.

Laufer, B. and Nation, I.S.P. (1995) Vocabulary size and use: Lexical richness in L2 written production. *Applied Linguistics* 16 (3), 307–322.

Leech, G., Rayson, P. and Wilson, A. (2001) *Word Frequencies in Written and Spoken English*. London: Longman.

Malvern, D. and Richards, B. (1997) A new measure of lexical diversity. In A. Ryan and A. Wray (eds) *Evolving Models of Language* (pp. 58–71). Clevedon: Multilingual Matters.

Meara, P.M. and Bell, H. (2001) P_Lex: A simple and effective way of describing the lexical characteristics of short L2 texts. *Prospect* 16 (3), 5–19.

Miralpeix, I. (2007) Lexical knowledge in instructed language learning: The effects of age and exposure. *International Journal of English Studies* 7 (2), 61–83.

Nation, I.S.P. (1986) *Vocabulary Lists: Words, Affixes and Stems* (revised edn). Wellington, NZ: English Language Institute.

Pang, F. and Skehan, P. (2014) Self-reported planning behaviour and second language performance on narrative retelling. In P. Skehan (ed.) *Processing Perspectives on Task Performance* (pp. 95–127). Amsterdam: John Benjamins.

Qian, J. (2014) Get it right in the end: The effects of post-task transcribing on learners' oral performance. In P. Skehan (ed.) *Processing Perspectives on Task Performance* (pp. 129–154). Amsterdam: John Benjamins.

Read, J. and Nation, I.S.P. (2006) An investigation of the lexical dimension of the IELTS Speaking Test. *IELTS Research Reports* 6.

Skehan, P. (2009a) Lexical performance by native and non-native speakers on language learning tasks. In B. Richards, M. Daller, D. Malvern, P. Meara, J. Milton and J. Treffers-Daller (eds) *Vocabulary Studies in First and Second Language Acquisition* (pp. 107–124). Basingstoke: Palgrave.

Skehan, P. (2009b) Modelling second language performance: Integrating complexity, accuracy, fluency, and lexis. *Applied Linguistics* 30 (4), 510–532.

West, M. (1953) *A General Service List of English Words*. London: Longman.

Suggestions for further reading

Bell, H. (2009) The messy little details: A longitudinal case study of the emerging lexicon. In T. Fitzpatrick and A. Barfield (eds) *Lexical Processing in Second Language Learners* (pp. 111–127). Bristol: Multilingual Matters.

Moreno Espinosa, S. (2005) Can P_Lex accurately measure lexical richness in the written production of young learners of EFL? *Porta Linguarum* 4, 7–21.

Read, J. (2005) Applying lexical statistics to the IELTS speaking test. *Research Notes* 20, 12–16.

Skehan, P. (ed.) (2014) *Processing Perspectives on Task Performance*. Amsterdam: John Benjamins.

4 Lexical Signatures

Introduction

This chapter describes two programs that together make up the Lexical Signatures suite. Part 1 describes V_LexSig and Part 2 is devoted to SigSorter.

Part 1. V_LexSig v1.0

V_LexSig is a small utility program that takes as input two data sources. The first is a set of target words (this list will normally be a short list of 8–12 target words which are of interest to the researcher). The second data source is a text which may contain some of the target words or not. The program returns a binary description of the text in terms of the target word list. So, for example, if your target word list consisted of:

planning   permission   erect   dwelling   building   house   controlled   council   consent   forest

and the text to be analysed is:

The real question, one that nobody seemed to be asking, was what were the bears doing in the wood in the first place? It was obvious that the house in the woods had been built without planning permission. The wood was an officially designated Area of Outstanding Natural Beauty, and all new building in an area of that sort was very carefully controlled. You couldn't just build a house there. My! you couldn't even build a wooden shed there, let alone a whole house. And if you did build a house, then you were supposed to make sure that it conformed with the special guidance on building that the Council had issued only last year. Vernacular architecture. That was the word. And this house was definitely not in the approved vernacular style ...

then V_LexSig will return a string of binary digits that looks like this:

1 1 0 0 1 1 1 1 0 0

This coding tells us that the text contains the words *planning, permission, building, house, controlled* and *council,* but not the other words on the target word list.

The binary coding provides a very compact and economical way of describing texts, and allows us to easily identify the lexical similarities and differences between them.

V_LexSig works with a single text. The companion program, SigSorter, works with collections of lexical signature descriptions generated by V_LexSig, and allows you to perform some simple counts and sorting operations on sets of texts described in this way.

Using V_LexSig

You will find the V_LexSig program on the Lognostics Tools website, available at: http://www.lognostics.co.uk/tools/V_LexSig/V_LexSig.htm.

(1) The V_LexSig workspace screen is shown in Figure 4.1. V_LexSig requires two pieces of data – a short list of words and a text. V_LexSig will work comfortably with short texts generated by L2 speakers, up to about 500 words in length. It will also work in languages other than English.

(2) You may need to do some editorial tidying of the text that you want to work with. For example, you may want to mark some words as lexical phrases, rather than separate words. Use an underscore to do this: e.g. *planning_permission.*

(3) You can type the target wordset directly into the program, or copy and paste it from another source. This list will usually be a list of 8–12 words. Longer lists are possible, but the data they generate will be increasingly hard to make sense of, and for this reason long lists are probably best avoided. You should provide a short name to identify your word list. This identifier will be included in the report that V_LexSig provides.

The short text for analysis should be in .txt format. Copy and paste the text you want to analyse into the larger text box. If you prepare the text using a word processor, you should save it in a plain text format. Next, provide a short identification code for this text in the box marked **name of the text**.

Your text may include some characters that you want to ignore. A list of common punctuation marks is included in the box labelled **ignore these characters**. If your text contains other characters that you want to ignore you can add them to this list.

(4) Click on the **Start** button to process the text. Click on the **Clear** button to reset the workspace.

(5) The V_LexSig report page is shown in Figure 4.2. This report shows that ThreeBears.txt was tested against Target Word List 'TList12'. This list

was made up of 10 words, and ThreeBears.txt included word1, word2, word5, word6, word7 and word8. Word3, word4, word9 and word10 did not appear in this text.

If you are examining a large number of texts, then you should open a text file and keep all the report strings for your texts in this file. Files of this sort can be processed using the **SigSorter** program described in the next section.

(6) Click on the **New text** button to analyse another text.

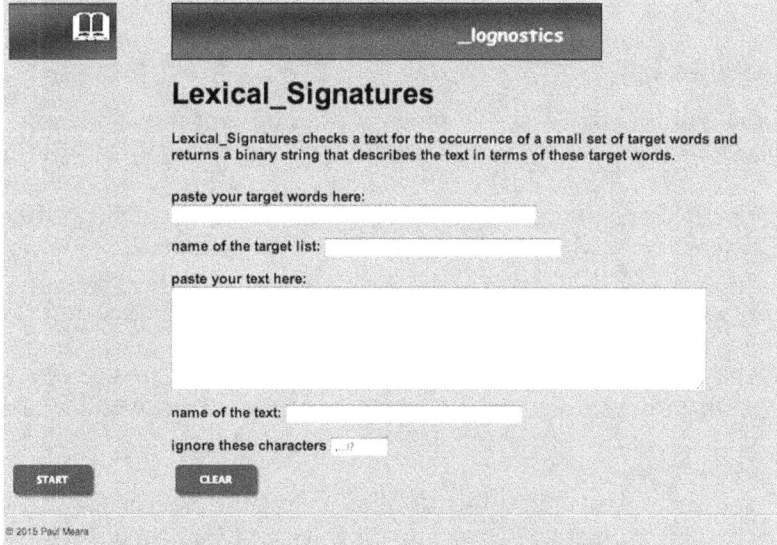

Figure 4.1 V_LexSig workspace

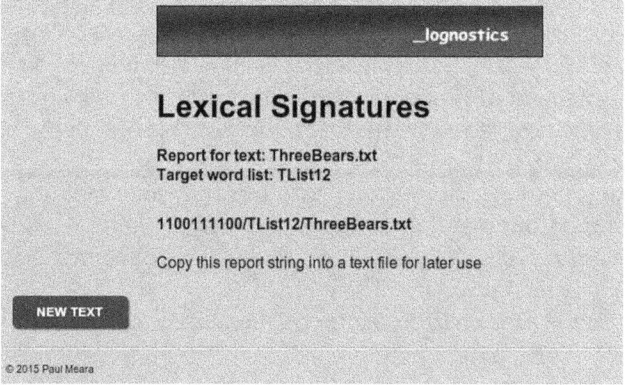

Figure 4.2 V_LexSig report page

Lexical Signatures 69

Part 2. SigSorter

SigSorter is a companion program to V_LexSig. It helps you perform some simple counts and sorting operations on sets of texts described by Lexical Signatures. Therefore, you will need the output produced by V_LexSig as input for SigSorter.

Using SigSorter

You will find the SigSorter program on the Lognostics Tools website, available at: http://www.lognostics.co.uk/tools/V_LexSig/SigSorter.htm.

(1) The SigSorter workspace is shown in Figure 4.3.
(2) Data preparation: SigSorter works with a text file that contains a set of report strings generated by the V_LexSig program described in the previous section. The data should look something like this:

1101111100/TList12/ThreeBears01.txt
1110111100/TList12/ThreeBears02.txt
1100011100/TList12/ThreeBears03.txt
1100011100/TList12/ThreeBears04.txt
1101111100/TList12/ThreeBears05.txt
1100011100/TList12/ThreeBears06.txt
1100111101/TList12/ThreeBears07.txt
1100111111/TList12/ThreeBears08.txt
1100111110/TList12/ThreeBears09.txt
1100111111/TList12/ThreeBears10.txt

Each line consists of a report string comprised of three parts separated by a slash (/). The first part contains a binary description of the relevant text. The second part consists of the name of the Target Word List that was used to generate the report string. The third part is a string which identifies the text that was being assessed. For example, in the list above, we have 10 texts that were all assessed using Target Word List TList12. This list contained 10 target words, so the binary descriptions contain 10 digits.

Normally you will be using report strings that have been prepared using the V_LexSig program, but you can prepare your data by hand if you need to do so.

(3) Enter a name for the dataset that you want to analyse.

Then enter the name of the Target Word List that you used to generate the original data.

Finally, copy and paste your dataset into the large box on the workspace.

(4) Click the **Submit** button to process these data.
(5) The SigSorter report screen is shown in Figure 4.4.

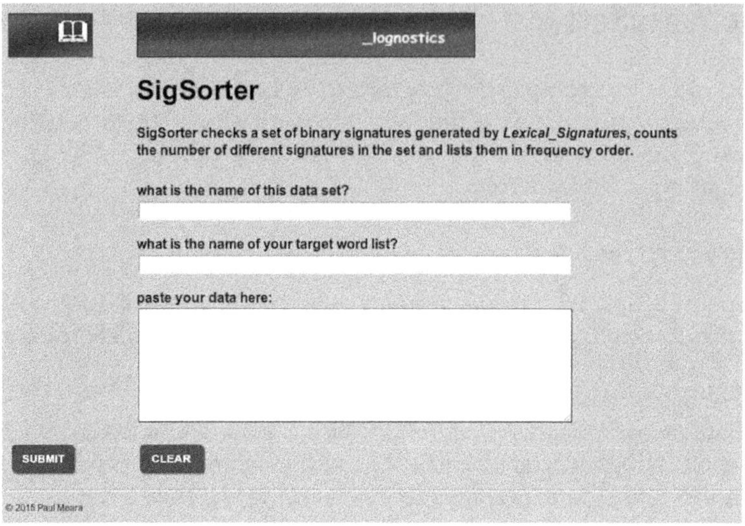

Figure 4.3 SigSorter workspace

This report page tells us that SigSorter has processed a dataset called ***ThreeBears***, and that this file was constructed using Target Word List ***TList12***. The report also tells us that six different signatures were identified in the dataset, and these signatures are listed in order of their frequency in the dataset. In this report, one signature occurred three times, two signatures occurred twice and there were three unique signatures that occurred only once in the dataset.

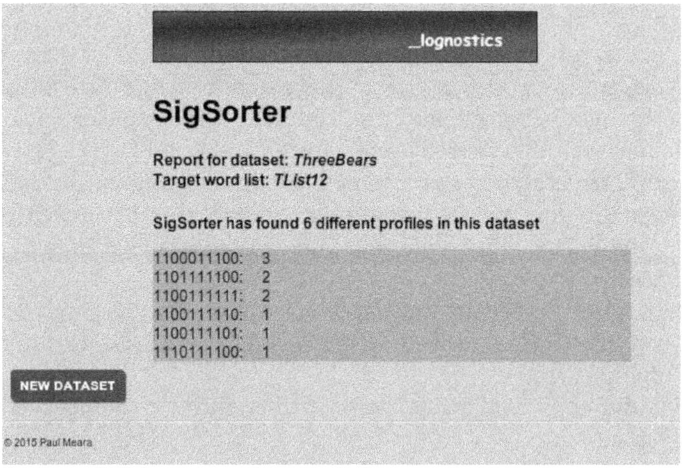

Figure 4.4 SigSorter report page

Copy and paste this signature list to a text file if you want to save it for further analysis.
(6) Click on the **New dataset** button if you want to analyse another set of texts, or if you want to work with a new Target Word List.

The technical bits

The programs described in this chapter are simple cgi scripts that process text files, and they do not have any special requirements or dependencies.

Background Reading

> Meara, P.M., Jacobs, G. and Rodgers, C. (2002) Lexical signatures in foreign language free-form texts. *ITL Review of Applied Linguistics* 135–136, 85–96.
>
> ## Abstract
>
> This paper presents an investigation into the extent to which the lexical choices made by learners of a second language (L2) are distinctive. It follows on from an earlier paper by the same authors in which a neural network was successfully trained to mark a set of texts produced by L2 learners to the same standard, within broad categories, as had been awarded by experienced human markers. For this present paper, we examined a set of L2 texts and searched them for unique lexical choices ('lexical signatures'). The results suggest a possible explanation for the success of the neural-network trial, and may have some practical implications for determining the levels of achievement reached by L2 learners.
>
> ## Introduction
>
> This paper is concerned with the idea of 'lexical signatures'. When we write, whether in a first or second language (L1 or L2), each of us makes lexical choices, and these choices reflect our ability to operate effectively in a language. The choices we make tell readers or listeners about ourselves, and provide them with clues about our language skills. Skilled readers can easily recognise a literary author's particular style, for example, or whether a text is intended for children. Several factors contribute to style, but a very large factor is the author's choice of particular words.
>
> A great deal of work has been carried out looking at the way writers choose words and how their style can be characterised in lexical terms (see, for example, Holmes (1994), for an overview of the question of

authorship attribution). It is normally assumed, however, that this type of analysis can only be applied to very advanced writers – typically novelists or poets. Our interests lie in an area which has not been studied in this way before: the lexical choices that L2 speakers make in ordinary tasks. In particular, this paper is concerned with how far and how easily lexical choices (lexical signatures) can be identified in texts written by L2 learners.

In some of our previous work, we have been struck by the diversity of lexical choice made by L2 learners. For example, in a collection of 77 short letters written as part of a low-level English language examination, we counted a total of 1270 different words, of which only three occurred in all the texts. This was despite the fact that the contents of the letters were very highly constrained by the examination question, which simply asked the writers to confirm arrangements for a visit to a factory. This finding suggests that even at relatively low levels of proficiency, L2 learners are far from uniform in their lexical choices.

The question we are interested in here is how easily we can identify lexical signatures in L2 writers. Obviously, at the most basic level, texts produced by L2 writers differ from one another, and some texts contain words which are not included in other texts. In fact, given any set of free-form texts, it is almost always possible to find some words which occur in only one text. In our examination texts, for example, more than half of the 1270 words in the entire corpus occurred in only one text: obviously, these words uniquely identify a text. In a way, however, this is not a particularly interesting finding. A great deal of work is required to identify these words and, in the final analysis, there is not much to be said about them other than that they are used by only one writer. A more interesting question is whether we can find patterns of lexical choice among words which occur more frequently in a set of texts. These words are much easier to identify, and because they tend to be more common words, they appear to be less serendipitous than the words which occur in only one text.

The work that follows is based on a set of 59 essays in French, produced by non-native-speaking learners of French, undergraduates at a British university. For reasons which will become apparent later, we originally planned to work with 64 texts, but five were lost due to reasons beyond our control, and we were unable to replace these missing texts from our student cohort. The essays were based on a task which requires the students to describe and analyse a picture produced by the Scottish Tourist Board, which had appeared in the French press. The picture shows a framed, sepia-coloured photograph of a young man and a woman holding hands in a remote Scottish glen, while the text, tastefully set against a tartan background, exhorts people to spend their holidays in Scotland and provides details of where to apply for a brochure. This task tends to produce unimaginative responses, which are very similar in content and style.

How can we describe the lexical choices in texts of this sort in an interesting way? The methodology we have developed is basically very simple. First we choose a small set of target words which we then use to describe each text. For example, suppose we decide that we are interested in the words:

page, blanc, couleur, pas, office, comme   **Word List A**

Now, let us suppose that some of these words appear in Text X while others do not. We can now derive a binary part-description of Text X in which words that occur are represented as 1s, while missing words are represented by 0s. In this way, the description of Text X with respect to Word List A might be:

1 1 1 0 0 0

We read this as showing that target words 1–3 occur in the text, while target words 4, 5 and 6 do not.

This notation is very compact, and it allows us to carry out a number of simple comparisons between sets of texts in an efficient way. Specifically, the notation offers us a straightforward method of exploring the idea that L2 writers make unique lexical choices, even in unpromising and undemanding tasks.

Method

The 59 texts produced by the students were first assembled into a single corpus. All the words that appeared in the corpus were listed (a total of 2272 unlemmatised words), and the number of texts containing each word was catalogued. These data are summarised in Figure 1. This figure shows the number of different words occurring in a single text, the number of different words occurring in two of the texts, the number of words occurring in three of the texts, and so on up to the number of words appearing in all 59 texts. Figure 1 clearly indicates that most words occur in a small number of texts, suggesting that there is relatively little lexical overlap between texts.

We can now test the claim that L2 writers tend to make unique lexical choices by taking a set of N words from this list, and checking their occurrence in the texts. How big should N be? Given 59 texts, the

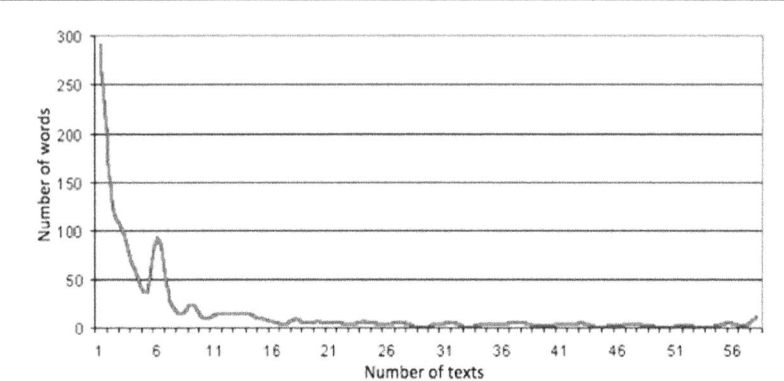

Figure 1 The number of different words appearing in *N* texts

strongest possible test of our conjecture would be to take a set of only six words. Six words gives us $2^6 = 64$ possible patterns of choice: that is, given six words which can either be present in a text or not, there are a total of 64 possible patterns (ranging from 0 0 0 0 0 0 to 1 1 1 1 1 1 in binary notation). Our conjecture that L2 learners tend to produce unique lexical signatures suggests that we ought to find a very large number of the 64 possible combinations among our data.

We tested this idea in the following way. First we selected three sets of 50 words. Set H (= High Frequency) were 50 words that occurred in many of the texts, specifically between 32 and 50 texts; Set M (= Middle Frequency) were 50 words which occurred in about half the texts, specifically between 19 and 29 texts; Set L (= Low Frequency) were 50 words which occurred in only a few texts, specifically between 10 and 13 texts. Fifty words was an arbitrary choice, large enough to produce interesting data but small enough to be manageable. These wordsets are listed in Table 1. It is important to note that most of the words are common French terms. We are not dealing with arcane items here: the few unusual words such as *tartan* and *Nessie* reflect the specific content of the advertisement.

From each set of 50 words, we developed 25 randomly selected subsets, each subset consisting of six words (clearly, there is some overlap between the subsets). This gave us a set of 75 subsets, examples of which are listed in Table 2. Twenty-five of the subsets come from Set H, 25 from Set M and 25 from Set L.

Next, we generated binary descriptions of the texts, in terms of each of the subsets. This gave us a set of 59 binary descriptions for each of the 75 subsets. By way of an example, Table 3 shows the complete data for Set H, Subset 1.

Table 1 Three sets of randomly selected words

Set H: words appearing in a large number of texts
sur réalité nessie charme peut cette plus sont avec aussi se son image homme entre blanc page par ce vous femme très tourisme ensorcelant office guide jaune couleurs mot être paysage printemps comme mais mots elle deux gens tout rattrapera pas photo pays noir dessous réveille tartan bas lettres ils

Set M: words occurring in about half the texts
bon montagnes gratuit partie adresse couleur vacances fond bien petit même centre remplir ou bleu impression aide rouge questions donne chapeau monstre couple nom grande petite haut sa beaucoup vert voit temps lac nous jupe où peu encore phrase si internet ont trouve gauche assez porte but romantique veut

Set L: words occurring in few texts
vêtements petits facile grandes beau trouver ceux nature air lecteur idée fois blanches faut beauté quand choses mystère traditionnel vieux tous grand documentation pense va titre vie sens doit leur peinture traditionnelle côté non plein aider utilisé style quelques écriture tradition livre cela donc lire puis soleil allé quelque je

Table 2 Examples of the six-word target subsets

Target subsets from Wordset H

ils: lettres: par: elle: femme: peut:	noir: office: nessie: sont: page: homme:
se: noir: tourisme: bas: plus: son:	photo: réveille: comme: ensorcelant: femme: rattrapera:
noir: page: printemps: photo: ensorcelant: deux:	page: blanc: couleurs: pas: office: comme:
par: paqe: lettres: dessous: pas: réveille:	qens: charme: lettres: femme: mot: quide:
blanc: photo: son: homme: ce: entre:	très: blanc: mots: dessous: jaune: charme:

Target subsets from Wordset M

petite: couleur: bien: nous: grande: ont:	montagnes: ont: bien: encore: grande: chapeau:
fond: voit: couple: centre: bleu: chapeau:	remplir: gratuit: temps: impression: centre: nous:
couple: questions: sa: chapeau: monstre: gauche	assez: peu: encore: lac: donne: sa:
porte: voit: gauche: temps: jupe: questions:	voit: peu: chapeau: vert: grande: porte:
ou: où: monstre: couleur: rouge: chapeau:	veut: haut: bleu: si: couple: bon:

Target subsets from Wordset L

leur: choses: livre: beauté: quand: idée:	mystère: fois: choses: tradition: doit: je:
tradition: pense: soleil: tous: documentation: quand:	idée: côté: quelques: cela: documentation: donc:
donc: blanches: vieux: puis: traditionnel: peinture:	pense: mystère: cela: plein: écriture: va:
quand: traditionnelle: je: doit: beauté: air:	grand: petits: non: utilisé: style: donc:
doit: leur: beau: vie: traditionnelle: ceux:	traditionnelle: pense: sens: idée: plein: aider:

We can now ask two questions of these data:

(1) How many distinct data patterns (distinct signatures) can be found?
(2) How many of these distinct signatures are unique?

76 Part 2: Measuring Lexical Variation, Sophistication and Originality

A distinct signature is one which is different from all the other signatures in at least one place. Not all distinct signatures are unique: a small number of the signatures are produced by more than one writer.

The answers to the above questions for the data in Table 3 turned out to be 32 distinct patterns, of which 21 are unique. But, clearly, a better overall picture can be obtained by averaging out the figures for a large number of different subsets. We therefore repeated this type of analysis for each of the 25 subsets from Set H, Set M and Set L, making a total of 75 separate analyses. This process is summarised in Table 4, while Table 5 summarises the outcome.

What do these results show us? At the most superficial level, the data show that there is some degree of variation among the texts as described by the lexical subsets. On average, for Set H and for Set L, approximately one-third of the 64 possible binary combinations are actually used up, while for Set M the figure rises to half of the possible binary combinations. For Set H, 80% of the combinations that are used

Table 3 Binary descriptions of 59 texts: Subset H1

0 0 0 0 1 1 \text01	0 1 1 1 0 1 \text21	1 0 1 1 1 1 \text41
0 0 1 0 0 0 \text02	0 1 1 1 1 0 \text22	1 0 1 1 1 1 \text42
0 0 1 0 0 1 \text03	0 1 1 1 1 1 \text23	1 0 1 1 1 1 \text43
0 0 1 0 1 0 \text04	0 1 1 1 1 1 \text24	1 1 0 0 1 0 \text44
0 0 1 1 0 0 \text05	0 1 1 1 1 1 \text25	1 1 0 0 1 1 \text45
0 0 1 1 0 1 \text06	0 1 1 1 1 1 \text26	1 1 0 1 1 1 \text46
0 0 1 1 0 1 \text07	0 1 1 1 1 1 \text27	1 1 0 1 1 1 \text47
0 0 1 1 1 1 \text08	1 0 0 0 0 1 \text28	1 1 1 0 1 1 \text48
0 0 1 1 1 1 \text09	1 0 0 0 0 1 \text29	1 1 1 0 1 0 \text49
0 0 1 1 1 1 \text10	1 0 0 1 0 1 \text30	1 1 1 0 1 0 \text50
0 0 1 1 1 1 \text11	1 0 0 1 1 1 \text31	1 1 1 0 1 0 \text51
0 1 0 0 0 1 \text12	1 0 1 0 0 1 \text32	1 1 1 0 1 0 \text52
0 1 0 0 1 1 \text13	1 0 1 0 0 1 \text33	1 1 1 1 0 1 \text53
0 1 0 1 0 1 \text14	1 0 1 0 1 1 \text34	1 1 1 0 1 1 \text54
0 1 0 1 1 1 \text15	1 0 1 0 1 1 \text35	1 1 1 1 1 1 \text55
0 1 0 1 1 1 \text16	1 0 1 1 0 0 \text36	1 1 1 1 1 1 \text56
0 1 0 1 1 1 \text17	1 0 1 1 0 1 \text37	1 1 1 1 1 1 \text57
0 1 0 1 1 1 \text18	1 0 1 1 1 0 \text38	1 1 1 1 1 1 \text58
0 1 1 0 1 1 \text19	1 0 1 1 1 1 \text39	1 1 1 1 1 1 \text59
0 1 1 0 1 1 \text20	1 0 1 1 1 1 \text40	

Table 4 Summary of the data collection and analysis

Assemble a small corpus of texts and enumerate the words in the corpus
Select 50 words occurring in most texts (Set H)
Select 50 words occurring in about half the texts (Set M)
Select 50 words occurring in few of the texts (Set L)
Generate 25 subsets of six words from Set H
Generate 25 subsets of six words from Set M
Generate 25 subsets of six words from Set L
Generate 75 binary descriptions of the texts, one for each subset
Calculate the number of different binary descriptions generated by each subset
Calculate the number of unique binary descriptions generated by each subset

Table 5 Mean distinct and mean unique signatures (59 texts, subset size = 6)

	Distinct signatures	Unique signatures	Ratio of unique to distinct signatures
Set H	20.88	16.88	80.8
Set M	35.60	21.24	59.7
Set L	21.20	10.72	50.6

are indeed unique. For Sets M and L, the figures are lower – 59% and 50% of the patterns we find are unique.

These average figures actually mask a great deal of variation, and this is summarised in Table 6, which shows the best and the worst figures produced by each lexical subset at each of the frequency levels.

It can be seen from Table 6 that, even under exacting conditions (sets of only six words), a surprisingly large number of unique signatures can be identified. This suggests that if we relaxed our constraints it might be possible to improve the number of unique signatures we find. In order to test this idea, we ran a new set of analyses, in which we used subsets of seven, eight, nine and 10 words (2^7 allows for 128 distinct binary

Table 6 Performance of the best and worst subsets (59 texts, subset size = 6)

		Set H	Set M	Set L
No. different signatures	Best:	34	41	25
	Worst:	29	32	18
No. unique signatures	Best:	21	29	18
	Worst:	13	16	4

Table 7 Mean distinct and mean unique signatures for varying size subsets

No. distinct signatures

Subset size	6	7	8	9	10
Set H	20.88	28.88	41.76	45.80	48.88
Set M	35.60	43.56	49.72	54.40	55.12
Set L	21.20	26.20	31.04	36.32	39.68

No. unique signatures

Subset size	6	7	8	9	10
Set H	16.88	23.84	32.28	37.84	42.00
Set M	21.24	31.80	42.28	50.48	51.80
Set L	10.72	15.64	20.48	26.68	30.40

Best performance at identifying unique signatures

Subset size	6	7	8	9	10
Set H	21	35	39	48	57
Set M	29	41	51	7	57
Set L	18	23	29	32	40

patterns, 2^8 for 256 patterns, 2^9 for 512 patterns, and 2^{10} for 1024 patterns). The results are summarised in Table 7.

These data suggest that in some circumstances it is very nearly possible to select a set of 10 commonly occurring words that will uniquely identify a text. At this level, for Sets H and M, the best subsets uniquely identify more than 90% of our cases. Some good subsets occur with smaller subsets from these sets. We suspect that a genetic algorithm approach might allow us to identify these very good discriminators with ease. Set L seems to be a less good source of target words, although even here the worst subset managed to identify 35 distinct signatures, of which 28 – almost 80% – were unique.

Discussion

The analyses reported here arose from a discussion of some of our earlier work in which we suggested that lexical signatures might be used together with neural networks in order to evaluate the writing of non-native speakers (Meara *et al.*, 2000). In that work, we used subsets of 10 words, and found that we could almost always train a network to recognise the distinct signatures and assign them an appropriate mark. With hindsight, this result is not as astonishing as we thought it was. We suggested at the time that it was surprising to achieve this degree of reliability with the very small amount of information from the texts we were evaluating. However, one of our colleagues suggested that 2^{10} was such a large amount of information that our binary descriptions were in reality much richer than we thought. The analysis reported here seems to bear out this judgement. It may be that the neural network we used for that work was, above all, identifying levels of lexical uniqueness, and that this uniqueness correlated well with the subjective evaluative impressions of the human markers. That, in itself, in no way negates the interest or potential of the results, but they do need further investigation.

In the meantime, we think we may have stumbled across a rather important finding, which may have implications in areas other than the one for which our work was intended. Presumably, very low-level learners do not show the degree of variation we have reported here, if only for the reason that their L2 vocabulary is more limited. This raises the question of whether unique lexical signatures could be used as a way of measuring progress in the learning of a second language. It seems plausible that less proficient learners, whose lexicons are limited in size, would tend to make similar lexical choices, and their lexical signatures would tend, therefore, not to be unique. On the other hand, learners with a good grasp of their second language, and a more extensive vocabulary, would be more likely to produce unique signatures. This suggests that it ought to be possible to compute a uniqueness index for learners, by calculating the number of times a small randomised lexical sample of their output matches samples found in a criterion group. We believe that this idea might provide an alternative approach to the problem of how written texts produced by non-native speakers could be evaluated in online settings.

References

Holmes, D.I. (1994) Authorship attribution. *Computers and the Humanities* 28 (2), 87–106.

Meara, P.M., Rodgers, C. and Jacobs, G. (2000) Computational assessment of texts written by L2 speakers. *System* 28 (3), 345–354.

Reflections on Meara *et al.* (2002)

This paper picks up a theme which will be discussed in more detail in the next chapter (V_Unique). At the time we wrote this paper, we were just beginning to get interested in the idea of how we might measure productive vocabulary. Although most researchers were avidly pursuing measures based on type/token counts, our feeling was that measures of this sort were not really sensitive enough to be used as a proxy measure for productive vocabulary size. Instead we started to look for other properties that might characterise texts generated by a large vocabulary.

Our first idea was that we would expect texts generated by beginners to be very similar to one another, whereas texts generated by more advanced learners ought to be more varied. This idea sounds very simple, but in practice it turned out to be quite a difficult idea to work with. One of the reasons for this is that 'difference' is not an intrinsic property of a text. You can only measure how 'different' a text is by comparing it with other texts. However, there were no established methods for comparing the lexical contents of texts. It would have been possible to draw up a list of all the words contained in a set of texts, and to identify words which occurred in only one or two of them (the V_Lists program described in Chapter 1 would allow you to do this in a fairly straight-forward way). We might then have compared these lists of words, although it is not immediately obvious what comparisons you would want to make with data of this sort. Perhaps more advanced learners would generate more words not used by other people? They do, but the more texts you use for comparison, fewer words turn out to be genuinely unique, so this obvious measure turns out to be highly dependent on the size of the group, and not very stable anyway. In any case, it was not obvious how we could make a link between specific word choices and overall productive vocabulary size. For example, suppose we have a task where L2 speakers are describing a man fishing in a river: one writer says he is fishing for *trout* while another says he is fishing for *salmon*, and no other writer uses these words. It is not immediately obvious that rare word choices of this sort actually tell us very much about the writers' vocabulary.

We made a number of small-scale studies of L2 writers which suggested that even at intermediate levels it was very unusual for L2 writers to choose the same words as every other writer in a group. This paper was a first attempt at formalising this idea. The counterintuitive idea that the non-occurrence of a word in a text might be as important as the occurrence of a word in a text arose from a conversation with David Malvern. Malvern pointed out that even short binary descriptions carried huge amounts of information. He suggested that it might make sense to view a set of texts as objects located in a multidimensional space defined by the presence or absence of a small number of words, and he further suggested that descriptions of this sort really need to be as short and as economical as possible. Lexical Signatures was designed to allow us to investigate some of the questions that Malvern's suggestions hinted at.

In the event, we found that the really interesting words in a set of texts were not the words which were only used by one or two people – these occurred so rarely in the text set that they provided very little information. Similarly, words which were used by almost everybody also failed to discriminate between texts, and so these words were also not interesting. However, words which occurred in about half of our text set **were** interesting. These words tended to be not very unusual words but relatively high-frequency words, often words in the 1K frequency band. These were words that you would definitely expect even low-level students to know, and yet there was considerable variation in the way these words occurred (or not) in texts. It turned out that very small sets of these middle-frequency words produced a very large number of unique signatures in the groups we tested, and that for a group of around 64 writers, almost all the writers produced a unique signature when we tested as few as 10 words.

This was not quite what we had expected: if everyone is producing different lexical signatures, then it is unlikely that we would be able to assess their writing simply by looking at these many different signatures. However, we thought that it might be possible to do a more sophisticated analysis using neural network analysis of the signatures. Some preliminary (and only partially successful) work of this sort was described in Meara *et al.* (2000). More recently, however, we have become interested in a different approach, one that was hinted at in the 2002 paper, but not developed at the time.

This new approach is based on the idea that lexical signatures, although varied, are not entirely random. We might expect to find that a cluster of high-level L2 texts might have signatures which were different from the signatures which are characteristically found in weaker L2 texts. The way we spot these characteristic differences is to classify two sets of texts and find a binary signature which maximises the difference between the two groups. We do this using a *genetic algorithm* approach. The methodology for doing this will not be familiar to most readers, so we explain it here in detail.

Suppose that we have two sets of L2 texts. We compute a lexical signature for each text, based on a small set of words that occur in about half the texts. Let us say that these signatures consist of a sequence of 10 binary digits. The texts will have been classified beforehand – let us say that half of them score less than 60% in some examination scheme, while the other half score higher than 60% in this scheme. Call the first set Set A and the second set Set B.

Next, we select a small number of random binary signatures – we can usually work with 10 of these. Then we score each of the texts against each of the random signatures. The easiest way to do this is to score 1 point for each binary digit in the text signature that corresponds to the equivalent digit in the random signature. For example, if the first random signature was 1111000010, and the signature generated from Text A is 0011001111, then the random signature would score five points. We then add up the scores collected across all the texts in Set A and across all the texts in Set B, and compute the difference for the two sets. Doing this for each random signature in turn allows us to rank the signatures in terms of how effective they are at distinguishing between the two text sets and we can use these difference scores to rank the random signatures in order. Some of the signatures will probably work moderately well, others less so.

The next step is to keep the best random signatures and reject the others. So let us say that we keep the top two random signatures. The eight rejected signatures are replaced by copies of the two best ones, but in each of these new signatures one digit is flipped from a 1 to a 0 or a 0 to a 1. Thus, if the highest scoring random signature is 1111000010, we would get a series of slightly modified signatures, say 0111000010, 1011000010, 111110010 and 1111000011. These new signatures are then used to evaluate the texts again, and a new set of improved signatures is used to evaluate the texts.

This process is repeated a number of times. Each time, the best random signature will be slightly better than the previous best signature. Eventually a signature emerges which maximises the difference between the two groups.

The question which then arises is whether the best signature can discriminate between new texts that were not included in the original dataset. As far as we can see, the answer to this question is usually yes, although we have not done this work with large datasets yet.

More Research is Needed ...

This section contains some ideas that could easily be worked up into small-scale research projects.

- How many binary different signatures – each eight words long – would we expect to find in a set of 64 texts?
- What are the characteristics of lexical signatures that do not appear in a text set?
- Do spoken texts produce more variant signatures or fewer than written texts?
- What is the minimum length of text that is necessary to generate interesting signatures?
- Is there a way to characterise some lexical signatures as 'good' and others as 'bad'?
- Is a proficient L2 writer more likely to produce a unique signature than a lower level learner?
- If you ask an L2 writer to do a task twice, will they generate the same lexical signature?
- If an L2 writer generates a unique signature in one text, what is the likelihood that they will also generate a unique signature in a second text?
- Are L2 writers with large receptive vocabularies more likely to generate unique signatures than writers with smaller receptive vocabularies?
- Do examiners rate texts that contain unique lexical signatures more highly than texts that do not?
- The discussion of lexical signatures in this chapter has all been in terms of L2 writers. Can you think of other groups that might be distinguished by their lexical signatures?

References

Meara, P.M., Rodgers, C. and Jacobs, G. (2000) Computational assessment of texts written by L2 speakers. *System* 28 (3), 345–354.

Meara, P.M., Jacobs, G. and Rodgers, C. (2002) Lexical signatures in foreign language free-form texts. *ITL Review of Applied Linguistics* 135–136, 85–96.

Suggestions for further reading

Farringdon, J.M., Morton, A.Q., Farringdon, M.G. and Baker, M.D. (1996) *Analysing for Authorship: A Guide to the Cusum Technique*. Cardiff: University of Wales Press.

Foster, D. (2000) *Author Unknown: On the Trail of Anonymous*. London: Macmillan.

Michaelson, S., Morton, A.Q. and Hamilton-Smith, N. (1979) Fingerprinting the mind. *Endeavour* 3 (4), 171–175.

Pennebaker, J.W. (2011) *The Secret Life of Pronouns: What our Words Say About us*. London: Bloomsbury.

5 V_Unique v1.0

Introduction

V_Unique was conceived as a minimal vocabulary test to assess lexical originality. It was created as a way to collect words quickly and efficiently from test takers and to compare these words to those already provided by other users in the same test. Until now, to our knowledge, the only way in which lexical originality has been studied is in learners' compositions, e.g. by determining the number of words that are unique to a text written by one learner of a group and are not present in any of the other texts by other students in the same group. Apart from some studies using this embedded measure (and the Lexical Signatures approach presented in the previous chapter) there has been scant research on uniqueness or originality (see Tzima & Miralpeix, 2015, this chapter). V_Unique can thus be useful both for learners and researchers to explore and better understand lexical originality.

Using V_Unique

You will find V_Unique on the Lognostics Tools website, available at: http://www.lognostics.co.uk/tools/V_Unique/V_Unique.htm

(1) V_Unique workspace looks like Figure 5.1.
(2) The 'about you' section asks you to provide an ID code and some further information about yourself. The ID code can be any combination of letters and numbers.
(3) The program asks you to provide 10 words that best describe the person that appears in the picture on the right of the screen.
(4) When you have finished providing all the words, you will be able to compare your words with those provided by 100 native speakers (**Test1** button), 100 upper-intermediate/advanced learners (**Test2** button) or all the other people who have taken the test so far (**Explore** button).
(5) V_Unique generates a report that looks like Figure 5.2.

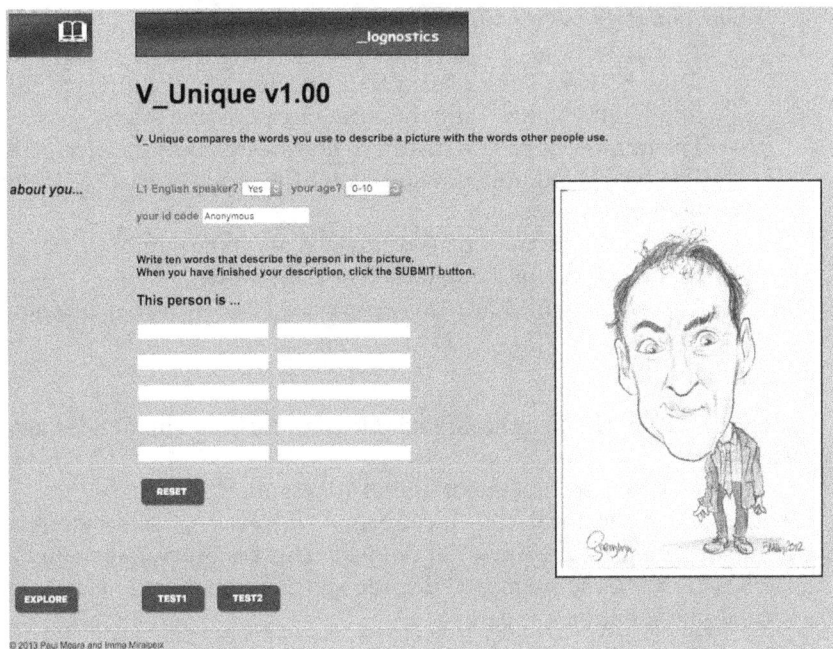

Figure 5.1 V_Unique workspace

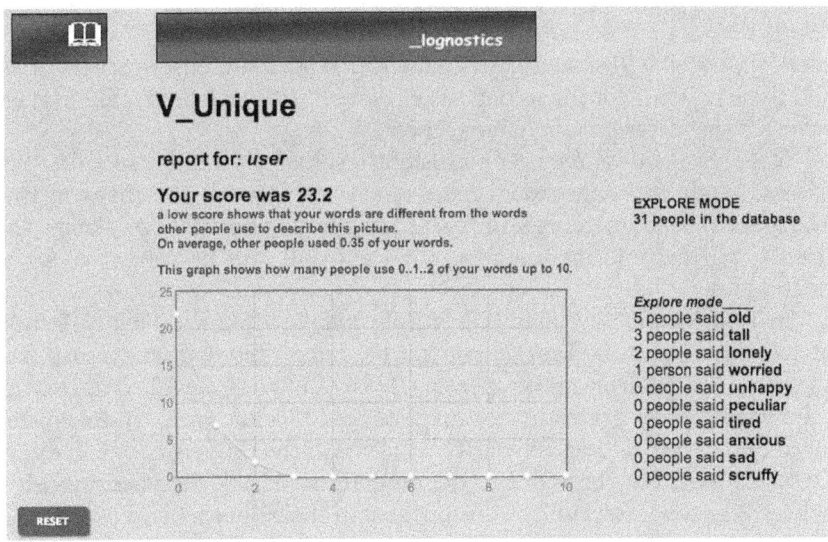

Figure 5.2 V_Unique report page

(6) The report gives you different kinds of information:
- Your score: the Technical Bits section (see below) explains in detail how the score is calculated, and lists some cautions to bear in mind if you are using these data in a research study.
- The number of people that have previously taken the test.
- The average number of words you have provided that were also used by other people.
- A list of the words you have provided, with the number of people that have previously used each of these words.
- A graph showing how many people use 0, 1, 2 ... of your 10 words.

The technical bits

V_Unique scores the data that are submitted to the program in the following way:

Each dataset consists of a maximum of 10 responses.

In **Explore Mode**, the dataset is compared with every other dataset that has been submitted to V_Unique. V_Unique computes the average number of matches between the submitted dataset and the stored datasets. So, for example, if you submit these data:

tall, dark, handsome, clever, wise, thoughtful, earnest, old, trustworthy, kind

and the stored data consist of the two datasets:

tall, old, sad, lonely, anxious, unhappy, worried, tired, scruffy, peculiar
sad, old, kind, badly-dressed, old-fashioned, bald, untidy, weird, scary, clever

then V_Unique will score two matches for the first stored dataset (*tall, old*) and three matches for the second stored dataset (*old, kind, clever*). The average score for this dataset is therefore $(2 + 3)/2 = 2.5$.

Note that you will *not* get consistent results for a dataset submitted in Explore Mode. Since the stored dataset keeps on growing and changing, the average number of matches will change. As the stored dataset gets larger, the results will become more stable, but they will still be subject to some fluctuation.

In **Test Mode**, the submitted data are compared with a stable collection of 100 other datasets. **Test1** compares the submitted dataset against data generated by 100 adult native speakers (NSs) of English. **Test2** compares the submitted dataset against data generated by 100 adult upper-intermediate/ advanced learners of English, mostly students at the University of Barcelona. Other datasets may be added to the program as reliable data become available. Any new datasets will be documented in the online manual. You should use V_Unique in Test Mode if you are collecting data for experimental purposes.

Broadly speaking, we find that the degree of overlap between datasets is surprisingly small. It is rare to find two people submitting exactly the same dataset, and it is very rare to find a test taker who submits a dataset consisting of 10 words that no-one has used before. In practice, we find that most people generate datasets that have between two and four shared words with other datasets in the program, and that the scores tend to cluster around the lower end of this range. This range is rather small, and for this reason the scores that V_Unique reports are actually a logarithmic transformation of the raw scores, which stretches the data out over a 100-point scale, and gives more weighting to low scores.

The formula used for this transformation is:

$$\text{Score} = 100 * \log(M + 1)$$

where M is the raw mean score.

Table 5.1 shows how this formula converts raw scores into reported scores. Raw scores above nine are in theory possible, but can be discounted in practice.

Note that a low score shows that your words are different from the words other people use to describe the picture, whereas a high score indicates that your words are similar to those used by other people.

Note also that if you are working with group data, then you should *not* take an average of these reported scores. The reason for this is that $(\log(x) + \log(y))/2$ is not the same as $\log((x + y)/2)$. So,

$$(\log(2) + \log(6))/2 - 0.539$$

while

$$\log((2 + 6)/2) = 0.602$$

If you need to compute average scores, then you will need to 'unwrap' the reported scores, using the formula:

$$\text{Score} = (10^R) - 1$$

where R is the reported score. You can then compute a proper average score for the group, and apply the logarithmic transformation to this new average if you need to. In practice, it is probably safer to avoid this procedure, and to use a non-parametric statistic instead.

Table 5.1 Example of raw scores converted into reported scores

Raw score	0	1	2	3	4	5	6	7	8	9
Reported score	0	30.1	47.7	60.2	69.9	77.8	84.5	90.3	95.4	100

Background Reading

> **Tzima, F.E. and Miralpeix, I. (2015) Lexical originality: Towards new forms of assessment. Adapted from Unpublished MA thesis, 2013. University of Barcelona.**
>
> ## Introduction
>
> The purpose of this research is to present a rationale for assessing Lexical Originality in a different way from that which has been used until now. The study also puts forward a proposal on how this assessment could be implemented and presents some preliminary results that help to determine the viability of the proposal, which can also be taken as a point of departure for further research on the topic.
>
> After providing a theoretical framework focusing mainly on lexical sophistication (LS) and originality (LO), this paper presents a study conducted with data elicited from two groups of participants: 100 Catalan/Spanish learners of English as a foreign language (NNSs) and 100 native English speakers (NSs), who were asked to describe a picture with 10 adjectives. After exploring the data that this picture elicited, two different originality indexes were computed (O1 and O2), which allowed us to shed some light on issues that had not been examined in previous literature.
>
> ## Literature review
>
> ### What are lexical sophistication (LS) and lexical originality (LO)?
>
> According to Laufer (1991) and Laufer and Nation (1995: 309), lexical sophistication (LS) is 'the percentage of "advanced" words in the text' and it refers to the proportion of rare or difficult words that a learner uses in a text sample. Lu (2012), among others, states that it is one of the three components of lexical richness – the other two being lexical density (LD), which is the ratio of lexical words in a text, and lexical variation (LV), the number of different words as opposed to the total number of words that a learner uses.
>
> Lexical originality (LO) has been defined as 'the percentage of lexemes used by one writer and none of the other writers in the group' (Laufer, 1991: 442). Linnarud (1986) referred to it as 'lexical individuality' (LI). Therefore, LO is different from LS because in the former what matters is the number of words unique to a learner compared to the group s/he belongs to. In LS, the words in a text are usually judged against general vocabulary frequency lists: the more infrequent the words a learner uses are, the more 'advanced' or 'sophisticated' the vocabulary of this particular learner is. In the case of originality, the more words a learner uses that

no other people from the group have used, the more original his/her vocabulary is.

While there is a wide agreement on most of the measures to assess lexical variation and density, there is a lack of consensus on measuring how 'advanced' or 'original' vocabulary is. The lack of agreement may have to do with the fact that variation and density are intrinsic measures, while originality and sophistication are extrinsic measures (Meara & Bell, 2001). Intrinsic measures, such as the type/token ratio (TTR) and D (Malvern et al., 2004), take into account only the vocabulary present in the learner's text itself. In contrast, extrinsic measures assess the learner's vocabulary taking into consideration aspects external to the text (e.g. how frequent the words in the text are in standard frequency lists). Therefore, extrinsic measures may vary from study to study depending on the criteria adopted by researchers in each case.

How have LS and LO been assessed?

In this section, we aim at showing how LS and LO have been measured in previous research. Apart from reviewing pertinent literature, our purpose is also to make evident that the differences between LS and LO can actually be quite subtle and may blur in some cases. Table 1 offers a summary of the literature that is relevant for the present study: the left column shows whether we are dealing with LS or LO; the middle column presents the different measures; and the right column provides examples of studies using this form of assessment.

The first point to highlight from the studies in Table 1 is that just three of them measure LO (Laufer, 1991; Linnarud, 1986; Meara et al., 2002). Two of them – Linnarud (1986) and Laufer (1991) – measure LO in data that are also analysed with other measures, such as those of LS. Linnarud (1986) assessed the LS and LO of Swedish learners of English and English NSs and found that the native group scored higher in both. In this study, the words defined as sophisticated were the ones presented from Grade 9 onwards in the Swedish school. Regarding LO, it was concluded that 'the lexis of the native speaker is much more original than that of the non-native' (Linnarud, 1986: 53).

Laufer (1991) analysed whether implicit teaching of vocabulary leads to significant lexical growth and if the proficiency level of the learner plays a role in this process. To accomplish this aim, she assessed the compositions of two groups of university students, one group after the first semester and the other at the end of the second semester, and compared the results to the first composition they all had written at the beginning of the course. Throughout the year, the participants were provided with new vocabulary implicitly, either through the teachers' lectures or by homework that included reading. Students were assessed on

Table 1 Summary of the studies and measures on LS and/or LO

What is measured	How it is measured	Examples of studies
LS	Guiraud Advanced Daller et al. (2003)	Tidball and Treffers-Daller (2007) Daller and Xue (2007)
	Vocabulary Profile Laufer and Nation (1995)	Muncie (2002) Morris and Cobb (2003) East (2006) Miralpeix (2007)
	Lambdas (P_Lex) Meara and Bell (2001)	Moreno Espinosa (2005) Miralpeix (2007) Skehan (2009)
	Various frequency lists	Linnarud (1986)* Harley and King (1989) Laufer (1991)* Lu (2012)
	Teachers' judgements	Bardel et al. (2012)
LO	Lexical Signatures Meara et al. (2000)	Meara et al. (2002)

Notes: *Also measured LO.

the basis of frequency lists. Since the study dealt with university learners, the list that was used in order to judge a word as advanced or not was an existing list of academic words that was created by considering the vocabulary used in university textbooks. Then, the formula used to calculate the percentage of LS was the number of advanced lexemes multiplied by 100% and divided by the total number of lexical words. The study also analysed the texts produced by each participant for LO, LV and LD: LO behaved similarly to LV and LD. Results also showed that the students whose vocabulary was already advanced did not show remarkable improvement.

Linnarud (1986) calculates LO as the number of lexical words unique to the writer divided into the total number of lexical words in the composition and multiplied by 100; Laufer (1991) uses as the denominator of the formula the total number of tokens. Therefore, the two studies analyse the LO of a text with similar formulae. However, Meara et al. (2002) use a different approach to LO (already presented in Meara et al., 2000): they aim at identifying a number of words that occur in a group of texts and train a neural network (NN) to analyse individual texts in terms of the presence/non-presence of these words. It was found that a few wordsets are good at discriminating between texts in a large number of cases and they proceed to study unique lexical choices (lexical signatures) made by L2 writers. It was observed that networks identified levels of lexical uniqueness that correlated with the subjective evaluation of human markers.

To our knowledge, there are no other studies dealing specifically with LO. The other studies in Table 1 are concerned with LS and they measure it mainly in five different ways, which we summarise in the following paragraphs. A first group of studies assessed how 'advanced' or 'sophisticated' lexis is by introducing a modification to a LV measure such as Guiraud index (i.e. number of types divided into the square root of the tokens: types/√tokens). Therefore, Daller *et al.* (2003) propose the 'Guiraud Advanced Index' (GA): the new formula of GA considers only the 'advanced' types (advanced types/√tokens) and they take as 'advanced' those words not found in high-frequency lists, which results in a more qualitative estimation. Another study that explores GA is by Daller and Xue (2007), who investigate the oral proficiency of Chinese learners of English – one group studying in China and the other in the UK. Their findings suggest that GA discriminates between groups, which is consistent with previous studies. The authors emphasise the fact that it is of great importance that the lists used for the assessment are appropriate for the context to be tested. Similarly, it is also acknowledged that the word lists used were not ideal for their study, since they were not compiled from oral speech samples. The measure has also been tested in French by Tidball and Treffers-Daller (2007).

The second group of studies include those using the Lexical Frequency Profile (LFP; Laufer & Nation, 1995). Profiles had been used for some time in the 1990s, but they became more popular later on, as they could be automatically computed with the help of programs that work with predetermined lists of words, based on frequency criteria (e.g. Morris & Cobb, 2003; Muncie, 2002). Researchers' opinions on the LFP vary: East (2006) points out that it may be providing a measure of sophistication but not necessarily of accuracy; Daller *et al.* (2003) emphasise the fact that it cannot be used to assess languages that do not have reliable word lists; and Bardel *et al.* (2012) argue that its weakness may lie in the fact that it does not deal with cognates and thematic words appropriately.

As the LFP is 'much less reliable and much less sensitive than Laufer and Nation claim' (Meara & Bell, 2001: 8), Meara and Bell (2001) proposed a new extrinsic measure – Lambda – which is presented as a more reliable measure of sophistication. A third group of studies on LS use Lambdas to describe how often infrequent words are used in texts. Daller *et al.* (2003) highlight that P_Lex, the program used to analyse texts in these terms, can only work for languages with standard lists (similarly to what happens with the LFP), which can be a limitation. However, the fact that sophistication can be expressed with a single value is considered an advantage, as opposed to the four figures a profile entails. Different studies have used P_Lex to evaluate the LS of learners' productions, e.g. Moreno Espinosa (2005), Miralpeix (2007) and Skehan (2009).

The fourth group of studies presented in Table 1 is formed by works that have used different frequency lists from those of Nation or that have focused on some word categories in these lists. For instance, Lu (2012) provides five different formulae to measure LS and relies on a predetermined list (BNC word list; Leech *et al.*, 2001). One of these formulae is Verb Sophistication-I, which concentrates on the verbs used by the learners, and it is found by dividing the number of sophisticated verbs in a text by the total number of verbs. This focus on verbs involves a more specific distinction and Harley and King (1989) have used it to compare native to non-natives students of French. Nevertheless, in their evaluation of lexical measures, Wolfe-Quintero *et al.* (1998) question the verb sophistication formula used in Harley and King (1989) and suggest finding others that are not affected by text size.

Finally, Bardel *et al.* (2012) use teachers' judgements to re-evaluate the lexis in French and Italian elicited from Swedish L1 learners in a previous study by Lindqvist *et al.* (2011). The initial study judged the vocabulary used by these learners according to the frequency lists of the Lexical Oral Production Profiler (Lindqvist *et al.*, 2011), which were compiled from learner language and NSs' language samples. However, thematic words and cognates that were originally regarded as difficult and infrequent words turned out to be considered basic and easy by the teachers in the study. Consequently, vocabulary was reclassified, the measurement improved and more transparent results were obtained. The number of low-frequency words was reduced after the teachers' re-evaluation of words' difficulty levels and this new classification also resulted in a clearer discrimination of the groups of learners that were tested in previous studies. Authors claim that teachers' judgements appear to be 'a good tool to determine basic and advanced vocabulary in L2' (Bardel *et al.*, 2012: 287).

At this point, we think that we already have enough information to introduce several reflections. First of all, it has usually been assumed that LS was more reliable than LO, because LS assesses learners independently of other people's profiles and according to predetermined standard lists that are fixed. When it comes to LO, the individual's vocabulary is assessed depending on the profiles other people have and, consequently, this results in an unstable and constantly changing picture of one's vocabulary. That is, LO does not actually depend on each individual learner, but on the group of individuals s/he is compared to.

Nevertheless, in light of the studies presented in this section, it seems that the 'predetermined standard lists' usually need to be adapted to properly assess LS. What is more, they do not usually work well without adaptation and they can also change from study to study. In addition, scores also seem to be more reliable when they are not independent from other people's profiles, or when teachers' judgements on word difficulty are taken into consideration (as in Bardel et al., 2012). Results then tend to be more valid – e.g. more homogeneous within groups at the same proficiency level. Thus, we often assess LS taking into account a group, which is a typical feature of LO (see Table 2).

Table 2 What we mean by 'sophistication' and 'originality'

Concept	What does it mean?	According to what?
LS	'Infrequent'	In general frequency lists from corpora (e.g. BNC, etc.)
	'Infrequent'	In adapted lists • Sometimes adapted/devised having a group in mind (e.g. easy or difficult for learners)
LO	'Infrequent', 'unique'	In relation to what the group you belong to does, often in the same task (e.g. composition)

Note: ---- 'Closely related, not always clear differences'.

Even in the case of using adapted lists, general frequency judgements are not free of criticism: Aizawa et al. (2001) do not directly measure LS or LO but test intermediate-level Japanese learners' of English ability by making judgements of word frequency and comparing it to English NSs'. Results indicated that judgements by natives were not similar to the standard list order and that the ratings of both groups showed great variance for some items. Therefore, the study shows that frequency judgements do also have their own intricacies. It is concluded that there is no current methodology that can assess frequency in depth and there is a need for new ideas and improved methodologies.

Maybe then it is time to develop a way to assess LO that tries to avoid problems repeatedly encountered in the literature and concentrates on what we have learned until now. An attempt to do so is presented in the next section.

A different approach to LO

Sophistication and originality are concerned with the 'rarity' of words used by the learner. As Wolfe-Quintero et al. (1998: 114) have pointed out, this 'may depend on how the sophisticated words are defined' and, of course, according to whom. The purpose of this paper is to measure originality in a different way from other studies so far.

From the studies in the previous section, we think that an efficient way to approach LO:

- May be useful for (or applied to) different languages, even those that have no available standard frequency lists (Daller *et al.*, 2003).
- May give the possibility of having the measure also for the learners' L1 or for NSs of the target language: cognates played a role in Bardel and Lindqvist (2011), also Meara and Bell (2001) talk about possible L1 effects. Furthermore, Linnarud (1986) finds significant differences between NS's lexical individuality and that of learners.
- Should take context into consideration. At least, we have all these indications:
  – Daller and Xue (2007) would have liked to judge oral data against oral corpora instead of written corpora;
  – thematic words need a different treatment (according to Bardel & Lindqvist, 2011);
  – task effects can play a role (Meara & Bell, 2001; Skehan, 2009).
- Could concentrate on certain word categories rather than focus on whole texts: Harley and King (1989) used verbs.
- Should not make use of subjective judgements: Aizawa *et al.* (2001) showed they could be dangerous.
- Should use frequency counts in some way: using frequency as criteria cannot be discarded (the notion of LO is intrinsically related to it), although we might need some different frequency counts from those of available frequency lists.
- Could be useful to study originality in relation to other vocabulary dimensions.

Therefore, in contrast to the majority of studies that have dealt with texts, this new approach will focus on the production of single words (adjectives) by learners and NSs. The analysis of the data will also be different: participants' LO will not be determined by considering pre-existing lists compiled by previous researchers, but rather the yardstick will be data provided by participants in a particular task. Word frequencies will still constitute the main criterion to characterise a learner's vocabulary as more or less original, but they will not be extracted from standard frequency counts: the reference will be the adjectives elicited from a group to describe a certain picture. By exploring the evaluation of LO in this way, the current study wants to make a contribution to L2 vocabulary description and assessment from a different perspective.

Research questions

In the light of what we have explained so far, and taking as a point of departure the production elicited from participants to describe a picture of a man, this study addresses two research questions:

(1) Which words do NSs and upper-intermediate/advanced EFL learners produce in a picture-elicitation task?
  (a) To what extent are the words produced by each group the same/different?
  (b) To what frequency bands (from a standard corpus) do the words elicited belong?
(2) Can we discriminate between groups using lexical originality (LO) scores?
  (c) Between NSs and EFL learners.
  (d) Between EFL learners.

Method

Participants

Data were collected from 248 participants, of which a final sample of 200 formed part of the study. They were divided in two groups: one ($N = 100$) consists of Catalan/Spanish learners of English as a foreign language (B2–C1 level) at the University of Barcelona (UB), and the other ($N = 100$) consists of English NSs. The NSs are visiting students at UB or other institutions in the city. This group also includes some other participants ($N = 10$) not living in Catalonia at the moment the study was conducted. The average age is 23.6 and 22.6 for learners and NSs, respectively.

Instruments

Participants were required to fill in a questionnaire in English, which asked some information about themselves: age, sex and linguistic profile. On the same sheet of paper, they were asked to write 10 adjectives that best described a man in a picture they were provided with.

Procedure

Data were collected in the students' classrooms by their teachers (sometimes with the help of the researcher) or before class by the researcher. Those NSs who did not live in Catalonia at the time of the data collection were sent the questionnaire and instructions to do the task through email. There was no time limit for the completion of the task and participants were not allowed to use dictionaries or any other materials for help.

Data analysis

After data collection, information from the questionnaire and words provided by the participants were processed in Excel files. Before starting to analyse the data, some decisions had to be taken concerning the words/participants to include in the study.

All spelling errors were corrected. Adjectives that were used with the wrong prefix or suffix were changed into their proper form (e.g. *disproportioned* was changed into *disproportionate*); one form was consistently adopted in words with two different spellings; lexical inventions and influences from the participants' mother tongue were excluded (e.g. *big-frented*; *'frente'* is *'forehead'* in Spanish) and all compound adjectives, including the ones not properly written with a hyphen, were rewritten hyphenated so as to avoid problems with processing tools. Nouns and verbs were also removed. In cases of doubt, the online version of the Oxford British Dictionary was consulted.

After editing the data, participants with less than eight adjectives were discarded from the final sample and 100 people were chosen for each group. We included all testees that provided 10 adjectives and some that produced nine or eight. The final data consisted of two corpora: one with adjectives provided by learners (NNSs) and one by the adjectives provided by NSs. As the number of NSs who gave 10 adjectives was higher than that of learners, the learners' corpus consisted of 950 tokens and that of NSs of 980. Table 3 shows the final number of participants together with the number of adjectives elicited per group.

In order to explore the corpora and perform the necessary analyses to answer the research questions proposed, the following tools were used:

- V_Words v2.0 (Meara, 2015b): to compute the number of types, tokens and obtain frequency lists.
- V_Lists v1.0 (Meara, 2015a): to obtain information on types co-occurring in different lists.

Table 3 Number of participants in each group and adjectives provided

	NS		Learners	
	Participants	Adjectives per person	Participants	Adjectives per person
	80	10	62	10
	20	9	26	9
	–	–	12	8
Total	100	980	100	950

Apart from these tools, the Range program (Heatley et al., 2002) was used to further analyse and describe the two corpora and the results were pictured in Excel diagrams.

In order to compute the first originality score (O1), participants of each group were awarded points for each word they provided; the points for each word corresponded to the frequency of the words in the corpus of the group the participant belonged to (NS or learner). Hence, the higher the score, the less original participants were.

To obtain the second originality score (O2), adjectives in the NS corpus were divided into four lists according to their frequency. List 1 included the most frequent words while List 4 was formed by hapaxes. Each learner was assessed by comparing the words s/he produced with these four new lists using Range. A profile that showed the distribution of words the learner used was created for each learner. Examples of possible profiles could be:

	List 1	List 2	List 3	List 4	Off-list
Learner_1	2	2	0	3	3
Learner_2	3	0	3	4	0

With the aim of further comparing the two corpora and of finding ways in which learners resembled (or not) NSs in their production, a cluster analysis was performed on these 100 profiles.

Apart from that, each learner participant was given a score depending on which list the words s/he used belonged to. For each word that was found in List 1, List 2, List 3 and List 4 they were given 0, 1, 2 and 3 points, respectively; for off-list words the points awarded were 4. Hence, the higher the score, the more original participants were. With the examples above, the O2 scores for these participants would be the following:

Learner_1: 23 (0 + 2 + 0 + 9 + 12)
Learner_2: 18 (0 + 0 + 6 + 12 + 0)

In order to answer our Research Question 2, both scores (O1 and O2) were assessed for normality and SPSS v21 was used for the statistical analyses. An independent samples t-test was conducted on O1 scores between learners and NSs (Research Question 2a). A one-way between-groups analysis of variance on O2 scores was performed with learners' subgroups to confirm whether O2 scores could significantly distinguish between clusters (Research Question 2b).

Results

Corpora description: The words participants produced

This section provides the results to answer our first research question. We wondered up to what extent are the words produced by NS and EFL learners the same or different (Research Question 1a). Table 4 gives an overview of the amount of tokens, types and hapaxes (words that appear just once) in each corpus. As can be seen in the table, and taking into account that the NS corpus contains 30 tokens more than the learners' corpus, the NS group produces considerably more types and hapaxes than learners.

If we focus on the comparison of the types elicited from both groups, NS tend to produce more different types than the learners' group (246 versus 126); 163 types co-occur in both corpora. Figure 1 presents these data in percentages.

Table 5 shows the most frequent words in the two corpora. Note that among the top most frequently used words, the two groups only have one in common (*big-headed*) and the top most frequent word for the NSs (*old*) appears much less often than the first two words in the learners' group (*big-headed* and *ugly*). However, if we take the words produced

Table 4 Number of tokens, types and hapaxes in the corpora

	NSs	Learners
Tokens	980	950
Types	364	286
Hapaxes	223	164

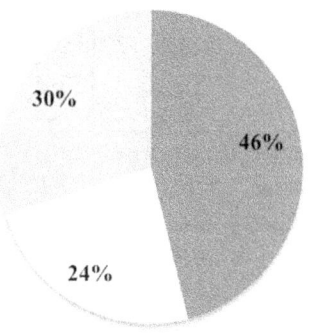

Figure 1 Percentages of types in the corpora in each group

Table 5 Words produced by 10 participants or more

NSs		Learners	
Word	Frequency rate	Word	Frequency rate
Old	32	Big-headed	67
Creepy	31	Ugly	47
Balding	26	Thin	28
Big-headed	25	*Angry*	27
Disproportionate	24	*Weird*	27
Angry	23	Short	24
Curious	21	Bald	22
Scary	20	*Old*	22
Weird	19	*Strange*	20
Middle-aged	16	Scary	17
Strange	15	Serious	14
Awkward	14	Intelligent	13
Messy	13	Crazy	12
Confused	12	Dirty	11
Intense	11	Mad	11
Funny	10	Shy	11
		Slim	11
		Bad-tempered	10
		Middle-aged	10
		Smart	10

at least 10 times in each group, then six of them appear in both lists (in italics).

Finally, in order to see which frequency ranges the words elicited belonged to (Research Question 1b), we classified them using Range (Heatley *et al.*, 2002). This program gives us a description in terms of how frequent words are in the language. Figure 2 indicates that the frequency profiles of the adjectives that both groups produce look alike; that is, both groups produce words mostly in the first two bands (up to the 2000 most frequent words in English). 52.55% of the words NSs produced are found in these bands versus 57.37% of the learners' production. About half of the words in each group are to be found in the next bands (from 3K onwards), taking into account that even NSs do not tend to produce words not included in the first six to seven bands. Note that

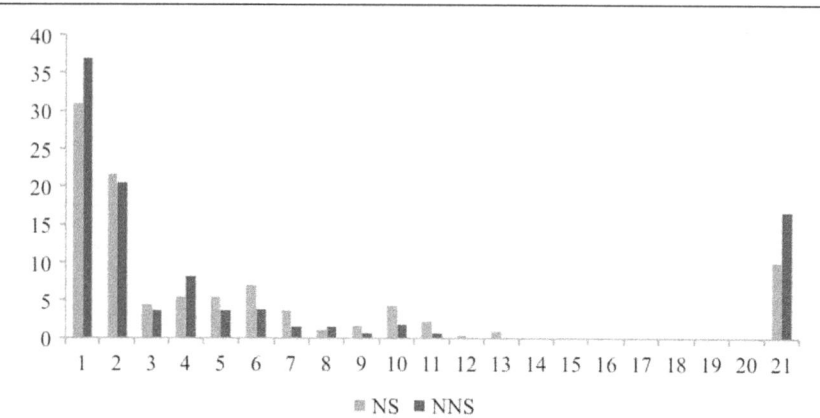

Figure 2 Range coverage for adjectives produced by NSs and learners

words in the 21st band are those the program could not classify in any of the lists.

Lexical originality scores

O1: Scores in relation to what participants in the same group produce

Figure 3 presents O1 scores in the NSs' group and the learners' group. With O1 scores, we rated participants according to the frequency of words in the group that participants belonged to (in this case, the higher the scores, the less original the participants' production; it meant that

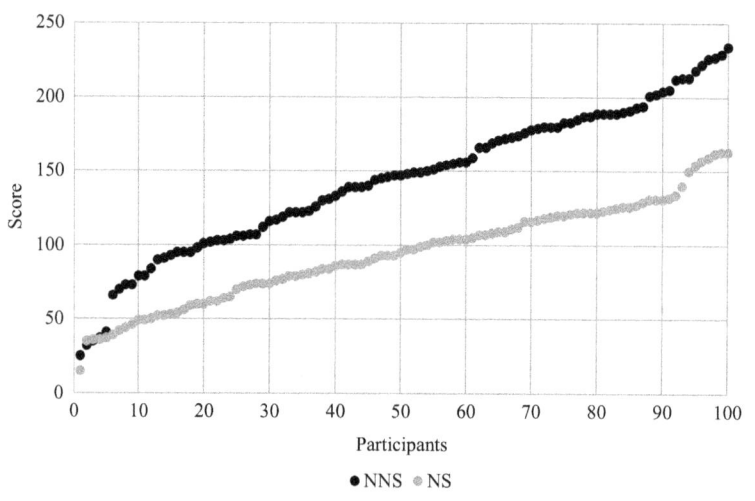

Figure 3 O1 scores for 100 learners and native speakers

more people produced the same words). As observed in the figure, learners' scores are usually higher; i.e. less original.

An independent samples t-test showed that there were significant differences between NSs' O1 scores (mean = 94.26, S.D. = 33.66) and learners' scores (mean = 143.84, S.D. = 49.20), $[t(198) = 8.317, p = 0.001]$, with a medium effect size (eta-squared = 0.26).

O2: Learners' scores in relation to NSs' production

Profiles were obtained for each of our learners as explained in the Data Analysis section. These profiles consisted of five bands in decreasing frequency order: the first contained words used very often by NSs, while the last was formed by words NSs had not used. A cluster analysis was conducted with the 100 profiles of learners in our study. This analysis aimed at finding typical profiles among our learners' group that may help us to identify the similarities and differences between the lexical choices made by the learner group compared with those of the NS group. The analysis distinguished between three clusters or subgroups, with the shapes shown in Figure 4.

It can be appreciated that the three subgroups behave similarly in the first three bands in each cluster; although in Cluster 3 participants produce more words in all these first three bands. However, for the fourth and fifth bands a different picture emerges. Cluster 1 has the highest mean for the fourth band; in Cluster 2 the means gradually increase and the highest mean is in the band that contains words not produced by NSs (exclusive of learners); learners in Cluster 3 provide similar amounts of adjectives in the two last bands.

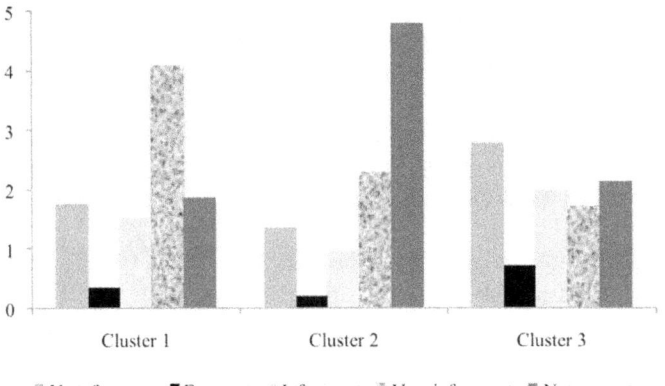

Figure 4 The clusters resulting from the cluster analysis

As we have introduced in the Data Analysis section, the O2 scores awarded to each learner depended on whether the words s/he produced were frequent or not in the NS corpus. Therefore, those commonly produced by NSs were awarded fewer points than those infrequently produced by NSs (hence the higher the score, the more original they were). As O2 scores presented a normal distribution, a one-way between-groups analysis of variance was conducted to explore the difference in O2 scores for learners. The categorical independent variable was the cluster learners belonged to (C1, C2 or C3). There was a statistically significant difference at the $p < 0.05$ level in O2 scores for the three clusters C1 ($N = 37$, mean = 23.08, S.D. = 3.56), C2 ($N = 28$, mean = 28.14, S.D. = 3.08), C3 ($N = 35$, mean = 18.43, S.D. = 4.04), as $[F(2, 97) = 56.3, p = 0.001]$. Taken together, the results indicate that, when we judge learners' production against that of NSs, different groups emerge (with statistically significant differences between them) and that O2 scores could discriminate between more or less original learners.

Discussion and conclusion

Several aspects should be considered in relation to our first research question (i.e. range and type of words elicited in the two groups). In this picture-elicitation task in which participants were asked to provide adjectives for a specific picture, the two corpora compiled presented some variability: they consisted of types that were common in both groups, but also of quite a lot of words that appeared only once in each corpus. Generally, the group of learners showed less diversity than the NSs concerning the types that they produced and learners tended to coincide in the same adjectives more often. This result is not unexpected since NSs of a language normally do have a larger vocabulary than learners and therefore a bigger repertoire to choose from. Even if a learner is very proficient, s/he may still lack words that a NS knows and uses. However, the fact that NSs produced more diverse words than learners does not mean that learners produced a narrow range of words; as shown by the results, the learners' corpus was also characterised by a considerable variety of vocabulary and a high amount of hapaxes exclusive to this corpus.

What is interesting from this description of the two corpora is that it offers a quantification of the amount of variability in both groups: when people (NSs or not) are asked to provide words for a picture, a certain amount of variability is expected, although we do not know up to what extent the words provided may vary. As Figure 1 shows, we have some evidence of the overlap we may expect between learners and

NSs and this may be extrapolated to similar tasks with learners of similar proficiency levels. We can also use it as an indication to start thinking about other possible indexes and more specific ways of approaching LO.

Concerning how frequent in the language the words produced were, both groups showed a similar behaviour: about half of the words in each corpus are frequent common words and the rest are infrequent. That is, the distribution of the words in the corpora according to predetermined standard lists is very similar in both groups (as shown by the analysis with Range). In this case, a list compiled for this specific type of task could have provided other information about the participants' behaviour, different from the profiles that resulted from other standard frequency external lists. What we have learned from this analysis is that a LS measure based on standard frequency lists would probably not have been able to distinguish learners' words from those of NSs', as participants in each group can share similar profiles. It is also worth noting that, even if the corpus does not consist of texts but of a collection of words as is the case here, the frequency profile resembles that of texts and presents a similar pattern (we do not find less common words more often than usual vocabulary).

Regarding the second research question (i.e. if and how scores can discriminate between NSs and learners or among learners), several considerations can be made. First, scores were given to participants according to the frequency of the words in their own group (O1). In contrast to the lexical frequency profiles we have just mentioned – which looked alike – this score was able to reveal significant differences in the LO of the two groups, the NSs' being the most original. It is interesting to see that, even though the two groups behaved similarly according to the extrinsic lists, once we studied the words in relation to adjectives produced specifically for that task, a different picture emerged and significant differences were found. This raises two interesting points. The first is whether this scoring method can also be effective to explore similarities and differences in the vocabularies of learners at different levels (Linnarud (1986) found a highly significant correlation between lexical individuality and grades). The second is that if this has been achieved with 10-word samples, long compositions may not actually be necessary to obtain a LO index, as long as a reference corpus for a particular task is available. Reference corpora of this sort would also be relatively easy to compile, even for those languages that do not have frequency lists available (Daller & Xue, 2007).

After calculating participants' O1 scores – according to the words given by their group peers – learners' O2 scores were computed taking as a reference NSs' production. The first question to discuss here is if it is licit to assess learners in relation to NSs, despite all the differences that exist between the two populations (see Cook, 1999). It seemed to us that it could be a way to start exploring LO and that other reference corpora could possibly also be obtained from learners at different levels. Furthermore, a corpus can also be compiled from very competent multilingual L2 users and be used as reference data. The second question concerns the scoring procedure: the NS corpus was used to obtain the frequency lists against which to judge learners' production. In this case, more points were awarded if the word was not common in the reference corpus, although other possible scoring methods may contemplate awarding more points to those learners whose words appeared more often in the NS corpus, as this would mean that his/her choices were more 'native-like'. However, this could actually be measuring something different from originality. It was seen that O2 scores had the potential to discriminate between different subgroups of learners (e.g. distinguishing between those that used words commonly used by NSs and those that did not, like those in Cluster 2). From the shapes of our cluster profiles, we have also learned that when the NS corpus is used as a reference, the frequency distribution of words in our learners' profiles does not exhibit a typical Zipfian curve (Zipf, 1935). This finding on a question that had been unexplored until now should be taken into consideration for further research.

Beyond the scoring method adopted, LO measures can be very helpful to L2 learners from a pedagogical perspective. Becoming aware of the words being used by other learners (at the same or higher level) or NSs in comparison with their own repertoire can be a motivation to expand each student's own vocabulary; this may also lead to an improvement in accuracy and precision to express oneself. Additionally, this information can also be useful for L2 teachers and material developers, as well as for researchers studying lexical acquisition, who may more thoroughly investigate LO development in relation to dimensions such as vocabulary size or organisation.

Limitations and further research

The purpose of the present research was to explore a new way of assessing LO. We would like to acknowledge here some limitations we have found in our work and propose ways of overcoming them in the future, as well as some ideas for further research.

First of all, the number of participants is limited to 100 in each group. A bigger sample of learners and NSs, which would result in a larger pool of adjectives and bigger corpora, could have provided a better model to work with and offer greater help to determine other possible ways to measure LO. More data will hopefully be gathered in further research and corpora will be enlarged. Another limitation is the fact that data were collected for just one picture. Our purpose was to explore the data that a simple task like the one proposed would elicit. However, findings cannot be generalised without testing other (similar) pictures, as results may be different in terms of variability, partial overlap between learners and NSs, etc. This remains to be seen in future studies.

A possibility we have not examined in this study either is what 'normal progression' would look like for learners at different proficiency levels (e.g. do they become more NS-like in their selection as proficiency improves or is it the case that it cannot actually be known due to the amount of variation?). Obtaining the same sort of data in longitudinal research or at different proficiency levels – even if fewer adjectives could be elicited from poor learners – would help us study how LO develops.

Acknowledgements

We would like to thank Michael Kennedy and Drs M. Luz Celaya and Júlia Barón for offering help with data collection.

References

Aizawa, K., Mochizuki, M. and Meara, P.M. (2001) Intuition about word frequency: What does it tell us about vocabulary knowledge? *Research Reports of the Faculty of Engineering. Tokyo Denki University* 20, 75–82.

Bardel, C. and Lindqvist, C. (2011) Developing a lexical profiler for spoken French and Italian L2: The role of frequency, cognates and thematic vocabulary. In L. Roberts, G. Pallotti and C. Bettoni (eds) *EUROSLA Yearbook 11* (pp. 75–93). Amsterdam: John Benjamins.

Bardel, C., Gudmundson, A. and Lindqvist, C. (2012) Aspects of lexical sophistication in advanced learners' oral production: Vocabulary acquisition in L2 French and Italian. *Studies in Second Language Acquisition* 34 (2), 269–290.

Cook, V. (1999) Going beyond the native speaker in language teaching. *TESOL Quarterly* 33 (2), 185–209.

Daller, H. and Xue, H. (2007) Lexical richness and the oral proficiency of Chinese EFL students. In H. Daller, J. Milton and J. Treffers-Daller (eds) *Modelling and Assessing Vocabulary Knowledge* (pp. 150–164). Cambridge: Cambridge University Press.

Daller, H., van Hout, R. and Treffers-Daller, J. (2003) Lexical richness in the spontaneous speech of bilinguals. *Applied Linguistics* 24 (2), 197–222.

East, M. (2006) The impact of bilingual dictionaries on lexical sophistication and lexical accuracy in tests of L2 writing proficiency: A quantitative analysis. *Assessing Writing* 11 (3), 179–197.

Harley, B. and King, M.L. (1989) Verb lexis in the written compositions of young L2 learners. *Studies in Second Language Acquisition* 11 (4), 415–439.

Heatley, A., Nation, I.S.P. and Coxhead, A. (2002) *RANGE Program*. See http://www.victoria.ac.nz/lals/about/staff/paul-nation.

Laufer, B. (1991) The development of L2 lexis in the expression of the advanced learner. *Modern Language Journal* 75 (4), 440–448.

Laufer, B. and Nation, I.S.P. (1995) Vocabulary size and use: Lexical richness in L2 written production. *Applied Linguistics* 16 (3), 307–322.

Leech, G., Rayson, P. and Wilson, A. (2001) *Word Frequencies in Written and Spoken English*. London: Longman.

Lindqvist, C., Bardel, C. and Gudmundson, A. (2011) Lexical richness in the advanced learner's oral production of French and Italian L2. *International Review of Applied Linguistics in Language Teaching* 49 (3), 221–240.

Linnarud, M. (1986) *Lexis in Composition: A Performance Analysis of Swedish Learners' Written English*. Malmö: Liber Förlag.

Lu, X. (2012) The relationship of lexical richness to the quality of ESL learners' oral narratives. *Modern Language Journal* 96 (2), 190–208.

Malvern, D., Richards, B., Chipere, N. and Durán, P. (2004) *Lexical Diversity and Language Development: Quantification and Assessment*. Basingstoke: Palgrave Macmillan.

Meara, P.M. (2015a) *V_Lists*. See http://www.lognostics.co.uk/tools/V_Lists/V_Lists.htm

Meara, P.M. (2015b) *V_Words*. See http://www.lognostics.co.uk/tools/V_Words/V_Words.htm

Meara, P. and Bell, H. (2001) P_Lex: A simple and effective way of describing the lexical characteristics of short L2 texts. *Prospect* 16 (3), 5–19.

Meara, P.M., Rodgers, C. and Jacobs, G. (2000) Computational assessment of texts written by L2 speakers. *System* 28 (3), 345–354.

Meara, P.M., Jacobs, G. and Rodgers, C. (2002) Lexical signatures in foreign language free-form texts. *ITL Review of Applied Linguistics* 135–136, 85–96.

Miralpeix, I. (2007) Lexical knowledge in instructed language learning: The effects of age and exposure. *International Journal of English Studies* 7 (2), 61–83.

Moreno Espinosa, S. (2005) Can P_Lex accurately measure lexical richness in the written production of young learners of EFL? *Porta Linguarum: Revista Internacional de Didáctica de las Lenguas Extranjeras* 4, 7–22.

Morris, L. and Cobb, T. (2003) Vocabulary profiles as predictors of the academic performance of TESL trainees. *System* 32 (1), 75–87.

Muncie, J. (2002) Process writing and vocabulary development: Comparing Lexical Frequency Profiles across drafts. *System* 30 (2), 225–235.

Skehan, P. (2009) Modelling second language performance: Integrating complexity, accuracy, fluency, and lexis. *Applied Linguistics* 30 (4), 510–532.

Tidball, F. and Treffers-Daller, J. (2007) Exploring measures of vocabulary richness in semi-spontaneous French speech: A quest for the Holy Grail? In H. Daller, J. Milton and J. Treffers-Daller (eds) *Modelling and Assessing Vocabulary Knowledge* (pp. 133–149). Cambridge: Cambridge University Press.

Wolfe-Quintero, K., Inagaki, S. and Kim, H.Y. (1998) *Second Language Development in Writing: Measures of Fluency, Accuracy, and Complexity*. Hawaii: University of Hawaii Press.

Zipf, G.K. (1935) *The Psycho-Biology of Language: An Introduction to Dynamic Philology*. Boston: Houghton Mifflin.

Reflections on Tzima and Miralpeix (2015)

This study is to be viewed as an exploratory piece of research on lexical originality (LO). The idea of 'uniqueness' in individuals' vocabularies has not been much studied, nor do we know about LO in L2 acquisition except from very few studies carried out a long time ago. Tzima and Miralpeix (2015) have generated evidence on some preliminary questions, although many remain still unanswered. In this section, we would like to comment on complementary ways to evaluate LO using the same type of data as in the study, offer some initial results from supplementary research with different input pictures, and suggest avenues for future investigation on vocabulary acquisition using picture-elicitation tasks.

In addition to the measurements presented in this paper (O1 and O2 indexes), there are other possible ways of evaluating the vocabulary elicited in this sort of task in order to further study LO. The paper introduced two scoring methods that focus on the frequency of the words that appear in the reference corpus. An alternative complementary approach could be scoring LO in terms of the number of matches, i.e. how many words coincide in a test taker's set and in sets produced by other previous test takers. The calculation could also be done taking into account a specific proficiency group (e.g. a group of learners at a particular level, very proficient learners or NSs). This type of scoring is the one adopted by the current version of V_Unique (see the 'Using V_Unique' section at the beginning of this chapter).

The work presented in Tzima and Miralpeix (2015) also throws up a number of other practical questions for which it is mandatory to collect new data. One of these questions is whether the description presented in Tables 4 and 5 (number of types, hapaxes, top-of-the-list words …) would be similar for other pictures and how many participants should be tested in order to get stable data for particular input pictures. In the same vein, we could ask whether the vocabulary profile we get in Figure 2 would show a similar distribution when we elicit adjectives from images depicting different characters. In order to throw light on these issues, data were collected from 44 EFL learners with two other pictures: one of a man (different from that used in the paper presented) and one of a woman. Learners were at the same proficiency level as those in the previous study and were asked to do exactly the same task.

Table 5.2 shows that the percentage of types and hapaxes is higher with a smaller number of learners and that a larger sample of participants is needed to get more stable data. However, the number of words with a frequency of 10 (or higher) is around the 2% (again, quite small), indicating that there is not a tendency for EFL participants to produce the same words even when they all have the picture of the same character to describe. It is rather the

Table 5.2 Results from three different learners' corpora

	Picture 1 (N = 100)	Picture 2 (N = 44)	Picture 3 (N = 44)
Tokens	950	415	421
Types	286 (30.10%)	196 (47.23%)	164 (38.95%)
Hapaxes	164 (17.26%)	135 (32.53%)	95 (22.56%)
Words frequency ≥ 10	20 (2.10%)	8 (1.93%)	8 (1.9%)

opposite: there is high variability (hapaxes may amount to a quarter of the pool of words elicited).

Regarding the LFP of the data collected, we saw in the paper that with 100 participants about 50% of the words elicited could be classified as 1K or 2K words, and that we needed up to bands of 6–7K to account for approximately 75% of the data. In the new picture showing an older man, 75% of the adjectives belonged to the first 2000 words, and the first four bands accounted for a 90% of the words elicited. The percentages varied slightly with the new picture of the woman, but still about a 90% of the words produced belonged to the first bands up to 4K. This indicates that 44 participants may not be sufficient to elicit a pool of words that is reliable and representative of the language that could be elicited. Still, as in the paper, data were distributed following a Zipfian curve even in a corpus with fewer tokens, and even if the elicited production was not a text but a list of content words.

In addition to LO, a descriptive task like the one presented in V_Unique may have the potential to be used to measure other dimensions of vocabulary knowledge. The first obvious question is whether the words produced can give any indication of how big the vocabulary size of the test taker is (i.e. if there is a possibility of using it as an indication of vocabulary size). Like the Lex30 test (Fitzpatrick & Meara, 2004), which was originally created to study word associations and lexical organisation, V_Unique may also help to assess recall ability. The second point is that, taking into account that words are elicited in this task in a particular order, the data generated might be used to study lexical availability, a dimension that has often been overlooked in vocabulary studies (see Jiménez Catalán, 2014; Chapter 9, this volume). V_Unique may offer two possible ways to explore availability: on the one hand, a lexical availability score can be derived from the words produced; on the other hand, semantic relations between words could be made explicit by semantic networks as proposed by Ferreira and Echeverría (2010). Likewise, we may ask if this kind of data would be useful to support Ferreira and Echeverría's idea that EFL learners distinguish only large semantic categories, while NSs organise words into very specific subcategories.

More Research is Needed ...

This section contains some ideas that could easily be worked up into small-scale research projects.

- How many participants do we need to collect data from to get stable data for a particular picture?
- Do lexical frequency profiles vary for different stimuli, or are they broadly stable?
- Do advanced learners tend to consistently use less frequent responses in this task?
- What would longitudinal data from the same participants over a certain period of time look like?
- Can the task be used to discriminate between learners at different levels of proficiency?
- What is the typical overlap between different response sets? Does this value differ with proficiency?
- Would the test elicit the same vocabulary if we asked test takers to be as original as possible in their responses?
- What sort of words would participants produce if they were asked to do the same task in their L1?
- Do the resulting scores correlate with other lexical measures?
- How do the results of this test relate to other dimensions of lexical competence?
- How could this type of research be used for pedagogical purposes?

References

Ferreira, R. and Echeverría, M.S. (2010) Redes semánticas en el léxico disponible de inglés L1 e inglés LE. [Semantic networks in the available vocabulary of L1 and L2 English speakers]. *Onomázein* 21 (1), 133–153.

Fitzpatrick, T. and Meara, P.M. (2004) Exploring the validity of a test of productive vocabulary. *Vigo International Journal of Applied Linguistics* 1, 55–74.

Jiménez Catalán, R.M. (ed.) (2014) *Lexical Availability in English and Spanish as a Second Language*. Berlin: Springer.

Tzima, F.E. and Miralpeix, I. (2015) Lexical originality: Towards new forms of assessment. Adapted from Unpublished MA thesis, 2013. University of Barcelona.

Suggestions for further reading

Blackwell, A.A. (2005) Acquiring the English adjective lexicon: Relationships with input properties and adjectival semantic typology. *Journal of Child Language* 32 (3), 535–562.

Henriksen, B. and Haastrup, K. (2000) Describing foreign language learners' productive vocabulary use and development. In I. Plag and K. Schneider (eds) *Language Use, Language Acquisition and Language History* (pp. 150–171). Trier: Wissenschaftlicher Verlag Trier.

Leech, G., Rayson, P. and Wilson, A. (2001) List 5.3: Frequency list of adjectives in the whole corpus (by lemma). In *Word Frequencies in Written and Spoken English*. London: Longman. See http://ucrel.lancs.ac.uk/bncfreq/lists/5_3_all_rank_adjective.txt

Mulder, K. and Hulstijn, J.H. (2011) Linguistic skills of adult native speakers, as a function of age and level of education. *Applied Linguistics* 32 (5), 475–494.

Ridgeway, D.W., Waters, E. and Kuczaj, S.A. (1985) Acquisition of emotion-descriptive language: Receptive and productive vocabulary norms for ages 18 months to 6 years. *Developmental Psychology* 21 (5), 901–908.

Slatcher, R.B., Chung, C.K., Pennebaker, J.W. and Stone, L.D. (2007) Winning words: Individual differences in linguistic style among U.S. presidential and vice presidential candidates. *Journal of Research in Personality* 41 (1), 63–75.

Part 3
Estimating Vocabulary Size

6   V_YesNo v1.0

Introduction

V_YesNo is based on the Eurocentres Vocabulary Size Test (EVST; Meara & Jones, 1990), one of the very first programs to come out of the vocabulary research group that developed at Birkbeck College London during the 1980s. The program grew out of a need for some 'quick and dirty' tests that could be used to efficiently describe the level of proficiency of L2 speakers taking part in experimental studies. At the time we developed EVST, there were no standard tests of this type. People usually described their experimental participants in terms of how many years of study they had completed, or by using ill-defined descriptions like 'beginner' or 'upper intermediate'. These terms were useful for broadly categorising participants, but they tended to mean different things in different contexts, and were not very useful for discriminating between students who were formally at the same level, but had very different levels of proficiency.

The original EVST program appeared to be a radically innovative approach to vocabulary testing in an L2 at the time it appeared, although it actually borrowed heavily from a methodology which had previously been used by Anderson and Freebody (1981) to test vocabulary in L1 speakers. In reality, the idea that vocabulary might be a good surrogate measure for overall proficiency in a foreign language was not as innovative as it appeared. The idea first crops up in a series of papers by Vivian Henmon, published in *The Journal of Educational Psychology* early in the 20th century (Henmon, 1917, 1920). Henmon's work dealt with Latin, but the idea that it might also work for modern foreign languages surfaced again in a thesis by Einar Ryden, briefly reported in an article in *The Journal of Educational Psychology* in 1948. Ryden did not use imaginary words as a way of correcting for guessing: that idea was sketched out by John Higgins and reported in a paper that appeared in 1995, but was actually based on research carried out in the 1970s (Higgins, 1995).

The main advantage of the Yes/No format was its stunning simplicity. At the time, the most common type of vocabulary test was the multiple choice test format. Typically, test takers were presented with a target word in a short sentence context, and asked to indicate which of a set of four or five possible meanings was appropriate for the target word in this context. Tests of this type were widely used by examination boards, but they had a number of disadvantages which made them less suitable for research purposes. One disadvantage was that multiple choice tests were difficult to construct, as they usually required extensive validation. A second disadvantage was that these tests were 'messy', in the sense that it was not always clear what an item tested, since correct answers depended not just on testees' knowledge of the target words, but also on their ability to read and understand the sentence contexts. A third disadvantage was that the multiple choice format does not allow us to test lots of words in a short time. We resolved these issues by simply presenting testees with a long list of words, one at a time, and asking them to indicate whether they knew the meaning of the word or not. We provided a check against cheating by including a number of items which did not actually exist as words. Participants who claimed to know a lot of these words had their scores reduced appropriately. Another advantage came from the way computing technology was developing at the time. Home computers were just becoming available as we were developing EVST – the first versions we wrote ran on a Sinclair ZX81 – and this new technology allowed us to write a computerised test that was an early example of computer adaptive testing. A final advantage was that students seemed to like the test, and would often take it two or three times, in the hope of maximising their scores. This was not something that we had experienced with our earlier attempts at test writing!

The Yes/No test (as it came to be called) turned out to be a surprisingly powerful tool, and it far exceeded our original expectations for it. In particular, we found that there was a fairly good correlation between scores on a Yes/No test and other language skills which were much more difficult to test. People with good grammar skills tended to have high vocabulary scores, the same was true of people with good reading skills, and people with high vocabulary scores tended to have better writing skills than people with weaker vocabulary scores. There was a lot of interest at the time in measures of overall L2 competence, (e.g. Oller, 1973) and we thought that the Yes/No vocabulary test would have a significant role to play in this area. In practice, there was considerable resistance to using vocabulary tests in this way – teachers, in particular, objected that using a vocabulary test to assess language skills would just encourage students to learn lists of words. Instead, cloze tests, which were easier to understand and somewhat less threatening to established practices, became the standard instrument for measuring proficiency where a 'quick and dirty' assessment was needed. At the same time, Paul Nation was developing his Vocabulary Levels Test (VLT; Nation, 1983), and it was this test which quickly became the 'industry standard' vocabulary assessment tool, following some detailed technical work by Beglar and Hunt (1999), by Schmitt *et al.* (2001), and the publication of Nation's very influential textbook *Teaching and Learning Vocabulary* in 1990.

In spite of this competition, the EVST test was successfully used as a placement test by some English language Schools in the UK, and a number of versions of the Yes/No approach also continued to be used in empirical research – particularly in the research that was being put out by the group at Swansea University. The method was particularly good at assessing high levels of vocabulary, while the VLT was more widely used at lower levels of proficiency. A further advantage of the Yes/No method was that it was readily adaptable to languages other than English, and during the 1990s we developed a whole series of tests covering the major European languages, and some of the minor ones as well, thanks to a grant from the EU's Lingua program. The methodology was also incorporated into the EU's Dialang project (Alderson & Huhta, 2005) as a way of guiding test takers to the right level of question difficulty.

Despite these early successes, the Yes/No test has played a somewhat limited role in vocabulary research. In part, this was because the scoring of Yes/No responses turned out to be much more difficult than we had anticipated, and this led to some very complex and competing alternatives being developed. Some critics objected in principle to the idea of using imaginary words in vocabulary tests and some objected to the idea of testing vocabulary knowledge out of context. There were also issues over what the Yes/No methodology was actually testing. Some critics felt that it 'merely' tested passive recognition of vocabulary, and that this was such a low-level skill that it was barely worth testing. Other critics felt that the approach failed to appreciate the complexity of vocabulary knowledge, and particularly the importance of partial knowledge and knowledge of multiple meanings of words. For instance, if you know that STREAM has something to do with water, but you do not exactly know what, can you really claim to know this word? Similarly, if you know collocations like *a stream of ideas* or *a stream of refugees*, but do not know the basic idea of flowing water, is STREAM really a part of your vocabulary? There were also issues over test takers' willingness to say YES to a word they were not sure about – some people readily say YES, where others are more cautious. Japanese learners, for example, are very cautious about claiming that they know a word, whereas speakers of some other L1s will very frequently claim to know words that vaguely resemble words they might know. Some critics argued that perhaps we should actually reward people for guessing, rather than punishing them, since we know that good language learners make extensive use of guessing when they encounter new words in context. Eyckmans (2004) provides a good discussion of these issues.

In short, the Yes/No tests opened up something of a hornets' nest in vocabulary research, and many of the questions that they raised are still waiting to be answered. The basic Yes/No test included in this chapter will allow you explore some of these issues for yourself.

We have included in this chapter a short paper by Meara and Jones (1988). This paper is typical of the very early studies using Yes/No tests, published

116 Part 3: Estimating Vocabulary Size

when we were still feeling our way with data of this sort. The commentary that follows this section highlights some of the issues that emerged later on, after we realised that the data provided by Yes/No test were much more complex than we had at first assumed.

Using V_YesNo

You can find V_YesNo on the Lognostics Tools website, available at: http://www.lognostics.co.uk/tools/V_YesNo/V_YesNo.htm. V_YesNo does not require data preparation before administering the test. The test is a self-contained program.

(1) The V_YesNo opening screen is shown in Figure 6.1.
    If you are not intending to keep the data for future reference, then you do not need to enter anything in the boxes.
    V_YesNo will record any data that are submitted to it. If you are likely to want to retrieve these data at some time – e.g. if you are planning to run the test with a large number of test takers as part of a larger project – then you should get each test taker to enter their name and a unique identifying code which will allow you to recover the data from storage later. The identification code can be any sequence of letters or numbers, as long as it is distinctive enough that it is unlikely to be used by anybody else. For example, if you work in Swansea University and are planning to run data collection over three years, then a code like SWAN15xxxxx, where xxxxx is a set of letters or numbers that identify the individual test takers, should be good enough to avoid conflicts with other people's data.
    Keep a record of any access codes that you use. You will need the codes if you want to retrieve your data from the V_YesNo database. Instructions for accessing the data in the V_YesNo database are provided at the end of this chapter.
(2) Click **Start** when you are ready to begin. This will bring up the main data capture screen (Figure 6.2). The main data capture screen for V_YesNo simply presents a set of instructions followed by a vocabulary item which the test taker may or may not know. The test taker just has to indicate this by clicking the appropriate response button. The next word will then be displayed. We usually find it helpful to emphasise to test takers that they should say YES only if they know the meaning of the target word: familiarity with a word form is not enough. We usually tell them that the test is not timed, and there is no advantage in doing the test as quickly as they can. Nevertheless, if they find themselves hesitating over a word, having to think about whether they know its meaning or not, then they should answer NO (**Next** button).

Some users tell their test takers that they should answer YES if they think an item might be an English word. We do not recommend this practice, as test takers should answer YES only when they are sure that they know what the word means, and click **Next** otherwise. Guessing is best avoided as saying YES to pseudo-words negatively affects the final score. Experience suggests that the test works better if the test takers are told that some of the words are not real words, and that they should not answer YES to items they do not know.

(3) There are 200 items in total. The small number in the bottom left hand corner of the screen indicates which stimulus word is being displayed. The program does not time the responses, so there is no advantage from doing the test quickly. Under normal circumstances, the test takes about

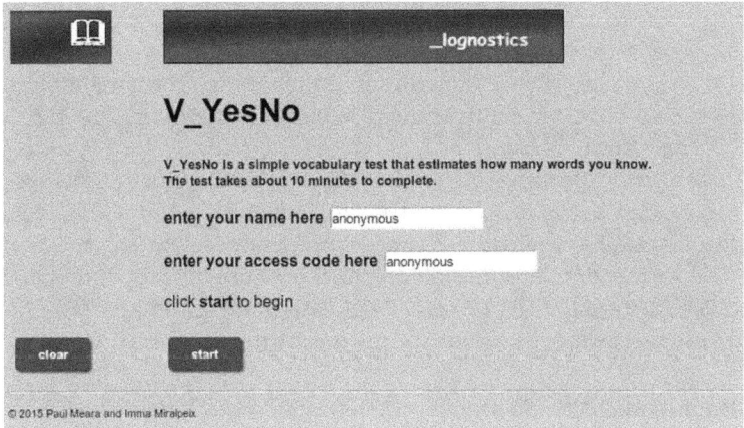

Figure 6.1 V_YesNo opening screen

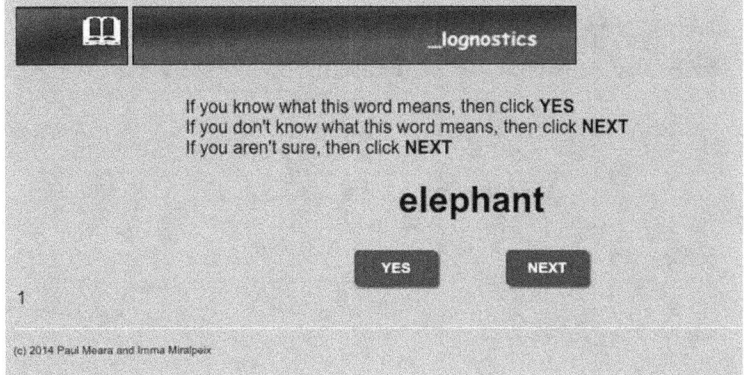

Figure 6.2 V_YesNo main screen

10 minutes. Test instances which take very much longer than this should be treated as suspicious.

(4) When you have responded to the final stimulus word, the program displays a report screen. The V_YesNo report screen is shown in Figure 6.3. The report screen has deliberately been kept as simple as possible so as not to confuse the test takers.

(5) Interpreting the report:
   - The score reported is an **estimate** of how many words the test taker knows. These scores can vary from 0 to 10,000 and should be treated with appropriate caution.
   - Educated native speakers and very fluent learners will score over 9000 on this test.
   - A score of 7500–9000 words indicates a very high level of proficiency.
   - A score of 4500–7500 words indicates a learner with a good level of competence.
   - A score of 2500–4500 words indicates an intermediate-level learner.
   - A score below 1500 words is typical of beginners. The test is not reliable at this level.

Generally speaking, the higher the scores, the more confidence you can have in them. It is very difficult to score more than 9000 words on this test unless you really do know the vocabulary being tested.

More detailed information on the scores provided by individual test takers is stored in the V_YesNo database (more information on how to access these data is provided at the end of this chapter).

The technical bits

V_YesNo is loosely based on the original EVST tests, in that it uses the same general format, but it is not an exact replica of this work. V_YesNo uses

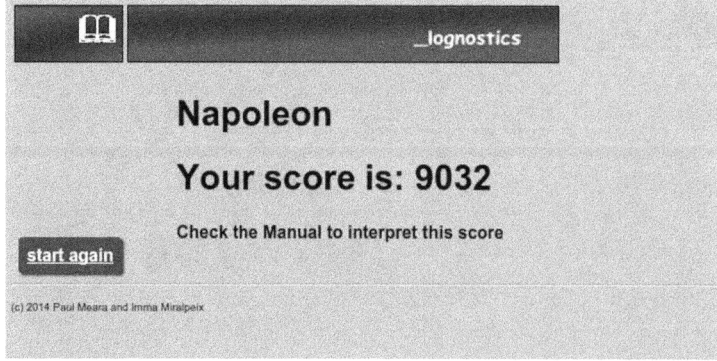

Figure 6.3 V_YesNo report screen

the same test items, and the same general approach to correction for guessing, but the overall structure is shorter and somewhat simplified relative to the EVST tests.

The approach adopted here is different from the original EVST tests in a number of ways. The principal difference is that the number of imaginary words in the stimulus set has been increased, so that real words and imaginary words occur in equal numbers. The main reason for this change is that it greatly simplifies the mathematics needed to score the responses. We have also found that the change reduces the amount of strategic guessing on the part of test takers.

The second difference is that the current version of V_YesNo is not 'computer adaptive' – every test taker gets the same set of stimulus words, and the program does not attempt to guess from their responses what levels need to be probed in more detail. The reason for this change is discussed in the commentary on Meara and Jones (1988) which follows this section.

The third difference is that we have adopted a scoring method that is rather different from the ones described in the earlier literature. The more recent versions of the Yes/No tests – notably X_Lex (Meara & Milton, 2003) – adopted a very simple method of correction for guessing in Yes/No tests as a way of avoiding some of the problems identified in Huibregtse *et al.* (2002) and Beeckmans *et al.* (2001). These simpler methods have not been entirely satisfactory, and for this reason V_YesNo has returned to a version of an earlier scoring method that was implemented in the original EVST tests. This method has the advantage that it avoids excessive penalisation for guessing, and is more generous towards guessing if the test taker gets most of the real words correct. That is, the amount deducted from a test taker's score for a single incorrect YES answer depends on the number of correct YES answers that they provide. Test takers who get most of the real words correct are penalised very lightly for a single incorrect YES answer, whereas those who get only a few real words correct are penalised more heavily. This approach is intuitively correct – some guessing is probably a good thing – but it is not properly backed up by theory. The approach does seem to work, but it should be treated as an 'engineering solution' rather than a theoretically motivated solution. The main advantage of this approach is that test takers can no longer get negative scores, and this solves one of the major problems with earlier versions of our tests.

The method works by collecting two scores for each test taker: Hits are YES responses to real words, False Alarms are YES responses to imaginary words. There are 100 real words and 100 imaginary words in the test. The real words are a stratified sample across a vocabulary of 10,000 words, so each Hit suggests that the test taker knows about 100 words. However, this figure needs to be reduced if there is a large number of False Alarms.

In practice, the data are split into blocks of 20 words, with each block containing 10 real words and 10 imaginary words. For each block, we compute three scores:

- H is the number of Hits, i.e. YES responses to real words.
- F is the number of False Alarms, i.e. YES responses to imaginary words.
- A is a correction factor that is used to adjust the raw Hits in the light of the number of False Alarms.

The correction factor is computed as Equation (1):

$$A = 1 - (w(F)/w(H)) \qquad (1)$$

where $w(F)$ and $w(H)$ are taken from Table 6.1.

Table 6.1 Values for $w(F)$ and $w(H)$

x	0	1	2	3	4	5	6	7	8	9	10
w(x)	0	1	3	6	10	15	20	24	27	29	30

This formula generates an S-shaped logistic weighting function that penalises incorrect YES answers differentially, depending on how many correct YES answers a testee produces. For example, if the number of Hits = 4 and the number of FAs = 1, then a relatively large correction is applied. If the number of Hits = 10 and the number of FAs = 1, then a much smaller correction is applied.

Since there are 100 real words in the test, and the words are sampled from a vocabulary of 10,000 words, we can estimate how many words the testee knows by applying Equation (2):

$$\text{Vsize} = H * 100 * A \qquad (2)$$

where Vsize is the vocabulary size estimate, and A is the correction for guessing from Equation (1).

Cautions

It is very important that V_YesNo should not be used in high-stakes testing situations where a high degree of accuracy and reliability is required. The scores are indicative, and should not be used inappropriately. For example, it would be very unwise to use V_YesNo as an alternative to a more extensive battery of proficiency tests if you were trying to establish whether a candidate's English was good enough to allow them to pursue a high-level course in economics at university level. On the other hand, if a candidate who claims to have, say, an IELTS score of 7.5 was clearly performing at a much lower level than this score would lead us to expect, then you might use V_YesNo to confirm your suspicions that the 7.5 score may not be genuine. For obvious reasons, the authors accept no liability if you use V_YesNo for checks of this sort.

Background Reading

> **Meara, P.M. and Jones, G. (1988) Vocabulary size as a placement indicator. In P. Grunwell (ed.) *Applied Linguistics in Society* (pp. 80–87). London: CILT.**
>
> ## Background
>
> This paper describes a placement test which was developed for the Eurocentres Group during 1986–1987. The Eurocentres schools, like many other private sector language schools in the UK, work on a cycle of short courses each lasting for four weeks. This means that every four weeks there is a huge turnover of students, and a large number of new students have to be assessed and assigned to classes at an appropriate level. In most schools, this assessment is done by means of a complex battery of tests specially designed for this purpose, and generally referred to as placement tests. The tests currently used by Eurocentres, the Joint Entrance Test (JET), are fairly typical of this sort of test; they comprise a listening test, a comprehension test, a grammar test and a reading test, supplemented by an oral interview.
>
> The main problem with tests of this sort is that they take a long time to administer and mark. In a situation where time is at a premium because classes cannot be started until the placement procedure is completed this is obviously a serious shortcoming.
>
> The tests that we have devised differ radically from traditional placement tests. They are very quick to administer (typically they need only 10–15 minutes to complete) and because the whole test is run by a small microcomputer the test is self-scoring and does not need to be checked by a teacher. This represents a large saving in teacher hours, and greatly simplifies the placement procedure.
>
> ## The test
>
> The test we devised for Eurocentres is very different from a traditional placement test, in that it is basically a vocabulary test, and does not attempt to measure other aspects of the learners' knowledge of English. The justification for this approach is that there is a large body of evidence (for English as an L1) that vocabulary knowledge is heavily implicated in

all practical language skills, and that in general speakers with a large vocabulary perform better on a wide range of linguistic indicators than speakers with a more limited vocabulary (Anderson & Freebody, 1981).

However, our test is not just a traditional vocabulary test of the type familiar from Cambridge Proficiency examinations. Instead of testing a small number of vocabulary items with complicated multiple choice type tests, our test is an attempt to measure the absolute size of a learner's vocabulary in English. We do this by simply displaying a large number of English words on a computer screen and asking the testees to decide whether they know each of the words displayed or not. The computer program then uses some sophisticated mathematical techniques to estimate testees' actual vocabulary size. The principal advantage of this methodology is that the test is totally automated. It takes less than 10 minutes to run, and scores itself without any manual intervention.

It is obviously not possible to demonstrate this technique in printed format, but you will get a rough idea how the test works if you try the test in Table 1 before you go any further.

The test in Table 1 presents you with a list of French words and asks you to say which of these words you know. The words are actually a sample of words from the Deuxième degré of *Français Fondamental*, which comprises a total of approximately 2000 high-frequency French words, and if you have studied school French even to an elementary level you should have been able to recognise at least some of these words.

The test in Table 1 actually contains two types of item: real words (which you might have recognised) and imaginary, non-existent words (which you cannot possibly have recognised). This combination of real and imaginary words gives us four combinations of items and answers:

Type of Item	Real	Imaginary
Response YES	RY	IY
Response NO	RN	IN

Now suppose that you identified all the real words and rejected all the imaginary words in the test. In this case we would want to say that you reliably recognised the real words and, because these words are a sample from the set of 2000 words, we would probably want to say that you would be able to recognise reliably all 2000 words in the set.

Suppose, on the other hand, that you identified half the real words and rejected all the imaginary ones. In this case we would want to say that you could probably recognise 50% of 2000 word set, that is, about 1000 words.

Table 1 Look through the French words listed below. Cross out words that you do not know well enough to say what they mean. Keep a record of how long it takes you to do the test.

vivant	trouver	magir	rompant	mélange
livrer	ivre	fombé	moup	vion
lague	inondation	soutenir	siècle	torveau
prêtre	repos	ganal	harton	toule
goûter	foulard	exiger	avare	étoulage
poignée	équipe	missoneur	ajurer	barron
clage	toutefois	leusse	cruyer	hésiter
surprendre	lavire	sid	roman	chic
ornir	cerise	papiment	confiture	gôter
ponte	écarter	mignette	jambonnant	démenager

More interesting cases arise when people produce YES responses to imaginary words. Suppose for example, that you recognised all the real words but you also claimed to recognise half the imaginary words. In this case, we would want to argue that your score of 100% on the real words is too high; it needs to be reduced because your threshold for saying that you recognise a word is too low. The size of the adjustment depends on the number of IY responses you make – obviously if you make lots of IYs, then your acceptance threshold is very low and you are likely to produce RY responses by chance.

The mathematics of all this is not too difficult. In the 1950s, the Navy carried out a great deal of research on how well ASDIC operators could identify enemy submarines. They were interested in three types of behaviour: times when an operator correctly identified that a submarine was actually there; times when an operator failed to identify a submarine that was actually there; and times when an operator identified a submarine that did not actually exist. You will see that there is an obvious parallel between these three situations and the RY, IY and RN responses described above; all that is necessary is to replace 'submarines' by 'French words'. The mathematical model devised to handle the submarine situation (Signal Detection Theory) should also apply to our vocabulary recognition task.

The test which we devised for Eurocentres uses this basic principle, but is rather more complicated than the test outlined above. A schematic version of our test is shown in Figure 1. Basically, our test is divided up into a number of levels, each corresponding to a frequency band of 1000 words. The first part of the test starts off at the highest frequency band,

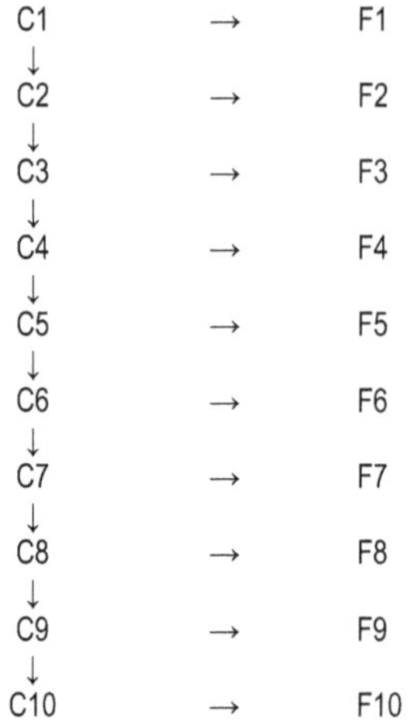

```
C1  →  F1
↓
C2  →  F2
↓
C3  →  F3
↓
C4  →  F4
↓
C5  →  F5
↓
C6  →  F6
↓
C7  →  F7
↓
C8  →  F8
↓
C9  →  F9
↓
C10 →  F10
```

Figure 1 The structure of test files

and assesses how many of these words a testee can be deemed to know by sampling 10 real words and 10 imaginary words. If the testees score highly on this band, then they are tested on the next band, and this process continues until performance drops below a preset threshold. At this point, the program works out a rough estimate of how many words we think each testee knows, and tests a further 50 words from the appropriate frequency band. So, suppose our testee scores 100% on Bands 1–4 but only 20% on Band 5, the program reckons that the testee knows somewhere between 4000 and 5000 words, and does its detailed testing on Band 4. The detailed testing phase actually tests one word in 20 at the appropriate level. Figure 1 shows the structure of test files, where we distinguish between Coarse files and Fine files:

- *Coarse files* (C1–C10) contain 10 items from the bottom end of a specific frequency band. The testee moves through the coarse files in turn, until her performance is too poor to allow her to continue, or until she successfully completes the final file C10.
- *Fine files* (F1–F10) contain 50 items from the specific frequency range, and thus allow us to test explicitly one word in 20. Once the testee finishes a fine file, her total vocabulary score is calculated.

Assessment

So far we have run three versions of the test with about 250 students from a wide range of language backgrounds, 109 at the Cambridge

Table 2 Correlations between the Vocabulary Test and JET

Cambridge	109 testees	Overall correlation	0.664
		Subgroups: French Ss	0.549
		German Ss	0.807
	Adjustments: 4 out of 5		
London	159 testees	Overall correlation	0.717
		Subgroups: French Ss	0.556
		Italian Ss	0.792
		Spanish Ss	0.723
		Portuguese Ss	0.756
		German Ss	0.790
		Non-IE Ss	0.735
	Adjustments: 9 out of 14		

Eurocentres School and two groups totalling 159 in London. For practical reasons, we have mainly been interested in correlating the results of our test with results of the Eurocentres JET test – i.e. we are interested in establishing how far our vocabulary test can be used as an alternative to JET placement test. The results of this work are summarised in Table 2.

There are a number of interesting points to note here. First, the correlations between JET and the vocabulary test (VOC) are generally high: in fact, given the diverse nature of the tests, the results are surprisingly high. Obviously, the correlation is not perfect, but given that JET is itself unsatisfactory in some ways, this is only to be expected. More interesting is the fact that the correlations vary slightly for different language groups. In general, correlations for homogenous language groups are better than correlations for mixed groups, and some linguistic groups produce very high levels of correlation indeed. This is not always the case, however. With the French speakers studied here, the correlations between the VOC and JET are consistently low. At the moment, we do not really know how to interpret these differences. One possible explanation is that the VOC test in its present format is systematically biased against speakers of particular languages, but it is equally possible that the JET test is biased in the same way. Some evidence for this latter view comes from another study (Meara & Buxton, 1987), in which very high levels of correlation between a VOC test and a more traditional multiple choice test were found with French speakers.

A further check on the effectiveness of the VOC test as a placement indicator comes from adjustments made to class registers one week after the original placements by JET. In the Cambridge study (109 cases) five students were reallocated to a different group on the basis of their actual performance in class. Four of these cases were moved to a higher level than their original placements, and in every case this move was in line with the placements produced by VOC. In the London trials (159 cases), a questionnaire was used to assess major discrepancies in the placements produced by JET. This trawl produced 14 cases; in nine of these cases, teachers' assessments agreed with the VOC score rather than the JET score. Not surprisingly, if these cases are excluded from the data, the overall correlation between JET and VOC increases.

Conclusion

This paper has described a relatively small-scale study which uses a measure of vocabulary size as a way of placing students at the start of their course. The data that we have presented suggest the test works well, although obviously a great deal more work will be needed before we can claim it is thoroughly reliable. The test in its present format, for example, is basically a test of visual familiarity, and it assumes that recognition of a word form is an adequate test of word knowledge. This assumption is clearly one that needs to be probed carefully. Obviously, formal recognition is a necessary but not sufficient condition for word knowledge but, by relying on recognition, the test probably overestimates true vocabulary knowledge. Whether this really matters or not is anybody's guess: it could be, for example, that passive recognition vocabulary is generally closely related to the size of the learners' active vocabulary, and that a more accurate estimate of vocabulary size could be obtained by suitably adjusting the raw scores found on the VOC test. Another problem arises from the imaginary words. The current version of the test uses imaginary words which are very carefully constructed so they share the physical characteristics of the real words in the same set. However, it is clear to us that some of the imaginary words are easier to handle than others: some can be rejected instantaneously, while others cause even native speakers in English to puzzle for a long time. We also think that some imaginary words cause difficulty to speakers from particular language backgrounds. Again, we do not know why this should be, but the problem is one that can easily be solved by further work.

At the moment, then, the best we can say is that the work we have done looks very promising and, if further developments live up to these promises, then it looks as though the tedious and time-consuming task of placing students at the start of a course could be greatly simplified and streamlined. A small contribution to *'applied linguistics in society'*, perhaps, but one that will be welcomed by many teachers.

However, the VOC test has other advantages besides these practical ones. One major advantage from the research point of view is the speed with which the VOC test can be administered. Since it only takes 10 minutes, there is no reason why it should not become a standard tool for assessing participants in empirical research. At the moment, the research literature uses only vague labels for describing people who take part in research: '50 first certificate students', '25 students following a pre-university course at Stanford', or '150 air force pilots' are typical examples of this sort of labelling. Clearly they are not very informative; it would be much more helpful to be told that we are dealing with, say, 150 air force pilots who scored mean a 4500 on the VOC test with a standard deviation of 50 words. The fact that the VOC test is so quick to administer makes this kind of standardisation a real possibility.

The VOC test is also interesting because it opens up areas of research which have not been accessible before. If the VOC test really does measure vocabulary size, then we can begin to ask questions like these:

- How fast do people learn new words?
- How much individual variation is there in the skill?
- Is it affected by other variables, such as L1, or L1 vocabulary size?
- How effective are different types of teaching programmes?
- Do intensive courses produce more vocabulary learning than less intensive ones?
- How quickly do learners who do not practise lose their vocabulary?
- Is the fallout rate such that it reaches a stable asymptote? i.e. is there a residue of words that you never really forget, no matter how little you practise?

These are questions that we hope to address in the future.

To sum up, then, the VOC started out as a practical research problem aimed at providing a solution to an organisational problem. In R&D circles, it is common to hear people talking about the practical spin-offs from the theoretical research: the VOCD test seems to be a clear case of theoretical spin-offs from the practical research. Maybe the real future of applied linguistics lies down this road?

References

Anderson, R. and Freebody, P. (1981) Vocabulary knowledge. In J.T. Guthrie (ed.) *Comprehension and Teaching: Research Reviews* (pp. 77–117). Newark, DE: International Reading Association.

Meara, P.M. and Buxton, B. (1987) An alternative to multiple choice vocabulary tests. *Language Testing* 4 (2), 142–154.

Reflections on Meara and Jones (1988)

Meara and Jones (1988) was the first public account of our work on Yes/No tests with L2 speakers. It was largely ignored by the academic community (Scholfield, 1995; Wesche *et al.*, 1996 were the only notable exceptions), but the work generated a certain amount of interest among language schools in London, where placement tests were a serious practical issue.

The work reported in this paper was probably a bit premature. It was commissioned by the Eurocentres Group rather faster than we expected, and we jumped into evaluating the practical applications of Yes/No tests as a placement test rather than evaluating the fundamental assumptions that Anderson and Freebody's work was based on. The commission from Eurocentres also meant that we did not have a free hand in evaluating the approach against a range of standard tests. Eurocentres wanted to know whether the Yes/No test produced results as good as the much longer in-house placement test that they were using at the time, the JET test. JET was not a standardised test, and it was not used outside the Eurocentres family, and this meant that the correlations we found between the Yes/No test and the subcomponents of the JET test were of limited interest to the wider community outside Eurocentres. Obviously, with hindsight, we should have run a whole series of other studies to evaluate whether the tests worked in other contexts. It is difficult to see, though, what other tests we might have used at the time.

In the event, the Yes/No project got bogged down in how to correct the scores for guessing. The formula used by Anderson and Freebody was the standard formula for correction for guessing, shown below as Equation (3).

$$P(K) = \frac{P(H) - P(FA)}{1 - P(FA)} \tag{3}$$

where $P(K)$ is the proportion of words that the test taker knows;
$P(H)$ is the probability of the test taker making a Hit response;
$P(FA)$ is the probability of the test taker making a False Alarm response.

However, a little bit of experimentation with this formula shows that it is problematical in a number of ways. The main problem is that the formula does not penalise False Alarms if the number of Hits is high. In the extreme case, where a test taker says YES to all the real words, no penalty applies however many False Alarms are recorded, and the test taker is credited with a full score. This is clearly not what was intended, but most people do not seem to have noticed this problem, and were not deterred from following Anderson and Freebody's lead. In an attempt to address this issue, we worked with alternative correction formulae based on Signal Detection Theory.

Again, with hindsight, this was a strategic error. Signal Detection Theory methods are not a standard part of the statistical toolkit provided to applied linguists, and this made the Yes/No methodology difficult for people to evaluate. It also discouraged them from evaluating some of the assumptions that we had made in applying Signal Detection Theory to vocabulary testing. For example, we can ask: Is it really valid to draw an analogy between recognising words and distinguishing a signal from background noise? Does it matter that non-signals in Signal Detection Theory models usually require a non-response, whereas our imaginary words required a specific NO response? How important is the fact that some imaginary words are much more likely to be identified as a known word than other words are? Is confidence that you know a word actually the same thing as really knowing it? We made a number of attempts to patch up the problems with Signal Detection approaches, but none of them really worked. Most ran up against the problem that about 10% of testees produced negative scores on the Yes/No test, a result which was difficult to interpret and did not inspire much confidence. Eventually, in our X_Lex tests, we abandoned the Signal Detection Theory models in favour of a more transparent approach to correction for guessing.

In spite of these problems, Meara and Jones (1988) highlighted a number of interesting questions which deserved further study. Probably the most important of these questions is why the tests work as well as they do. The 1988 paper explains how the test makes a rough estimate of the testees' vocabulary size, and then tests a band of words at the relevant frequency in order to firm up that estimate. Thus, if the program's coarse scoring reckons that a testee's vocabulary is about 5500 words, then it will test a lot of words from the 5K frequency band in order to firm up this estimate. However, if you think about it, this additional fine testing does not actually add very much information to what we know already. For most practical cases, knowing that a testee's vocabulary is in the region of 5500 is as much as we need to know. Making this estimate more accurate (e.g. claiming that the test taker knows 5442 words) looks good, but the accuracy is probably spurious. Most of the work has already been done when the program decided that the testee knows about 5500 words. What is surprising here is that the coarse scoring provided by EVST uses only 10 words at each 1000 word level, and yet still manages to provide data which classify testees into useful categories of proficiency. It is not at all clear how we can achieve this with such a very simple and very small vocabulary test.

The second question raised by the 1988 paper is the surprisingly large correlations that were found between vocabulary size and other aspects of language competence. Consistent correlations were reported between vocabulary size and other language skills in the region of 0.7 – this means that about half of the variation in the data can be explained in terms of participants' vocabulary size, a result which has been replicated in a large number of later studies. The obvious question that arises here is: Why does vocabulary knowledge play such a key role in language competence? Our best guess is that vocabulary size and the other aspects of competence are both strongly affected by general exposure to the L2. People who get a lot of exposure pick up a lot of words: for example, someone who reads a lot (and is therefore good at reading) will pick up a lot of words by way of incidental acquisition. It is not that having a large vocabulary makes you a good reader, rather that being a good reader leads you to engage in activity that makes it easy for you to acquire a large vocabulary. In this sense, it is not that vocabulary drives the other aspects of competence, but rather that almost any learning activity will provide opportunities for learners to develop their vocabularies. Measuring vocabulary size is just a very easy way to evaluate the extent of these opportunities.

The third question which arises from this paper is highlighted by the anomalous data recorded for L1 French speakers. Basically, there are very high correlations between JET scores and vocabulary scores for all the testees, but for L1 French speakers this relationship is much weaker than for other groups. This finding raises a number of questions about how the Yes/No tests work with specific L1 groups: Shillaw's (1996) work with L1 Japanese learners, and Al-Hazemi's (2001) work with L1 Arabic speakers suggest that there are some interesting cultural differences appearing in Yes/No data. The French data do not fit with this simple explanation, however. Our best guess is that the fact that there are large numbers of English words which closely resemble large numbers of French words affects the way L1 French speakers approach English words, and we suspect that this familiarity effect interacts with test takers' confidence in their judgements. This may also happen to L1 English speakers when faced with L2 French words. You can see this effect at work in Table 6.2.

It takes considerable confidence, and considerable familiarity with French morphology, to be able to say that none of these items is a French word – as English speakers, we are used to finding cognate words in French, and these items all look very plausible. Furthermore, if they *were* real words, then we would know exactly what they mean. This suggests that the construction of imaginary words for Yes/No tests may be a more subtle task than it looks at first sight. It also suggests Yes/No tests may not be an appropriate tool if you are working with test takers whose L1 and L2 share a very large number of identical cognates. For example, it might not be appropriate to use Yes/No tests to evaluate the L2 vocabulary size of L1 Spanish learners of Catalan, or L1 Norwegian learners of Swedish.

Table 6.2 Do you know the meaning of these French words?

| enjoyer | advent | dupliquer | indenter | invaluable |

More Research is Needed ...

This section contains some ideas that could easily be worked up into small-scale research projects.

- How reliable are the estimates that V_YesNo generates?
- V_YesNo, like most vocabulary size tests, relies heavily on frequency counts. Can we improve on frequency counts?
- Do Yes/No tests based on adjectives or verbs provide better estimates than tests based on randomly sampled words? (*This project would involve comparing different lists of items. The program does not allow you to do this at the moment.*)
- What kind of errors do people make on a Yes/No test? Do people actually know the words they think they know?
- How do the scores generated by V_YesNo compare with scores generated by other tests of vocabulary size?
- How do measures of receptive vocabulary compare with measures of productive vocabulary?
- How do the scores generated by V_YesNo compare with scores generated by a test of productive vocabulary size? How does this relationship vary with the test takers' vocabulary size?
- How do the scores generated with V_YesNo relate to the Common European Framework?
- How well do scores on V_YesNo correspond to grades on public examinations?
- Why do Yes/No vocabulary tests produce odd results with L1 French speakers?
- Some people get very low scores on Yes/No tests. What are the characteristics of these people?
- Can we use V_YesNo with very young learners?
- Is V_YesNo suitable for use with dyslexic learners?
- Is it feasible to use the Yes/No approach to evaluate listening vocabulary?

Accessing the Data Collected by V_YesNo

V_YesNo stores all the data produced by each individual test taker. It is possible for bona fide researchers to have access to these data on request. The data stored by V_YesNo consist of each test taker's overall Hits, False Alarms and their score reported by the program. The data also include a list of key presses made by each individual test taker, and a record of whether these were YES responses to real words, YES responses to non-words, NO responses to non-words or NO responses to real words.

The data are saved in this format: 271146:mateo:6221::
YynYnYnyNyyNYyYyNYNYYYYNYNNNyNYNYYnYNYNNNNNNYYY
NNnNNNYYYNnnYNyYNNNNnYYnNNnNYNYYYYnYyNNYnnNNN
NnNynYNYnnNNYyNYyYYYnYNNNyNNYNnNYnNnnYNynYNYNNN
NyYYNnNYNNYYYYNnNNYNNNNYYYYNNNYnNYNYNYYNYnYYY
YNNNNNYyYNNNYYy

This report tells you that **mateo**, whose id code was **271146**, scored 6221 words. In the data string, a **Y** indicates that mateo correctly identified a real word, a **y** indicates that he incorrectly identified an imaginary word as a word he knows. Similarly, a **N** response indicates that mateo identified an imaginary word as one that he did not know, while a **n** response indicates a real word that he failed to recognise.

The **V_YesNo_Rdr** program allows you to access any data that you have submitted to the site. The program can be accessed from the Lognostics ToolBox site, available at: http://www.lognostics.co.uk/tools/V_YesNo/V_YesNo_Rdr.htm.

This program will allow you to recover any data for which you have an access code. Further details are available in the online Manual.

References

Alderson, J.C. and Huhta, A. (2005) The development of a suite of computer-based diagnostic tests based on the Common European Framework. *Language Testing* 22 (3), 301–320.
Al-Hazemi, H. (2001) Listening to the Yes/No vocabulary test and its impact on the recognition of words as real or non-real. A case study of Arab learners of English. *International Review of Applied Linguistics in Language Teaching* 38 (2), 89–94.
Anderson, R. and Freebody, P. (1981) Vocabulary knowledge. In J.T. Guthrie (ed.) *Comprehension and Teaching: Research Reviews* (pp. 77–117). Newark, DE: International Reading Association.
Beeckmans, R., Eyckmans, J., Janssens, V., Dufranne, M. and Van de Velde, H. (2001) Examining the yes–no vocabulary test: Some methodological issues in theory and practice. *Language Testing* 18 (3), 235–274.
Beglar, D. and Hunt, A. (1999) Revising and validating the 2000 Word Level and University Word Level Vocabulary tests. *Language Testing* 16 (2), 131–162.
Eyckmans, J. (2004) Measuring receptive vocabulary size. PhD thesis, University of Utrecht.
Henmon, V.A.C. (1917) The measurement of ability in Latin. Part I: Vocabulary. *Journal of Educational Psychology* 8 (9), 515–538.
Henmon, V.A.C. (1920) The measurement of ability in Latin. Part III: Vocabulary and sentence tests. *Journal of Educational Psychology* 11 (3), 121–136.
Higgins, J. (1995) The THNEED test. In J. Higgins (ed.) *Computers and English Language Learning* (pp. 116–118). Oxford: Intellect.
Huibregtse, I., Admiraal, W. and Meara, P.M. (2002) Scores on a yes–no vocabulary test: Correction for guessing and response style. *Language Testing* 19 (3), 227–245.
Meara, P.M. and Jones, G. (1988) Vocabulary size as a placement indicator. In P. Grunwell (ed.) *Applied Linguistics in Society* (pp. 80–87). London: CILT.
Meara, P.M. and Jones, G. (1990) *Eurocentres Vocabulary Size Tests*. Zurich: Eurocentres Learning Service.

Meara, P.M. and Milton, J. (2003) *X_Lex: The Swansea Vocabulary Levels Test*. Newbury: Express Publishing.

Nation, I.S.P. (1983) Testing and teaching vocabulary. *Guidelines* 5 (1), 12–25.

Nation, I.S.P. (1990) *Teaching and Learning Vocabulary*. Rowley, MA: Newbury House.

Oller, J.W. (1973) Cloze tests of second language proficiency and what they measure. *Language Learning* 23 (1), 105–118.

Ryden, E.R. (1948) Vocabulary as an index of learning in a second language. *Journal of Educational Psychology* 39 (7), 436–440.

Schmitt, N., Schmitt, D. and Clapham, C. (2001) Developing and exploring the behaviour of two new versions of the Vocabulary Levels Test. *Language Testing* 18 (1), 55–88.

Scholfield, P. (1995) *Quantifying Language: A Researchers' and Teachers' Guide to Gathering Language Data and Reducing it to Figures*. Clevedon: Multilingual Matters.

Shillaw, J. (1996) The application of Rasch modelling to Yes/No vocabulary tests. See http://www.lognostics.co.uk/vlibrary/

Wesche, M.B., Paribakht, T.S. and Ready, D. (1996) A comparative study of four ESL placement instruments. In M. Milanovic and N. Saville (eds) *Performance Testing, Cognition and Assessment. Selected Papers from the 15th Testing Research Colloquium* (pp. 199–210). Cambridge: Cambridge University Press.

Suggestions for further reading

Cameron, L. (2002) Measuring vocabulary size in English as an additional language. *Language Teaching Research* 6 (2), 145–173.

Harrington, M. and Carey, M. (2009) The on-line Yes/No test as a placement tool. *System* 37 (4), 614–626.

Meara, P.M. (1990) Some notes on the Eurocentres Vocabulary Tests. In J. Tommola (ed.) *Foreign Language Comprehension and Production* (pp. 103–113). Turku: AFinLA Yearbook. See http://www.lognostics.co.uk/vlibrary/

Meara, P.M. (1994) The complexities of simple vocabulary tests. In F.G. Brinkman, J.A. van der Schee and M.C. Schouten-van Parreren (eds) *Curriculum Research: Different Disciplines and Common Goals* (pp. 15–28). Amsterdam: Vrije Universiteit. See http://www.lognostics.co.uk/vlibrary/

Mochida, A. and Harrington, M. (2006) Yes/No test as a measure of receptive vocabulary. *Language Learning* 23 (1), 73–98.

Shillaw, J. (2009) Putting Yes/No tests in context. In T. Fitzpatrick and A. Barfield (eds) *Lexical Processing in Second Language Learners* (pp. 13–24). Bristol: Multilingual Matters.

Stubbe, R. (2013) Comparing regression vs. correction formula predictions of passive recall test scores from Yes-No tests results. *Vocabulary Learning and Instruction* 2 (1), 39–46.

7   V_Size v2.01

Introduction

V_Size is part of our ongoing research into ways of assessing the productive vocabulary of L2 speakers. Most research in this area assesses the texts that L2 speakers produce in terms of their lexical richness – usually measured by looking at the type/token ratio of the text, or some variation of this ratio such as Malvern and Richard's vocd measure (e.g. Malvern *et al.*, 2004). Alternatively, they use profiles such as the lexical frequency profiles developed by Laufer and Nation (1995). V_Size belongs to the second category – it works with profiles, rather than with type/token ratios. Laufer and Nation's profiles are not particularly easy to work with, however, and it is difficult to summarise the data that they encapsulate in an economical and transparent way. V_Size is an attempt to do just that: it goes beyond the mere shape of the profile generated by a text, and asks what the profile tells us about the size of the productive vocabulary of the person who produced that text. Basically, the program allows us to look at a profile and make statements such as: 'this text looks as though it was generated by a person whose productive vocabulary is about 5500 words.' Obviously, this is a rather strong claim, and it requires some justification.

Briefly, the program makes use of a number of results that derive from Zipf's Law (Zipf, 1935). Zipf argued that language was one of very many things where a simple relationship could be found between the rank order of an event and the size of the event. For language, Zipf argued that the pattern of frequencies exhibited by words followed this law, and he claimed that there was a straightforward relationship between the number of times a word occurred in a corpus and its rank order in a frequency list generated from the corpus. In simple terms, Zipf claimed that some words are more frequent than others, and you could tell roughly how many times a word would occur in a large corpus by looking at its rank order. Zipf's work has been widely used in computational linguistics (e.g. Herdan, 1964). It was also taken up in an important paper by Ellegård (1960) which suggested that Zipf's ideas about text structure could be adapted for measurement purposes. Ellegård's paper makes an explicit distinction between 'theoretical' and 'observed' vocabularies, but the state of computing at the time meant that he was unable to exploit these insights effectively.

V_Size exploits these ideas in a very simple way: it assumes that Zipf's Law is basically correct, and that texts generated from a vocabulary of a particular size will tend to have a characteristic frequency profile. For example, a text generated by a speaker with a very small vocabulary will contain only very frequent words, whereas a text generated by a speaker with a very large vocabulary will have fewer very frequent words and more infrequent ones. Zipf's Law tells us how many more infrequent words we can expect to appear as a speaker's vocabulary grows. This allows us to generate a series of profiles that would be characteristic of the text produced by speakers with different vocabulary sizes.

V_Size uses these theoretical profiles to make an estimate of the productive vocabulary that was available to the person who generates an actual text. It does this by generating a profile for a specific text, and comparing this profile to a series of theoretical profiles stored in its memory. It reports which of these theoretical profiles is the best match to the actual profile, and estimates the vocabulary size of the author of the text.

Clearly, there are a number of assumptions here which need to be treated with caution. In practice, however, the profiles that are generated by these assumptions are an astonishingly good match for real texts, and the vocabulary size estimates generated by this type of comparison are plausible. This suggests that V_Size might be a good engineering solution to the problem of assessing productive vocabulary size, even if there is still considerable work to be done on the underlying theory.

Using V_Size

You will find the V_Size program on the Lognostics Tools website, available at: http://www.lognostics.co.uk/tools/V_Size/V_Size.htm.

(1) Your computer will display a window which looks like Figure 7.1. This is the V_Size workspace, where you have four different boxes: the first box is where you introduce the text for analysis; in the second you can give your text a name; and in the third box you will include all those words from the text that the program may not recognise and that you would like to classify as high-frequency items (see below). Finally, the last box contains the punctuation characters that you would like the program to ignore.
(2) Some preparation may be necessary before you submit a text to V_Size (you can do that on the opening screen or in a file before pasting the text).
For obvious reasons, we cannot include in the V_Size dictionary an exhaustive list of proper names, place names and numbers. If you replace

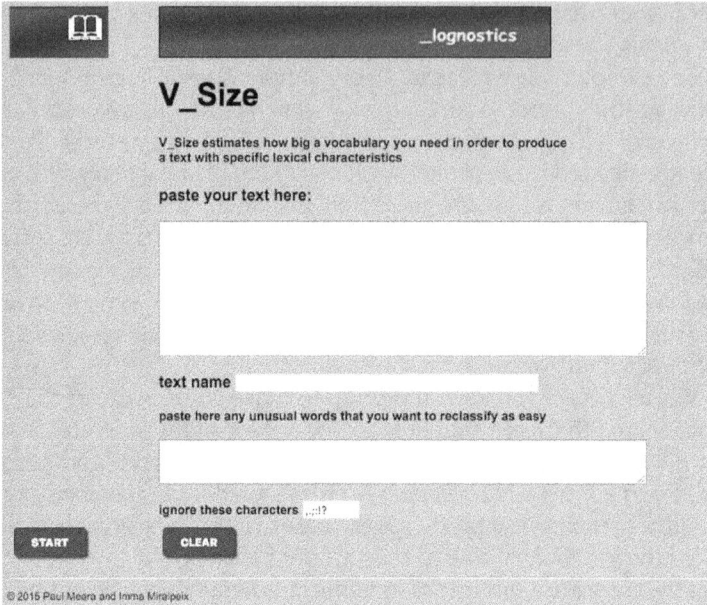

Figure 7.1 V_Size workspace

any items of this sort by PLACE, NAME or NUMBER as appropriate, then these items will automatically be scored as high-frequency words.

Some words may be objectively infrequent, but may have a high probability of occurrence in the context of a specific task. For example, if you ask people to write *The story of my life*, they will almost always include the word *born*. This is normally a low-frequency item, but in this context it **is** a high-frequency item, and you might want to recategorise it accordingly. Any words that you enter into the box underneath the main text box will automatically be reclassified by V_Size as high-frequency items.

You will also need to develop a formal policy on errors. Frequent words which are mis-spelled will be incorrectly labelled by V_Size as low-frequency words. You can resolve this problem either by correcting any spelling errors, or by listing any errors in the reclassification box.

(3) Once your text is ready, provide a name for it and introduce in the reclassification box all those words you would like the program to count as high-frequency words.
(4) Click on **Start** to obtain the vocabulary estimate for your text.
(5) V_Size produces a report that looks like Figure 7.2. In this example, the **estimated vocabulary size** indicates that the text called 'STORY' has been produced by a person who knows at least 3800 words productively. The report also shows the list of words that the program has classified as unusual. The graphic displays the empirical profile of your text ('data')

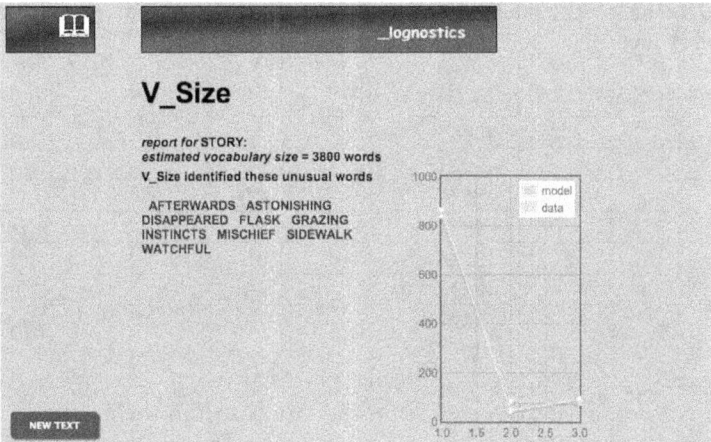

Figure 7.2 V_Size final report

and the theoretical profile that most closely matches your data ('model'). In the report screen of the program, the former appears in blue and the latter in yellow (dark line and clear line in the screenshot, Figure 7.2).
(6) At this point, you can click on the **New text** button to work with another text.

The technical bits

V_Size works by creating a profile for the text that you have submitted and this profile consists of three scores. The first score reflects the number of high-frequency words in the text – these are words that occur in the most frequent 1000 words of English together with their basic morphological derivatives. The second point reflects the number of slightly less frequent words in the text – these are words which occur in the second 1000 most frequent words in English and their basic derivatives. The third point reflects the total of all the other words in the text. The reference list used to make these assessments is based on the JACET lists (Ishikawa *et al.*, 2003) – this list is not strictly a frequency list of English words, but it seems to work better than alternatives such as the BNC list.

V_Size does not just count the words in your text to generate its profile. Instead, it takes a large number of randomly sampled lists of 100 words from your text, and computes the average values of these samples. The profile that V_Size evaluates is the average of these random samples. The reason for this approach is that the sort of texts we typically evaluate with V_Size tend to be short, and this means that the presence or absence of one or two words can significantly distort the profile. Using randomised samples smooths out these distortions, and makes the profiles more stable.

Table 7.1 Theoretical profiles for a 1000 word text generated from vocabularies containing 1000, 2000, 3000, 4000, 5000, 6000 and 7000 words

No. words in vocabulary	Expected 1K words	Expected 2K words	Other words
1000	1000	0	0
2000	908	92	0
3000	863	87	50
4000	832	84	84
5000	811	81	108
6000	793	80	127
7000	780	79	141

Next, V_Size compares the profile generated by your text against a set of stored profiles. These theoretical profiles are based on the assumption that the occurrence of words in texts is roughly determined by a Power Law of the sort described by Zipf (1935).

To build a theoretical profile, we first decide how many words our vocabulary contains – call this value V. Next we randomly select 1000 'words' to build our text. In fact, these words are numbers that vary between 1 and V. Low numbers are assumed to represent high-frequency words, and larger numbers are assumed to represent lower frequency words. By weighting the selection using a logarithmic transformation, we can generate a 'text' which contains a large number of high-frequency words, and smaller numbers of lower frequency words, just as real texts do. A selection of these theoretical profiles are shown in Table 7.1.

V_Size has a number of these profiles, spaced out at 100-word intervals. Each profile is based on the average of 1000 datasets. When the program has computed a profile for the data you submit to it, it goes on to compare the stored profile that is the best match for the data. Suppose, for example, that the data you submit generate the profile [831,83,56]. This profile looks very close to the stored profile for a 4000-word vocabulary [832,84,54]. If none of the other profiles is closer than this, then V_Size will return 4000 words as its best estimate of the vocabulary size that underlies the profile.

Note that the highest score returned by V_Size is 7000 words. It is theoretically possible to generate profiles for larger vocabulary sizes, but the program becomes less effective at discriminating between texts as the underlying vocabulary gets larger.

Background Reading

> **Gesa, F. (2015) How many words do you know? Measuring the L2 productive vocabulary size of EFL learners. Adapted from unpublished MA thesis, 2014. University of Barcelona.**

Introduction

Research on L2 vocabulary acquisition has traditionally distinguished between receptive and productive vocabulary size (see Melka, 1997; Waring, 1997). As the former has been much more fully investigated than the latter, there are a number of testing tools that both teachers and researchers can use to evaluate and measure receptive vocabulary size. There is, however, a serious shortage of tools that can be used to estimate productive vocabulary size in L2 learners. The present paper aims to explore the performance of a recently created tool (V_Size; Meara & Miralpeix, 2006), which estimates productive vocabulary size from learners' output.

Literature review

Vocabulary size and L2 learning

Vocabulary size – the number of words that a person knows in a given language – is a crucial feature in the attainment of native-like proficiency in a target language. The implications of having a large vocabulary are quite evident:

> all other things being equal, learners with big vocabularies are more proficient in a wide range of language skills than learners with smaller vocabularies, and there is some evidence to support the view that vocabulary skills make a significant contribution to almost all aspects of L2 proficiency. (Meara, 1996: 37)

Vocabulary size makes a great contribution to overall L2 proficiency and to several aspects of L2 learning/acquisition. For example, Miralpeix (2008) points to different reasons why vocabulary size has been considered a key factor in the process of learning a new language, one of them being that there is a strong relationship between vocabulary size and how well one understands, reads, writes and speaks the target language. In other words, if someone knows only a few words in a given language, s/he will not be able to communicate fluently and meaningfully.

There is some evidence that vocabulary size is directly related to different language skills. Hirsch and Nation (1992) argued that learners need at least 5000 words in order to read comfortably. What is more, Hu and Nation (2000) recommend a higher percentage (98–99%) to almost guarantee successful guessing. This connection can be extended to speaking. According to Koizumi (2005: 15), 'more than half (60–61%) of speaking ability is explained by productive vocabulary knowledge and one-fifth (19%) is predicted by the ability to use lexical knowledge'. Thus, a strong link has been established between the number of words a learner knows and their speaking skills. A more recent study by Staehr (2008) found a strong link between receptive vocabulary size and listening, reading and writing. Test results from 88 Danish learners of English who were finishing Grade 9 in six Danish schools exhibited moderate to strong correlations: vocabulary size and listening ($r = 0.69$); vocabulary size and reading ($r = 0.83$); and vocabulary size and writing ($r = 0.73$); all ps being significant at the 0.01 level.

There are also some other hints in the literature that productive vocabulary size is an important contributor to L2 performance. For example, it is related to the lexical richness and lexical sophistication of L2 texts: Laufer and Nation (1995) found significant correlations between productive vocabulary, as measured by the bands in the Lexical Frequency Profile (LFP), and the use of a greater variety of words. Results from the study suggest that 'we can reasonably expect learners' vocabulary size as measured by a vocabulary test [the LFP] to be reflected in the learners' productive use of the language' (Laufer & Nation, 1995: 319). Meara and Fitzpatrick (2000) studied receptive vocabulary size and lexical sophistication through a word-association test (i.e. Lex30). They found a correlation between size and sophistication of 0.841 level ($p < 0.001$), and conclude that 'this indicates that subjects with a large receptive vocabulary also tended to produce a relatively high number of infrequent words in the Lex30 test, and that scores on one of the tests can largely be predicted from the other' (Meara & Fitzpatrick, 2000: 24).

It seems, therefore, that vocabulary size (both receptive and productive) has an important role in the development of L2 learners' proficiency and in their ability to communicate successfully in the L2. However, any exploration of the specific effects of productive vocabulary size is seriously hampered by the lack of tools to estimate it properly.

The measurement of productive vocabulary size

Nation (1990: 5) defined productive vocabulary as 'the ability to write the needed vocabulary at the appropriate time'. This definition is quite similar to the one proposed by Nattinger (1988: 62), who defined productive vocabulary as 'the retrieval of words from memory by using them in appropriate situations'. Knowing a word productively differs from knowing it receptively as it also implies the ability to perform a set of operations with that word: for example, 'to decide to use or not use the word to suit the degree of formality in a situation' or 'to say it with correct pronunciation' (Nation, 2001: 28). In order to know a word productively, different aspects need to be mastered: knowledge of spelling and pronunciation, shades of meaning, ability to use it properly with its collocates in grammatically correct constructions, etc. (Waring, 1997).

Laufer (1998) makes a distinction between **controlled productive vocabulary** and **free productive vocabulary**. She defined a test of controlled productive vocabulary as one that 'entails producing words prompted by a task' (e.g. when the first two letters of a word in the context of a sentence are provided to the student), whereas free productive vocabulary 'has to do with using words at one's free will, without any specific prompts for particular words' (Laufer, 1998: 257).

Controlled productive vocabulary is considerably easier to assess than free productive vocabulary, and Laufer and Nation (1999) have developed a test that can be used to assess the former. The test uses the same vocabulary items that appear in Nation's Vocabulary Levels test, but it tests these words as gap-fill items in a sentence context. The test takers' responses are constrained by providing the first few letters of the expected response, as in the example below:

You must spend less until your deb_____ are paid.

Despite a number of criticisms of this methodology (e.g. Meara & Fitzpatrick, 2000), arguing that it is very difficult to obtain a meaningful estimate of productive vocabulary size using this approach, the Productive Vocabulary Levels Test has become the de facto norm for research on productive vocabulary size.

Free productive vocabulary is often assessed using Laufer and Nation's Lexical Frequency Profile (Laufer & Nation, 1995). This tool classifies the words in a text according to different frequency bands: 1K, 2K, AWL and NiL (not-in-the-list; i.e. words which do not belong to any of the previous categories). A more recent version of the LFP approach is the BNC-20 version of VocabProfile (Nation & Cobb, 2007), where the words in a text are analysed into 20 frequency-based bands (from 1K to 20K). The main problem with these analyses is that the profiles do not of themselves provide an overall estimation of learners' productive vocabulary size, and because the profile consists of a set of indices, rather than a single score, it is not straightforward to compare one profile with another.

V_Size (Meara & Miralpeix, 2006) is an attempt to extract a meaningful vocabulary size estimate from an LFP-type profile. It does this 'by comparing the curve of the learner's profile with the curves of theoretical ideal profiles generated by the logarithmic function' (Miralpeix,

2008: 173). These theoretical profiles are underpinned by Zipf's Law, which states that the frequency of a word in a corpus is inversely proportional to its rank in the frequency table (Zipf, 1935).

V_Size generates a large number of different profiles produced by vocabularies of different amounts of words and then finds the one that best matches the profile of the input text. V_Size v2.0 also reports the error of the adjustment (i.e. the figure describing the difference between the empirical profile from the input text and the theoretical profile which is found to be its best match). The reported error is usually very small. V_Size v2.0 analyses the input text by classifying its words into five different frequency categories: A (500 most common words); B (501–1000 words); C (1001–1500 words); D (1501–2000 words); and E (words not included in the 2000 most frequent words of the English language). The program can classify words according to two different frequency lists (BNC and JACET), but it also allows the user to re-classify words that the program identifies as 'difficult' because they are not found in these word lists. The main advantages of this approach are that: (1) it is inferential; (2) it works with five bands instead of four; (3) it chooses words at random to obtain the theoretical profiles; and (4) it is time saving (Miralpeix, 2008: 179). Castañeda-Jiménez and Jarvis (2014: 501) point out that V_Size 'is the only freely available computer program we [the authors] know of that outputs estimates of learners' productive vocabulary based on the texts they produce'.

Research questions

The present exploratory study uses V_Size to answer the following research questions:

- RQ1: Is there a difference between EFL learners' and native speakers' (NSs) productive vocabulary size estimates as measured by an oral narrative task?
- RQ2: Is there a difference in EFL learners' productive vocabulary size estimates when narrative tasks are assessed according to two different baselists (i.e. JACET 2000 list versus NSs' task-based frequency list)?

Methodology

Participants

Ten English as a Foreign Language (EFL) learners participated in the study. All of them were in their early/mid-twenties and they were university students who, at the time of testing, were at Level 4 (upper intermediate) at the Escola d'Idiomes Moderns (EIM), the language school of the University of Barcelona. For comparison purposes, data from 10 adult NSs of similar ages performing the same task were also collected and analysed.

Instruments

A cartoon by Heaton (1966) *'The Dog Story'* was used to elicit participants' speech. This cartoon consists of six pictures which show two children going for a picnic. Unfortunately, a small dog gets into their picnic basket. When the children arrive at their destination, the dog has eaten all the food, and they are left without their lunch.

In order to analyse the data, the total number of words (types and tokens) produced by learners in their retellings was calculated. To do so, a pruned version of the participants' narratives was inputted into an early version of V_Words (Meara, 2010; see Chapter 1). Frequency lists of the types used by learners and NSs were also compiled with this program.

The main instrument used to evaluate participants' productive vocabulary size was V_Size v2.0 (Meara & Miralpeix, 2006). V_Size is a computer program that gives an overall estimate of the productive vocabulary that was available to the person completing the task – in this case telling *The Dog Story*. V_Size v2.0 has two stored dictionaries which can be used to generate a profile for a text. In this study a decision was made to use the JACET 2000 frequency list (Ishikawa *et al.*, 2003), since it was compiled for pedagogical purposes and it was believed to be more suitable for the narratives that participants (EFL learners in a formal setting) produced. The alternative dictionary, based on the BNC list, does not appear to produce good results with learners at this level.

Procedure

Participants were presented with the cartoon with six vignettes and they were asked to retell the story that the images depicted. Participants had the drawings in front of them all the time while retelling the story. All oral narratives participants produced had to be slightly edited: as they were transcribed following CHILDES conventions (MacWhinney, 1995), false starts, immediate repetitions, words in learners' L1s, abandoned sentences and invented words were not considered in the analyses. The resulting pruned narratives were used to calculate the number of types and tokens and the productive vocabulary size estimates.

As mentioned above, participants' productions were first analysed according to JACET 2000 frequency list. The various words that the program was not able to classify were looked up in the JACET 2000 list and classified accordingly. The program has five frequency bands: Band A (500 most common words); Band B (501–1000 words); Band C

(1001–1500 words); Band D (1501–2000 words); and Band E includes all the words that do not fall into these previous categories. Proper nouns were classified as Band A items, while errors were discarded for the analysis. As the program saves all the words that the researcher classifies manually, the dictionary file was updated each time a narrative was analysed so as to avoid any discrepancy between the criteria followed to classify words.

The narratives were also analysed using a word list based on a set of descriptions of *The Dog Story* cartoon produced by a small group of native speakers of English. All NSs' retellings of *The Dog Story* were put together in a text file, which was analysed with V_Words and a frequency list was created. As our purpose was to set up Bands A, B, C, D and E for *The Dog Story*, the total number of types was divided by five and the same number of words was then allocated to each band. There were 410 types in total and 82 different words were allocated to each band. The resulting frequency list was copied and pasted into the file 'mydicfile' that V_Size has stored in its folder. This dictionary was used to repeat the analyses of learners' oral narratives.

Once all narratives were analysed, all results produced by the program (profiles, estimates and errors) were entered into IBM SPSS Statistics v21 so as to be later analysed statistically. A series of paired and independent-samples t-tests were run in order to answer the research questions that the present paper seeks to answer.

Results

V_Size's discriminatory power between EFL learners and NSs

In order to answer our first research question, normality was assessed according to the Shapiro–Wilk Test, since it is the test recommended for small samples of participants. As the data were found to follow a normal distribution, a series of independent-samples t-tests were run comparing vocabulary size estimates for EFL learners and NSs. A summary of the results is presented in Table 1.

Results of the independent-samples t-test showed that NS test takers produced significantly more words and that their productive vocabulary was more varied than that of EFL learners [tokens: $t(18) = 2.627, p = 0.017$; types: $t(18) = 3.126, p = 0.006$]. EFL learners' and NSs' productive vocabulary size estimates were significantly different [$t(9.231) = 4.159, p = 0.002$]. In addition, there was a significant difference in Bands A and E. The results of the independent-samples t-test run with 'V_Size A' indicated that EFL learners produced a significantly higher number of words classed in Band A than NSs [$t(11.975) = -3.628, p = 0.003$]. Regarding Band E, the opposite occurs, as NSs produced a significantly

Table 1 Descriptive statistics (RQ1)

Measure	EFL learners	NSs	Sig.
Types	$M = 61.50$ (S.D. $= 11.75$)	$M = 96.30$ (S.D. $= 33.19$)	✓
Tokens	$M = 129.20$ (S.D. $= 24.72$)	$M = 205.60$ (S.D. $= 88.58$)	✓
V_Size Estimate	$M = 1,200$ (S.D. $= 176.38$)	$M = 3,260$ (S.D. $= 1,556.49$)	✓
V_Size Band A	$M = 88.10$ (S.D. $= 2.56$)	$M = 80.40$ (S.D. $= 6.20$)	✓
V_Size Band B	$M = 5.40$ (S.D. $= 2.59$)	$M = 7.10$ (S.D. $= 2.73$)	✗
V_Size Band C	$M = 2.70$ (S.D. $= 1.25$)	$M = 2.90$ (S.D. $= 1.85$)	✗
V_Size Band D	$M = 0.90$ (S.D. $= 0.74$)	$M = 1.40$ (S.D. $= 0.84$)	✗
V_Size Band E	$M = 2.90$ (S.D. $= 1.91$)	$M = 8.20$ (S.D. $= 3.33$)	✓

Notes: All means (M), except for 'V_Size Estimate', 'types' and 'tokens', are expressed in percentages.
✓ indicates significant difference between the groups.

higher number of infrequent words than EFL learners [$t(18) = 4.368$, $p = 0.001$].

Appropriateness of baseline data

The second research question asked whether there was any difference between estimating learners' vocabulary according to different baseline lists (i.e. JACET 2000 or a task-specific list extracted from a corpus of NSs' story retellings). The estimates obtained when data were analysed according to the NS corpus list is presented in Table 2 (second column). Results obtained from the JACET list analysis are presented in the third column. A series of paired-samples t-tests were run and the fourth column in Table 2 indicates where significant differences were found.

Table 2 Descriptive statistics (RQ2)

Measure (EFL learners)	NS corpus list	JACET list	Sig.
V_Size estimate	$M = 2,490$ (S.D. $= 629.73$)	$M = 1,200$ (S.D. $= 176.38$)	✓
V_Size Band A	$M = 76.80$ (S.D. $= 5.43$)	$M = 88.10$ (S.D. $= 2.56$)	✓
V_Size Band B	$M = 11.30$ (S.D. $= 2.71$)	$M = 5.40$ (S.D. $= 2.59$)	✓
V_Size Band C	$M = 6.60$ (S.D. $= 2.67$)	$M = 2.70$ (S.D. $= 1.25$)	✓
V_Size Band D	$M = 2.90$ (S.D. $= 1.29$)	$M = 0.90$ (S.D. $= 0.74$)	✓
V_Size Band E	$M = 2.40$ (S.D. $= 2.12$)	$M = 2.90$ (S.D. $= 1.91$)	✗

Notes: All means (M), except for 'V_Size Estimate Corpus' are expressed in percentages.
✓ indicates significant differences between the two measurements.

One of the main differences observed is that the overall estimate that V_Size provided was significantly different depending on whether it was calculated according to the JACET 2000 Frequency List or the NSs' corpus list. The results of the paired-samples t-test revealed that EFL learners' productive vocabulary size estimates were significantly higher when the estimates were based on the NSs' corpus than when they were based on the JACET 2000 list [$t(9) = 6.238, p = 0.001$].

In addition, it can be observed that all bands (except for Band E) showed significant differences depending on whether EFL learners' narratives were judged according to JACET 2000 or according to the NS corpus. In Band A, EFL learners produced a larger number of frequent words when their narratives were assessed using JACET 2000 as the baseline than when assessing them according to NSs' productions [$t(9) = 6.547, p = 0.001$]. The opposite tendency was found in Band B, since more words pertaining to this band were produced when narratives were judged according to the NSs' corpus [$t(9) = -6.556, p = 0.001$]. The same tendency seen in Band B was evident in Bands C and D: in Band C, there was a statistically significant difference depending on the frequency list that was used [$t(9) = -3.513, p = 0.007$]. In Band D, this difference also proved to be significant [$t(9) = -4.243, p = 0.002$]. The comparison turned out to be non-significant as far as infrequent words (i.e. words allocated to Band E) were concerned. It should also be noted that the error V_Size reported was smaller when EFL learners' narratives based on *The Dog Story* were analysed using the NSs' corpus (M = 20.22, S.D. = 14.95) than when analysing them using the JACET 2000 Frequency List (M = 42.80, S.D. = 29.74); however, this difference did not reach statistical significance [$t(9) = 0.127, p = 0.901$].

Discussion and conclusions

Although the amount of data collected is still small, results from the study show that V_Size estimates can discriminate between NSs and upper-intermediate EFL learners in the task participants were asked to perform. The role of baseline data that V_Size uses was also investigated and the findings indicate that EFL learners' vocabulary size estimates differed significantly depending on how they were calculated. Additionally, the study revealed that judging narratives on the basis of NSs' corpus may have the potential to provide more meaningful estimates than evaluating them using a general frequency list. These results will be discussed in more depth in the following sections.

V_Size's discriminatory power between EFL Learners and NSs

According to the results from the statistical analyses, it can be concluded that V_Size estimates reliably discriminated between the two groups (upper-intermediate EFL learners and NSs) in *The Dog Story*. However, these results should be interpreted with appropriate caution, as the estimates V_Size offers will be different when other tasks are used, and they may not necessarily distinguish between texts at other proficiency levels.

There are a number of possible reasons why *The Dog Story* task seems to be a good discriminator for these students. An obvious interpretation is that the learner test takers in this study were indeed not competent enough to produce narratives with a vocabulary similar to that of NS test takers. Given the non-advanced level of the learner participants, this seems like a plausible interpretation of the results. The fact that V_Size discriminated between EFL learners and NSs may be due to the fact that the vocabulary the task typically elicits in NS test takers is still not known at the upper-intermediate level. The cartoon simply provides many opportunities for NSs to use vocabulary that EFL learners at this level of proficiency just do not know productively yet. It was observed in the data that NS participants very often described particular elements in the pictures for which learners may not have had the words; i.e. students' lexical choice was more restricted to complete the task accurately. The task seems to have required the use of some very specific vocabulary (e.g. 'crumbs', 'flask' or 'wagging'), and learner test takers who did not know these specific words may have been forced to adopt narrative strategies which were different from those of the NS test takers.

However, before we accept this explanation of the results, we also need to take into account the nature of the task that was used in the study. *The Dog Story* is a highly controlled task and participants had the story in front of them when retelling the plot. This may encourage them to describe detailed features found in the pictures in a way that is untypical of other types of production. The results might then be interpreted in the light of the research by Tavakoli (2009) and Tavakoli and Foster (2008), who claim that some variance in the participants' performance can be triggered by different aspects of task design: had the storyline been more or less complex, or had participants been asked to retell the story without seeing the pictures, the results may have been different. Still, the results suggest that that structured tasks with prompts can be useful when trying to estimate productive vocabulary size of different proficiency groups.

Appropriateness of baseline data

Our second research question concerned the effects of using different baseline data on the vocabulary size estimates. A comparison between the estimates based on different counts showed that the vocabulary size estimates generated by V_Size are significantly affected by the choice of baseline data, and can vary greatly depending on this choice. The data examined here suggest that general purpose frequency lists (such as the JACET list) might provide less appropriate baseline data than other specially adapted frequency lists, such as one derived from a corpus of words used for a particular task. This prompted us to examine in closer detail the error data reported by V_Size (the difference between the curve produced by our text and the closest matching theoretical). These error values were reduced when we used the NS lists as baseline data. In these cases, error figures were lower than when we used the JACET lists for the same purpose. Thus, we are led to the conclusion that judging EFL learners' productions with NSs' narratives as the baseline can provide more reliable results. When narratives were evaluated with JACET 2000 as the baseline, EFL learners' profiles were all very similar and it was hard to even visually distinguish between them. However, when the same narratives were judged with NSs' productions as the baseline, learners' profiles started to become more easily distinguishable one from another. In this case, smaller errors of fit indicated that the match between theoretical and actual profiles were a bit more precise.

Although these results would suggest that every task should be evaluated on the basis of what highly proficient language users (or even NSs) are able to do in the same task, more research is necessary. Results are only applicable to the levels and task used in this study: bigger corpora are needed to verify and generalise the results of this modest investigation. However, this idea of assessing narratives according to what NSs or highly proficient users are able to produce in the same task has clear implications for teaching and assessment: learners' progress can possibly be better gauged according to a general set of standards which are produced for specific tasks, particularly as far as free production (oral or written) is concerned.

Limitations and further research

This paper presents some limitations that need to be acknowledged. The main limitation is that the number of participants involved in the study is very small. More than 10 participants in each of the groups would be needed to confirm whether the results obtained are consistent and can be extrapolated. Nevertheless, the results obtained are still indicative of tendencies that future studies should take into account; this piece of research can be taken as a starting point to carry out more detailed experiments. A second limitation is that this report analyses data from only a single task and a single task type. Clearly, further work using a wider range of task types is needed to properly evaluate the V_Size approach. A particularly interesting aspect is that the present study analysed data from oral narratives, and it is not clear whether the differences we report would also emerge from written data. Written texts are much more commonly used to evaluate L2 productive vocabulary than spoken data are. Henriksen and Haastrup (2000: 164) state that a written free production task is the most valid tool to test learners' vocabulary knowledge, and we might expect that written data collection tasks would indeed elicit texts with different lexical properties from those used here.

However, if the general approach developed in this paper turns out to be a robust one, then the V_Size methodology might open up a number of possible ways of investigating some important problems in L2 vocabulary research. For instance, we might be able to compare estimates of productive vocabulary size generated by V_Size with estimates of receptive vocabulary size generated by other tests. Substantial research has been conducted on this topic and discrepant ideas have been put forward (for example, see Fan, 2000; Melka, 1997). The scores provided by V_Size provide another way of critically exploring these ideas, and examining more closely the models that underlie them.

References

Castañeda-Jiménez, G. and Jarvis, S. (2014) Exploring lexical diversity in second language Spanish. In K.L. Geeslin (ed.) *The Handbook of Spanish Second Language Acquisition* (pp. 498–513). Chichester: Wiley Blackwell.

Fan, M. (2000) How big is the gap and how to narrow it? An investigation into the active and passive vocabulary knowledge of L2 learners. *RELC Journal* 31 (2), 105–119.

Heaton, B. (1966) *Composition Through Pictures*. London: Longman.

Henriksen, B. and Haastrup, K. (2000) Describing foreign language learners' productive vocabulary use and development. In I. Plag and K.P. Schneider (eds) *Language Use, Language Acquisition and Language History: (Mostly) Empirical Studies in Honour of Rüdiger Zimmermann* (pp. 150–172). Trier: Wissenschaftlicher Verlag Trier.

Hirsch, D. and Nation, I.S.P. (1992) What vocabulary size is needed to read unsimplified texts for pleasure? *Reading in a Foreign Language* 8 (2), 689–696.

Hu, M. and Nation, I.S.P. (2000) Unknown vocabulary density and reading comprehension. *Reading in a Foreign Language* 13 (1), 403–430.

Ishikawa, S., Uemura, T., Kaneda, M., Shimizu, S., Sugimori, N. Tono, Y., Mochizuki, M. and Murata, M. (2003) *JACET 8000: JACET List of 8000 Basic Words*. Tokyo: JACET.

Koizumi, R. (2005) Predicting speaking ability from vocabulary knowledge. *JLTA Journal* 7 (1), 1–20.

Laufer, B. (1998) The development of passive and active vocabulary in a second language: Same or different? *Applied Linguistics* 19 (2), 255–271.

Laufer, B. and Nation, I.S.P. (1995) Vocabulary size and use: Lexical richness in L2 written production. *Applied Linguistics* 16 (3), 307–322.

Laufer, B. and Nation, I.S.P. (1999) A vocabulary size test of controlled productive ability. *Language Testing* 16 (1), 33–51.

MacWhinney, B. (1995) *The CHILDES Project: Tools for Analysing Talk*. Hillsdale, NJ: Lawrence Erlbaum.
Meara, P.M. (1996) The dimensions of lexical competence. In G. Brown, K. Malmkjaer and J. Williams (eds) *Performance and Competence in Second Language Acquisition* (pp. 35–53). Cambridge: Cambridge University Press.
Meara, P.M. (2010) V_Words (v1.0) [computer software]. See http://www.lognostics.co.uk/tools/.
Meara, P. and Fitzpatrick, T. (2000) Lex30: An improved method of assessing productive vocabulary in an L2. *System* 28 (1), 19–30.
Meara, P.M. and Miralpeix, I. (2006) V_Size (v2.0) [computer software]. Swansea: Lognostics.
Melka, F. (1997) Receptive vs. productive aspects of vocabulary. In N. Schmitt and M. McCarthy (eds) *Vocabulary: Description, Acquisition and Pedagogy* (pp. 84–102). Cambridge: Cambridge University Press.
Miralpeix, I. (2008) The influence of age on vocabulary acquisition in English as a foreign language. Doctoral dissertation, Universitat de Barcelona.
Nation, I.S.P. (1990) *Teaching and Learning Vocabulary*. Rowley, MA: Newbury House.
Nation, I.S.P. (2001) *Learning Vocabulary in Another Language*. Cambridge: Cambridge University Press.
Nation, I.S.P. and Cobb, T. (2007) VocabProfile (vBNC-20) [computer software]. See http://www.lextutor.ca/vp/comp/
Nattinger, J. (1988) Some current trends in vocabulary teaching. In R. Carter and M. McCarthy (eds) *Vocabulary in Language Teaching* (pp. 62–82). New York: Longman.
Staehr, L.S. (2008) Vocabulary size and the skills of listening, reading and writing. *Language Learning Journal* 36 (2), 139–152.
Tavakoli, P. (2009) Assessing L2 task performance: Understanding the effects of task design. *System* 37 (3), 482–495.
Tavakoli, P. and Foster, P. (2008) Task design and second language performance: The effect of narrative type on learner output. *Language Learning* 58 (2), 439–473.
Waring, R. (1997) A comparison of the receptive and productive vocabulary sizes of some second language learners. *Immaculata; The Occasional Papers at Notre Dame Seishin University* 1, 53–68. Retrieved from http://www.robwaring.org/papers/various/vocsize.html (last accessed 15 June 2014).
Zipf, G.K. (1935) *The Psycho-Biology of Language: An Introduction to Dynamic Philology*. Boston, MA: Houghton Mifflin.

Reflections on Gesa (2015)

The study by Gesa uses an earlier version of V_Size which generated a five-point profile from a text. The five points were based on 500-word frequency slices. However, experimenting further with the V_Size program convinced us that using 500-word frequency slices was perhaps not the best way of constructing a frequency profile for a text. The 500-word slices were difficult to justify on theoretical grounds, and diverged significantly from current practice in the field. They were also difficult to handle in practice: if V_Size identified, say, *Australian* as a difficult word, and asked you to recategorise it, it was necessary to decide whether Category A (words 1–500),

Category B (words 501–1000), Category C (words 1001–1500) or Category D (words 1501–2000) was most appropriate. It was difficult to make decisions like this reliably without referring to a full frequency list, and even with a short text, if you had large numbers of words of this sort, it became something of a chore to run the program. In addition, since these 500-word categories are typically rather small anyway, adding or subtracting one or two items from them could significantly change the shape of a profile.

Further work with the original programs (e.g. Miralpeix, 2008) had shown that the proportion of 1K words in a profile was the most important contributor to the overall profile, and we did in fact develop a version of V_Size which used *only* this value to compute the overall V_Size estimates. There is some practical justification for this simplification in that work like Gesa's generally shows that the most important parts of the profiles are the very high frequency words and the very low frequency words – the proportions of words in the central sections of the profiles tend not to vary much, and do not contribute greatly to the vocabulary size estimates. Edwards and Collins (2011) argued that the 2K score can in fact be predicted from the 1K score in a proper Zipfian Model, and this meant that we needed to compute only the 1K and 3K+ values in a profile. These considerations led us to believe that a simpler profile might be more reliable than the five-point profiles used in the earlier versions of V_Size. Consequently, the profiles used in v2.01 consist of only three points, corresponding respectively to 1K words, 2K words and words that are not included in these two most frequent word bands. This change has the additional advantage that it makes the data less dependent on the word list chosen as the base-list for V_Size's calculations. Using a three-point profile also simplifies the computations and makes the estimates provided by the program more stable. Interestingly, it also means that the V_Size profiles more closely resemble the profiles that are implicit in Laufer's Beyond 2000 measure (Laufer, 1995).

V_Size v2.01 also differs from previous versions of the program in the way the program builds its profile for a text. V_Size v2.01 actually does this by computing the average of a large number of profiles based on a number of sets of 100 words selected at random from the original text. This procedure is essentially the same as the method adopted by Malvern and Richards in their computation of the vocd measure. It has the advantage that the profile of a text is less likely to change significantly if any one word is replaced by another. Generally speaking, the profiles generated by V_Size are astonishingly close to the profiles generated by Zipf's theoretical model, shown by the fact that the two curves reported by V_Size are usually extremely close to one another, and this inspires some confidence in the general approach.

There are a number of features in Gesa's data which suggest that the analysis needs to be looked at more carefully. The most important feature is that the overall vocabulary size estimates in Gesa's paper are surprisingly low – 1200 words for the learner group and 3200 words for the NS group.

Furthermore, the standard deviation for the NS group is relatively large, implying as it does that some NS test takers are using a very restricted vocabulary in this task. These data are rather different from other datasets that we have analysed using the V_Size program, where the vocabulary size estimates are generally much higher, and the difference between NS groups and learner groups are more marked. We think that Gesa's results may be partly due to the nature of the task – *The Dog Story* is clearly aimed at children, and this means that it might elicit an unusually simplified vocabulary in the retellings. Gesa's data are also unusual in that they are based on oral retellings rather than written texts. Spoken language is generally simpler than written language, and it is possible that this feature accounts for the surprisingly low vocabulary size estimates reported here. It is also possible that the Zipfian profiles that V_Size uses are not really appropriate for analysing oral texts. This seems unlikely, however. Ridley (1982) and Ridley and Gonzales (1994) have shown that NS oral texts are consistent with Zipf's Law. Nevertheless, these results do suggest that the vocabulary size estimates generated by V_Size may be very task dependent.

Findings for the second research question (see Table 2 in Gesa, 2015) suggest that the shape of the profile for a text, and therefore the V_Size estimate that is based on this profile, may be strongly affected by the base list that is used for the initial analysis of the text. Using a task-based word list extracted from a corpus of NSs productions, rather than a frequency count, reduces the proportion of very high frequency words in our profiles, and slightly increases the number of items in the lower frequency bands. These findings suggest two further avenues of research. The first of these would be the development of specific word lists for a set of standard tasks. Lists of this sort would allow us to estimate the productive vocabularies available to learners for specific tasks. Given the importance of tasks in current SLA research, it is very surprising that work of this sort does not appear to have been undertaken already. There is an obvious gap in the research here. The second approach worth exploring, given the absence of task-specific reference lists, would be to make vocabulary size estimates based on a general standard list such as the JACET list, rather than a strict frequency count such as the BNC list. The JACET list is not a strict frequency count: rather it is a frequency-based pedagogical word list which reflects the type of words that learners are typically exposed to in their learning. This is the approach we have taken in V_Size v2.01, which uses the JACET list to compute the profile of a text. V_Size v2.01 also allows users to override the JACET classifications if this is deemed appropriate under the circumstances. This seems to be a pragmatic response to the practicalities of dealing with data of the sort that L2 learners generate. However, it is not immediately obvious that Zipfian models do describe the output of learners when their texts are evaluated against word lists that are not strict frequency counts. It is possible that a non-Zipfian model might provide better fitting curve data – for example, it might turn out that a

Zipfian model systematically underestimates the real size of an L2 learner's vocabulary because L2 learners over-use high-frequency words. We can only have limited faith in the estimates provided by V_Size until issues of this sort are examined in more detail.

In the meantime, readers need to be aware that there is a large body of research that has criticised the use of lexical frequency counts for language instruction and assessment. Gardner (2007), for instance, claims that counts of this type are distorted due to the fact that they do not take meaning into account. She exemplifies this claim with the fact that these lists are often lemmatised and within the same lemma different frequency levels can be found (for example, 'climbed' might appear more often than 'climb'). She gives further evidence of the neglect of meaning by stating that the commonest words in a language tend to be polysemous (the 100 most frequent phrasal verbs in the BNC have 559 potential meaning senses, or an average of 5.6 per phrasal verb) and he argues that

> this line of reasoning brings into serious question the validity of computerised counts of individual word forms or computer-generated lists of individual forms for investigative or instructional purposes, especially if those words are of higher general frequency in a language. (Gardner, 2007: 252)

The limitation that frequency counts do not take meaning into account does not necessarily undermine the validity of the Zipfian models that V_Size uses, but it does sound a note of caution. Other shortcomings with Zipfian models have also been identified, such as the fact that the Power Law might not apply to the most frequent words or to the least frequent words in a language (Ferrer i Cancho, 2005; Ridley, 1982). This is not actually a recent objection, as this supposed imperfect adjustment is already acknowledged in Zipf's work and mentioned, among others, in Crystal's *Encyclopedia* (1987). Later studies like Fukś and Phipps (2006) and Kanter and Kessler (1995) present interesting information on the distribution of infrequent words, and there is research analysing more specifically what happens with the distribution of the most frequent words, that is, what takes place at the upper bound of the Zipfian curve (see, for example, Ninio, 2006, for an investigation of the statistical features of Hebrew motherese, which may have some implications for the input received by L2 speakers). Studies along this line of research make it evident that language also exhibits a certain degree of entropy. This randomness, more than challenging or questioning the general rules that language tends to obey, could be taken as an indication of where the general rule does not apply, or where it might be in need of some adjustments (e.g. by adding new parameters).

More research along the lines of Gesa's study is needed to show how general tendencies (such as those shown by Zipf's Law) could be exploited as a way of obtaining information about the learners' productive vocabularies.

V_Size is based on a theory of language that, in spite of not being faultless, might reasonably be expected to be used to obtain reliable estimates. However, as McNamara has acknowledged:

> Every test is vulnerable to good questions, about language and language use, about measurement, about test procedures, and about the uses to which the information in tests is to be put. In particular, a language test is only as good as the theory of language on which it is based, and it is within this area of theoretical inquiry into the essential nature of language and communication that we need to develop our ability to ask the next question. And the next. (McNamara, 2000: 86)

More Research is Needed ...

This section contains some ideas that could easily be worked up into small-scale research projects.

- At the moment, V_Size works only for English texts. What additional work would be needed for it to work with other languages?
- Do V_Size scores distinguish between learners at different levels of proficiency?
- We might expect V_Size scores to vary with increasing L2 competence, but what does this change look like, and how suddenly or slowly does it take place?
- How sensitive are V_Size scores to task?
- Are V_Size scores affected by the L1 of the person who generates a text?
- Is there a difference in the estimates for oral and written productions?
- Do V_Size scores correlate with other measures of productive vocabulary? Specifically, are V_Size scores related to the measures we get on V_Unique (Chapter 5) and V_Capture (Chapter 8). How do V_Size scores relate to Laufer and Nation's Controlled Productive Vocabulary Test?
- Do V_Size scores correlate with measures of receptive vocabulary? (e.g. do people with big scores on V_YesNo (Chapter 6) typically produce higher V_Size scores than learners with low V_YesNo scores?
- What is the best way to interpret a V_Size score?

References

Crystal, D. (ed.) (1987) *The Cambridge Encyclopedia of Language*. Cambridge: Cambridge University Press.
Edwards, R. and Collins, L. (2011) Lexical frequency profiles and Zipf's Law. *Language Learning* 61 (1), 1–30.
Ellegård, A. (1960) Estimating vocabulary size. *Word* 16, 219–244.

Ferrer i Cancho, R. (2005) The variation of Zipf's Law in human language. *European Physical Journal B* 44, 249–257.

Fuks, H. and Phipps, C. (2006) Toward a model of language acquisition threshold. In R. Wamkeue (ed.) *Proceedings of the 17th IASTED International Conference on Modelling and Simulation* (pp. 263–267). Anaheim, CA: Acta Press.

Gardner, D. (2007) Validating the construct of word in applied corpus-based vocabulary research: A critical survey. *Applied Linguistics* 28 (2), 241–265.

Gesa, F. (2015) How many words do you know? Measuring the L2 productive vocabulary size of EFL learners. Adapted from unpublished MA thesis, 2014. University of Barcelona.

Herdan, G. (1964) *Quantitative Linguistics*. London: Butterworth.

Ishikawa, S., Uemura, T., Kaneda, M., Shimizu, S., Sugimori, N., Tono, Y., Mochizuki, M. and Murata, M. (2003) *JACET 8000: JACET List of 8000 Basic Words*. Tokyo: JACET.

Kanter, I. and Kessler, D.A. (1995) Markov processes: Linguistics and Zipf's Law. *Physical Review Letters* 74 (22), 4559–4562.

Laufer, B. (1995) Beyond 2000: A measure of productive lexicon in second language. In L. Eubank and M. Sharwood-Smith (eds) *The Current State of Interlanguage* (pp. 265–272). Philadelphia, PA.: John Benjamins.

Laufer, B. and Nation, I.S.P. (1995) Vocabulary size and use: Lexical richness in L2 written production. *Applied Linguistics* 16 (3), 307–322.

Malvern, D., Richards, B.J., Chipere, N. and Durán, P. (2004) *Lexical Diversity and Language Development: Quantification and Assessment*. Basingstoke: Palgrave Macmillan.

McNamara, T. (2000) *Language Testing*. Oxford: Oxford University Press.

Miralpeix, I. (2008) The influence of age on vocabulary acquisition in English as a foreign language. PhD thesis, Universitat de Barcelona.

Ninio, A. (2006) Kernel vocabulary and Zipf's law in maternal input to syntactic development. In D. Bamman, T. Magnitskaia and C. Zaller (eds) *BUCLD 30: Proceedings of the 30th Annual Boston University Conference on Language Development* (pp. 423–431). Somerville, MA: Cascadilla Press.

Ridley, D.R. (1982) Zipf's Law in transcribed speech. *Psychological Research* 44 (1), 97–103.

Ridley, D.R. and Gonzales, E.A. (1994) Zipf's Law extended to small samples of adult speech. *Perceptual and Motor Skills* 79, 153–154.

Zipf, G.K. (1935) *The Psycho-Biology of Language: An Introduction to Dynamic Philology*. Boston, MA: Houghton Mifflin.

Suggestions for further reading

Edwards, R. and Collins, L. (2013) Modelling L2 vocabulary learning. In S. Jarvis and M. Daller (eds) *Vocabulary Knowledge: Human Ratings and Automated Measures* (pp. 157–184). Amsterdam: John Benjamins.

Egghe, L. (1999) On the law of Zipf–Mandelbrot for multi-word phrases. *Journal of the American Society for Information Science* 50 (3), 233–242.

Uemura, T. and Ishikawa, S. (2004) JACET 8000 and Asia TEFL Vocabulary Initiative. *Journal of Asia TEFL* 1 (1), 333–347.

8   V_Capture v1.0

Introduction

V_Capture is a program that was written with a view to investigating productive vocabulary size. It is based on an idea developed by biologists interested in counting the number of species in a test area, or the number of animals of a particular type in a test area. Some very sophisticated mathematical models have been developed in order to make research of this type possible. Most of them rely on the idea of capturing and then recapturing animals in traps on a number of different occasions. The mathematics uses the proportion of animals captured on both occasions to estimate the number of animals or species that you are interested in.

We wondered whether this same approach might apply to words. Obviously, the analogy is not entirely straightforward and, for that reason, the program we describe in this chapter needs to be treated with considerable caution. In spite of these reservations, we think that the capture/recapture approach is an interesting one for vocabulary researchers: it is fairly easy to implement, can be used with many different types of data, and allows you to move beyond the narrow confines of the data generated from single tasks.

Most of these issues are discussed in some detail in the paper by Meara and Olmos Alcoy which also forms part of this chapter. Meara and Olmos Alcoy's paper uses a very simple version of the capture/recapture method that is based on some very early work by Petersen (1896). Petersen's version used just two data collection events, but more recent work has developed more complex models that use multiple data collection events. It seems to us that these more complex models might be very effective tools for investigating the productive vocabulary of L2 speakers. For the moment, however, we are focusing on Petersen's simple two-event model, since this simple approach already raises a number of issues which need to be investigated further, and would make good topics for research at MA or PhD level.

Using V_Capture

You will find the V_Capture program on the Lognostics Tools website, available at: http://www.lognostics.co.uk/tools/V_Capture/V_Capture.htm.

(1) The V_Capture data entry screen is shown in Figure 8.1. It contains two data boxes, as V_Capture takes as its input two word lists (from two different texts). You need to enter the data from your two source texts into these boxes. The simplest way to do this is to drag and drop your word lists into the boxes. You can also enter your data by hand, but we do not really recommend this unless your datasets are very small (and they should not be).

(2) Data preparation: typically, the two word lists would come from work generated by a single L2 learner – for example, they might be a list of words generated by a student in two essays (see Laufer & Nation, 1995, for an example of how to process data of this sort using the Lexical Frequency Profile approach). To use this kind of data with V_Capture, you need to make a **type list** from the two texts – i.e. a list of all the

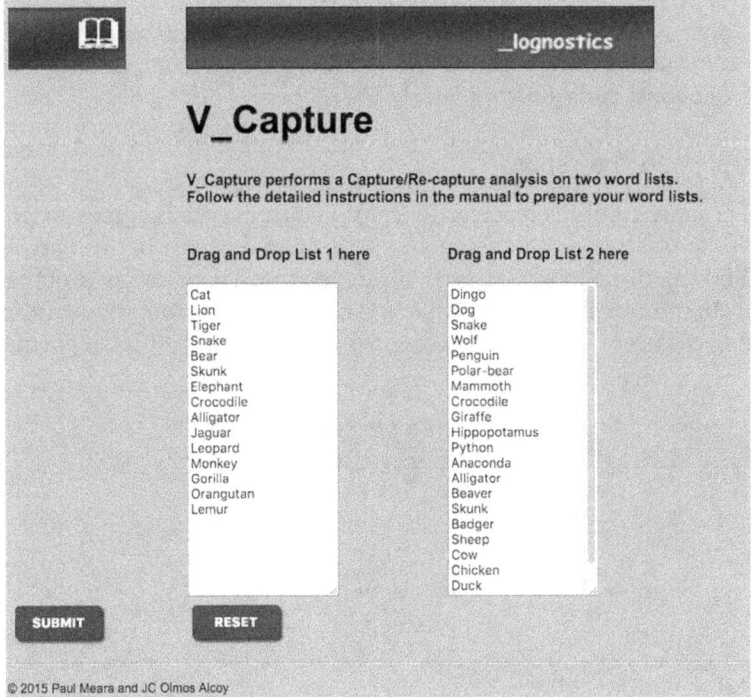

Figure 8.1 V_Capture data input page

different words contained in each text. The simplest way to do this is to use the V_Words program described in Chapter 1. V_Words takes a text or a list of words and returns a type list which contains all the different words that the text contains.

For reasons which are explained below, you should use V_Capture with type lists that are as large as possible. If your data contain fewer than 50 words, then you will need to be extremely cautious about how you interpret the results that V_Capture provides.

(3) When your data has been entered, then you can submit it for processing by clicking on the **Submit** button.
(4) V_Capture will return a report page that looks like Figure 8.2. This screen reports the main statistics from your two texts.

It tells you the **total number of words** collected in the two texts, how many **different words** have been found in this dataset and the **number of words** contained in Text 1 and Text 2 separately.

It also identifies which words occur only in Text 1, only in Text 2 or in both texts.

You will need all these data to make sense of the Petersen estimate reported in the last line of the report.

Note that you do not have to have exactly the same number of words in the two lists. However, it would be unusual to have two lists that were very different from one another. For example, it would be unusual to work with one list containing only 10 words and a second list containing 100 words.

Interpreting the report

The key part of the report made by V_Capture is the **Petersen estimate**. It helps to understand this estimate if you can make sense of the mathematical thinking that supports it. Petersen argued that a good estimate of the true number of animals in a site can be obtained from two independent capture events. At Time1, X animals are captured, and all of these animals are marked

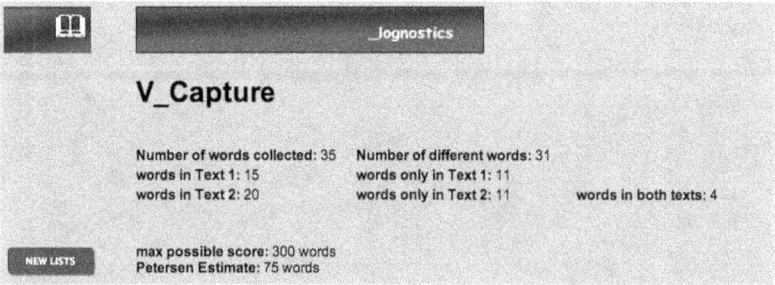

Figure 8.2 V_Capture report screen

in some way. For example, if you were counting frogs in a pond, then you could capture all the available frogs and mark them with a small blob of nail varnish. At Time2, you carry out an equivalent capture event, capturing Y frogs. Some of the animals captured at Time2 will also have been captured at Time1, and you can recognise these animals because they will still be carrying a blob of nail varnish. Let's call this group of animals Z. The two capture events give us three bits of data:

- X: the number of frogs captured at Time1;
- Y: the number of frogs captured at Time2; and
- Z: the number of frogs captured on both occasions.

Petersen argued that the proportion of marked animals that are captured at Time2 should equal the proportion of the total population that has been caught in both capture events, that is:

$$Z/X = Y/T$$

where T is the size of the target population that we are trying to assess. This equation is usually written in a slightly different format, which amounts to the same thing:

$$T = X * (Y/Z)$$

As an example, suppose that you capture 20 frogs at T1 and mark them. This gives you $X = 20$. At T2 you capture 15 frogs, of which five are marked. This gives you $Y = 15$ and $Z = 5$. Plugging these figures into the formula gives you

$$T = 20 * (15/5) = 60$$

You therefore estimate that there are 60 frogs in the pond, even though you only managed to capture a much smaller number of frogs on each separate capture occasion.

Cautions

It is tempting to treat the Petersen estimate as a vocabulary score, but this not as straightforward as it seems at first glance. There are a couple of points to note here. First, the maximum number of frogs is determined by $(X*Y)$. What this means is that you need to make a guess as to how many frogs there are before you start catching them. If your capture events are very short – say 10 minutes – and during this period you can only catch five of them, then the maximum value of T would be only $5 * 5 = 25$. If the real number of frogs in the pond were very much larger than this, then your estimate would fall massively short of the true figure. Clearly, you would need to have a much longer collection time, and collect many more than five frogs to get a reasonable estimate. In the case of L2 vocabularies, we are probably dealing with a total of many thousands of words. An intermediate-level learner probably has a vocabulary of around 4000 words. This means that you would need to collect at least 70 words to be in with a chance of estimating the learner's total vocabulary size. Anything less than that will produce estimates that are far too low. Secondly, estimate T is very strongly affected by the value of Z – the number of frogs (or words) that are caught on both occasions. If Z is small, then the estimate might be reasonably large, but as Z gets larger, then the value of T shrinks very quickly. For example, with the frog data described above, if we increase the number of marked frogs from five to 10, then the value of T halves to a mere 30. This has some serious implications for the type of data that you need to collect when you are using this method to estimate vocabulary sizes. L2 tasks only rarely generate data where the words a speaker produces are largely non-overlapping, and this needs to be factored in when you are deciding how many words you are going to collect from your subjects. For example, if you collected two datasets of 100 words, then the maximum Petersen estimate would be 10,000 words. However, if the data typically include 10 words that appear in both lists, then the Petersen estimate will fall to 1000 words – nowhere near enough to be a sensible estimate of a person's vocabulary size.

The best that we can do is to treat the Petersen estimate as a vocabulary size index rather than as a vocabulary size score. The index might work within the context of a particular task, but it will almost certainly not work across a range of different tasks. This means that you might be able to claim that two groups of students have significantly different Petersen scores on specific tasks and you might interpret this as showing that one group has a significantly larger vocabulary *for these tasks* than the other group does.

You would *not* be able to make a general claim about one group having a larger vocabulary than the other, and you would definitely not be able to make claims such as 'Group A has a mean vocabulary size that is 15% higher than the vocabulary size of Group B'. It *might* be possible to make claims of this sort if we could show that Petersen estimates on a set of specific tasks correlated very highly with other scores of productive vocabulary, but so far little work of this sort has been carried out.

Background Reading

> **Meara, P.M. and Olmos Alcoy, J.C. (2010) Words as species: An alternative approach to estimating productive vocabulary size.** ***Reading in a Foreign Language*** **22 (1), 222–236.**

Introduction

This paper addresses the issue of how we might be able to assess productive vocabulary size in second language (L2) learners. It discusses some previous attempts to develop measures of this sort, and argues that a fresh approach is needed in order to overcome some persistent problems that dog research in this area. The paper argues that there might be some similarities between assessing productive vocabularies – where many of the words known by learners do not actually appear in the material we can collect from them – and counting animals in the natural environment. If this is so, then there might be a case for adapting the capture/recapture methods developed by ecologists to measure animal populations. The paper reports a preliminary attempt to develop this analogy.

Paul Nation's (1990) Vocabulary Levels Test has perhaps been the single most important development in vocabulary acquisition research in the last 20 years. The test provides a rough estimate of a learner's receptive vocabulary size in the form of a vocabulary profile. Simple to use and easy to understand, it has been widely adopted by researchers around the world, and has rapidly become the de facto standard vocabulary size test. The vocabulary size estimates that it produces appear to be remarkably reliable and robust. This has led to the Vocabulary Levels Test being used in a very large number of empirical studies where vocabulary size is a critical variable, and particularly in studies that have examined the relationship between vocabulary size and reading ability in L2 learners. Inevitably, however, the development of a standard assessment tool of this sort opens up other areas of research, and the Vocabulary Levels Test is no exception to this generalisation. The availability of a reliable measure of receptive vocabulary size leads to some very interesting questions about the relationship between receptive vocabulary and active productive vocabulary. This issue is one that is extensively addressed in Nation's work.

The basic distinction between active and passive vocabulary is a staple idea that is widely taken for granted in introductory books on vocabulary acquisition, and in instructional texts designed to teach vocabularies. Some writers, for example, go as far as to list vocabulary items that need to be acquired productively and other vocabulary items that only need to learned for recognition purposes. Despite the fact that many researchers have written about this topic at a theoretical level (Corson, 1983, 1995; Laufer, 1998; Melka, 1997; Melka Teichroew, 1982, 1989), the idea of productive vocabulary remains a fundamentally elusive one. The main reason for this is that it has proved surprisingly difficult to develop simple and elegant tests of productive vocabulary size that have any degree of face validity, and this makes it difficult to answer, with confidence, questions such as *How are receptive and productive vocabulary related? Do receptive and productive vocabulary grow at the same rate? Are there thresholds in the development of a passive vocabulary?* Not surprisingly, perhaps, given the widespread use of Nation's Vocabulary Levels Test to assess receptive vocabulary, the approach most widely used in the recent research literature that investigates productive vocabulary in L2 learners is an adaptation of the original Vocabulary Levels Test usually known as the Productive Levels Test (Laufer & Nation, 1999). Laufer has used these two tests in combination to make some very interesting theoretical claims about the relationship between receptive and productive vocabulary, and how these two facets of vocabulary knowledge develop at different rates (Laufer, 1998). However, the data provided by the Productive Levels Test are much more difficult to interpret than the data provided by the original Vocabulary Levels Test, and in our view it is worth looking at alternative approaches to estimating productive vocabulary size. This is not to denigrate the usefulness of the Productive Levels Test approach, of course, but rather because we think that productive vocabulary may be a more complicated notion than it appears to be at first sight, one that would benefit from being examined from a number of different and perhaps unconventional points of view.

In our previous research we have developed three main ideas, which we think might allow us to 'triangulate' the idea of productive vocabulary size. For obvious reasons, most traditional studies of productive vocabulary require learners to produce short texts for evaluation, but this material is difficult to collect, particularly when you are dealing with low-level learners who are reluctant to produce extended texts. Our first solution to this problem was to move away from using written texts as the raw data for research on productive vocabulary size. We (Meara & Fitzpatrick, 2000) argued that ordinary texts generated by learners tended to contain very large numbers of highly frequent words, and very few infrequent words, which were the true indicators of a large productive vocabulary. We tried to get round this problem by getting learners to generate 'texts' derived from a set of word association tests called Lex30. These data typically consisted of relatively infrequent L2 words that could be profiled using standard vocabulary assessment tools such as Range (Heatley *et al.*, 2002), and we argued that these profiles provided a better picture of the scope of a testee's productive vocabulary than other, more traditional, test types did. Unfortunately, although the test scores tended to correlate with tests of receptive vocabulary size, it was not obvious how the profiles provided by the Lex30 test could be converted into proper estimates of productive vocabulary size.

In our second approach to estimating productive vocabulary (Meara & Bell, 2001), we returned to using texts generated by L2 writers, and attempted to develop an 'extrinsic' measure of vocabulary richness. This paper analysed sets of short texts produced by L2 learners, and for each text generated a curve that described the incidence of 'unusual' words in short segments of text. We then showed that these curves could be summarised in terms of a single parameter, λ, and argued that this parameter might be related to overall productive vocabulary size. This approach successfully distinguished between learners of English at different proficiency levels, but as with the Lex30 test, Meara and Bell were not able to establish a direct, quantifiable relationship between λ and overall productive vocabulary size.

In our third approach (Meara & Miralpeix, 2007) we attempted to estimate productive vocabulary directly by looking at the frequency distribution of words used by L2 writers, and comparing these profiles to a set of theoretical profiles derived from Zipf's law (Zipf, 1935). Meara and Miralpeix argued that it might be possible to estimate a learner's productive vocabulary size by identifying a theoretical vocabulary profile that closely matched the actual data produced by the learner. This general approach proved to be solid enough to distinguish between advanced and less advanced learners. More importantly, however, this approach actually allows us to quantify the productive vocabulary that seems to be behind a particular text. For example, it allows us to tentatively make statements like 'the text in Example 1 implies a productive vocabulary of around 6400 words'. This is a significant advance, which opens up a number of promising avenues of research, but it rests on a number of assumptions about the way L2 learners acquire words, which may not be fully justified.

Example 1 V_Size estimates that the following text was generated by a speaker with a productive vocabulary of at least 6400 words.

Once upon a time there was a dark and lonely wood, where three bears lived. The bears lived in a small cottage at the end of a dark and lonely road, where few people ever strayed. The bears liked it a lot. They did not get many visitors, but that was fine. The rest of the time they kept to themselves, and went about their business in a calm and peaceful way.

Father Bear was the one who liked the dark and lonely bit best. He was a philosopher by nature, who loved to read dark and lonely poetry written in the dead of Winter by Scandinavian poets who also lived in dark and lonely woods, and generally suffered from Angst. Mother Bear didn't have much time for Angst. She was practical and organised, and liked the dark and lonely wood because nothing ever happened there to disturb her domestic routine. Yes, it would have been nice if Father

> *Bear did a bit more of the cooking and cleaning, and yes, it would have been nice if Tesco had a branch at the edge of the wood, but it was better than having noisy neighbours who bothered you all the time. Baby Bear still hadn't decided if he liked the dark and lonely wood or not. It was scary at night, and it was easy to get lost in the wood if you forgot to leave your marks on the trees where the paths split. But Baby Bear had been to the town once too, and he definitely did not like it. Not one bit.*

Obviously, it would be very useful to have a tool that would allow us to estimate a learner's productive vocabulary size with some degree of confidence. For this reason, we have also been pursuing other approaches to estimating vocabulary size. Our hope is that these different approaches will all turn out to provide answers that are broadly similar and, if we could achieve this, then it might be possible to develop a reliable, practical test of productive vocabulary size, which would allow us to take further the ideas raised in Laufer's (1998) paper. This paper sketches an approach that is rather different from the approaches we have developed in our previous work, but one that we feel is very much in the spirit of Paul Nation's thinking-outside-the-box approach to vocabulary testing.

Estimating population sizes in the field

The main problem with estimating productive vocabulary size is that it is extremely difficult to get all the data that we need from our participants. If we were dealing with learners with very small vocabularies, then it might be possible to devise a set of tests that assessed whether our learners could produce each of the words in a short list of target words that we are interested in. In practice, however, this only works where we are dealing with very small vocabularies. In real testing situations, it is logistically impractical to test the entire vocabulary of a learner who has more than a very elementary vocabulary. In this paper, for example, we are interested in learners of Spanish. Threshold Level Spanish (Slagter, 1979) comprises a lexicon of around 1500 words, which gives learners only a very limited level of competence in Spanish. Testing vocabulary exhaustively at this level is difficult, although it is just about feasible with very cooperative participants. Testing the vocabulary of more advanced participants becomes increasingly difficult as their vocabulary grows. Consequently, if we want to test the vocabularies of even moderately advanced students, we have no option but to resort to sampling methods, and to extrapolate from the results we get when we test a small number of words. Obviously, the trick here lies in devising a sampling method that is appropriate and transparent. We may not be able to get L2 learners to produce for us all the words that they know, but we might be able to develop a testing methodology that allows us to extrapolate meaningfully from the words that we can elicit.

This problem is not unique to linguistics. Analogous problems also occur in other areas of study, and are particularly important in ecology, where we want to count the number of animals in a given habitat area. A typical problem of this sort is when we want to estimate the number of deer inhabiting a forest, the number of elephants occupying a national park, or the number of cockroaches infesting a hotel. Simply counting the animals is not straightforward: the animals are not cooperative and do not line up in a way that allows us to number them reliably. This makes it notoriously difficult to make good estimates of animal populations, a problem that can have serious consequences if we are trying to manage the population and control the number of animals that a particular environment can provide for or, as in the case of the cockroaches, if we are trying to eliminate them altogether.

Ecologists have developed a number of methods that allow them to resolve this problem. All of these methods rely on capturing a small number of animals, and then extrapolating this basic count to an estimate of the actual number of animals that could have been caught. The basic approach is known as the capture-recapture methodology, first developed by Petersen (1896), and further developed by Lincoln (1930). In this approach, we first develop a way of capturing the animals we are interested in, and standardise it. Suppose, for example, that we want to count the number of fish in a river. We could identify a suitable stretch of river to investigate, and then distribute traps that will catch the fish without harming them. We leave the traps out for a set time, overnight, for instance, and count the number of fish that we have trapped. We then mark these animals in a way that will allow us to identify them, before releasing them back into the wild. The next night, we carry out the same counting exercise, enumerating the fish trapped overnight. This gives us three numbers: N, the number of fish captured on Day 1; M, the number of fish captured on Day 2; and X, the number of fish that were captured on both occasions. Petersen argued that it was possible to extrapolate from these figures to the total number of fish in the stretch of river. Petersen's estimate is calculated as follows:

$$E = (N * M)/X$$

That is, Petersen's estimate of the size of the fish population is the product of the two separate counts divided by the number of fish counted on both occasions. A simple example will make this idea more concrete. Suppose that on Day 1 we count 100 fish in a 10-mile stretch of river, and we mark them all. On Day 2, we find 60 fish, 20 of which were also noted on Day 1. Petersen's estimate of the number of fish inhabiting the stretch of river would be

$$E = (100 * 60)/20 = 6000/20 = 300$$

If the river is actually 100 miles long, with similar conditions throughout, then our 10-mile stretch represents a 10% sample of the whole river, so we could extrapolate that there are about 3000 fish in the entire length of the river.

There are a number of points to make about this estimate. First, the estimate is quite a lot larger than the totals counted on either of the two data collection times. Secondly, it assumes that the way we counted the fish was a reasonable one, one that gave us a good chance of capturing the fish we want to count, and that the one-mile stretch we have selected represents in some way the entire river. Thirdly, the mathematics only works in a straightforward way if we assume that the two collection times are equivalent, and if each animal has an equal chance of being counted on both collection times. The population of fish needs to be constant from Day 1 to Day 2 – if half our fish were killed by otters, or died from poisoning overnight, then Petersen's model would simply not apply. Finally, we are assuming that the data collection on Day 2 is 'equivalent' to the data collection on Day 1, and so on. If these assumptions do not hold, then the model will not work, but if the assumptions are broadly correct, then these two capture events allow us to make a rough estimate of the number of fish in the river, even though we are not able to count every single one of them, and even though we only sampled a part of the entire river.

Petersen's method has been widely used in ecological studies, where researchers have been interested in estimating the size of elusive animal populations, and it turns out to be surprisingly accurate and reliable. Seber (1982, 1986) provided a number of examples of how the method has been used in practice.

The question we ask in this paper is whether it might be possible to adapt this approach to making estimates about productive vocabulary size. At first, it seems unlikely that this ecological approach would provide a good analogy for what happens with words. Words are not animals, and their characteristics are very unlike those of fish or elephants. Indeed, you could argue that words are not entities at all – rather they are processes or events, which need to be counted in ways that are different from the ways we use to count objects. Nevertheless, there seems to be a case for exploring this idea a little further before we reject it out of hand.

One immediate objection is that the method as we have described it so far seems to work well for counting individual animals, but when we count words we are not really interested in how many exemplars of a single word we find. More commonly we are interested in how many different word types we can identify in a text. This is more like counting the number of different animal species we find in our stretch of river, rather than the number of fish. Suppose that our first data collection event delivers 10 different types of animals, and we make a record of these 10 types. If our second data collection delivers 12 types of animals, of which eight were previously recorded, then Petersen's estimate of the number of species inhabiting the river is

$$E = (10 * 12)/8 = 120/8 = 15$$

This approach to measuring the number of different species in a site uses essentially the same mathematics as the earlier example, but counts the number of different fish types rather than the number of different fish tokens. This shift in focus seems to us to be an interesting one, which readily leads into better analogies with words. The main difficulty is that, while it is relatively easy to devise traps or hides that allow us to observe animals and count species, it is much less obvious as to how one goes about building equivalent traps for words. However, as a first stab, in this paper we are going to assume that a good way of trapping words is to get speakers to write short essays. Some of the problems with this assumption will be given further consideration in the final section of this paper.

Methodology

Participants

Twenty-four participants took part in this study. All of them were learning Spanish at the University of Dundee. Eleven of the participants were at a low-intermediate level, while the remaining 13 participants were considered by their teacher to be 'advanced.' These participants were all native English speakers. We acknowledge that these numbers are very small. We also acknowledge that there are some important differences between Spanish and other languages, which may have affected the results.

Data collection

The 24 participants were asked to write a description of a cartoon story. The story consisted of six pictures. In the first picture, a man and a boy are playing with a dog beside the sea. The boy throws a stick into the sea for the dog to fetch. The second picture shows this game being observed by a smartly dressed man with an umbrella. In the third picture, this man approaches the dog and shows it his umbrella. The fourth picture shows the smart man throwing his umbrella into the sea. Unfortunately, the dog ignores this. In the fifth picture, the man, the boy and the dog abandon the smart man, leaving his umbrella floating on the water. The final picture shows the smart man removing his clothes, presumably so that he can swim out to sea and rescue his lost umbrella.

Participants were given 30 minutes to write their accounts, and during this time they were not allowed to use dictionaries, or to confer with their colleagues. This same procedure was repeated a week later, when the participants were asked to write a second description of the same cartoon story. In both data collection events, participants wrote their stories by hand. The hand-written stories were then collected and transcribed into machine-readable format for further analysis. Example 2 illustrates the kind of material that was generated by this task. The use of a single time-limited task is an analogue of the method used to count fish in the river. We are not looking for a task that will elicit every single word a participant knows. Rather, we are trying to devise a word trap that will capture enough words for us to make a reasonable estimate of the participant's vocabulary.

Because the students are fairly low level, some leniency was used in the transcriptions. Orthographic errors were corrected, and grammatical errors were ignored. The transcriptions were submitted to a computer program that reported the number of word tokens and the number of word types for each text. In calculating these figures, a number of ad hoc decisions had to be made about how to handle different word forms in Spanish. Noun and adjective forms that varied in number or gender were considered as exemplars of a single word type. So, *guapa, guapas* and *guapos* were considered to be variants of a single type *guapo*. For verbs, the same principle applied, except that verbs in the same tense were considered to be examples of a single type, while irregular forms and different tenses were counted as separate types. Thus, *soy, eres* and *es* would count as three tokens of the word type *ser*, while *fuiste* and *seremos* would count as additional word types. In fixed expressions such as *por una parte, desde luego* or *por otro lado*, each word was counted separately. English words were not included in the transcripts, and words that were so badly spelled that they were unrecognisable were also deleted from the transcripts.

Example 2 **Below is a sample text elicited by the cartoon story.**

Hay un hombre y un niño cerca de un río y el hombre está mirando el niño, el niño está jugando con el perro y se tira un ayuda de andar de madera en el río.

El perro llega del agua con el ayuda de andar de madera y aparece un hombre, alto y delgado, con un ayuda de andar de madera, tiene la ropa muy formal y un sombrero. Este hombre nuevo está mirando el niño y el perro con un sonrisa.

El hombre original y el niño toman el madera del perro y el hombre formal empieza a enseñar a el perro su ayuda de andar de madera. El perro, el hombre original y el niño están mirando a el hombre formal.

El hombre formal empieza a tirar su ayuda de andar de madera en el río, con gran fuerza, se usa todo su cuerpo para tirar y el madera va muy, muy lejos en el río. El hombre original, el niño y el perro están mirando, sin movimiento, a el hombre formal.

Ahora el ayuda de andar de madera está en el río, muy lejos y el hombre original, el niño y el perro están andando fuera, ya tienen todos sus posesiones y están contentas. El hombre formal está muy descontenta, su madera está lejos y en el río. El hombre formal pregunta a el perro, el hombre y el niño para que queden y el perro trae el madera del río.

Ahora el hombre formal está solo y está mirando el ayuda de andar de madera pero al mismo tiempo está sacando todo su ropa para que nade a su madera. Su sombrero, zapatos, chaqueta y camiseta están en el suelo y ahora mismo el hombre formal está sacando sus pantalones.

Results

Table 1 shows the mean number of word tokens that the two groups generated for each of the two collection times. The table suggests that the texts of the advanced group tend to be longer than those of the less advanced group, but there is a striking difference between the text lengths of the intermediate group at T1 and T2. An analysis of variance in which the main effects were Group and Test Time confirmed that there was a significant group effect, $F(1, 22) = 24.19$, $p < 0.001$. Paired t-tests confirmed that the number of tokens generated by the intermediate group was significantly greater for the second narrative than for the

Table 1 Mean number of word tokens in two narrative description tasks

Group	T1 narrative	T2 narrative	Combined
Advanced			
Mean	190.23	199.15	389.38
S.D.	48.72	63.65	59.81
Intermediate			
Mean	99.19	133.63	232.81
S.D.	27.16	40.28	89.94

Table 2 Mean number of word types in two narrative description tasks

Group	T1 narrative	T2 narrative	Combined
Advanced			
Mean	72.91	73.73	33.55
S.D.	17.00	19.09	9.11
Intermediate			
Mean	43.36	52.36	25.82
S.D.	8.89	15.09	6.91

first, $t(10) = 3.37$, $p < 0.01$, although the Group × Test Time interaction is not significant.

These data are fairly straightforward to interpret. The difference between the groups is what we would have expected, since text length is generally a good indicator of L2 proficiency. The significant test effect for the intermediate group is more difficult to interpret, and will be discussed further in the next section of this paper.

Table 2 shows a more complex dataset that records for each participant the number of different word types they produced in each of the data collections, along with the number of word types that occurred in both narratives. The data suggest that the advanced group produces more word types than the intermediate group. It also suggests that for the advanced group the two tasks broadly elicited the same number of types, while for the intermediate-level group, the number of types elicited in the second data collection was significantly greater than the number of types elicited in the first data collection. A t-test confirmed that this difference was significant for the intermediate group, $t = 2.83$, $p = 0.017$. An analysis of variance in which the main effects were Group and Test confirmed that there was a significant overall difference between the advanced group and the intermediate group, but failed to show a significant test effect, or any significant Group × Test interaction.

For each participant, the raw number of types was plugged into the Petersen estimate formula, and the estimates generated in this way are reported in Table 3. The striking feature of these data is the very low degree of overlap between the two groups: A Mann–Whitney U-test confirmed that the Petersen estimates reliably distinguish the two groups, $U = 9.5$, $p < 0.01$.

Discussion

In this section, we will discuss some issues that arise out of the results reported in the previous section. Two important issues need to be

Table 3 Mean Petersen estimates based on the number of types in two tasks

Group	Petersen estimate
Advanced	
Mean	160.37
S.D.	38.51
Intermediate	
Mean	93.81
S.D.	31.30

highlighted. These are (a) the validity of the general approach, and (b) whether the Petersen estimates give us any additional information that is not available in the raw word counts. The final section will consider a number of smaller issues raised by the data.

The general approach

In the introduction to this paper, we speculated that we might be able to use methods developed for estimating animal population sizes as a way of estimating the extent of vocabulary resources in L2 speakers. The data reported in Section 4 suggest that this analogical extension of the species counting method has been partly successful, but not entirely so. The main finding is that the Petersen estimates generated from our raw data are clearly able to distinguish between the advanced and the intermediate groups, and that these estimates distinguish the groups rather better than the raw token counts and raw type counts do. In all cases, the Petersen estimates suggest that the participants' productive vocabulary is considerably higher than the actual counts we find in the raw data, and in this respect the method is clearly able to detect knowledge of vocabulary that is not immediately obvious in the raw data. However, as an estimate of overall vocabulary knowledge, the Petersen estimates are clearly not as helpful as we had hoped. The estimates suggest that our intermediate group has a productive vocabulary of about 90 words, and that our advanced group has a productive vocabulary of about 160 words. The figures suggest that the vocabulary of the advanced participants is nearly twice that of the intermediate participants, which seems plausible. However, the absolute figures are just ridiculously low, and clearly they cannot be interpreted at face value. We need to ask, therefore, why the estimates have not produced more realistic figures.

With hindsight, it is obvious that Petersen estimates are very highly constrained by the number of types that are 'trapped' by the data-gathering method. The maximum value of the estimate is in fact determined by the product of the two data collection counts, M and N. Thus, if we collect 100 types for M, and 100 types for N, the maximum value of E is 100 * 100 = 10,000. In practice, this maximum would only be achievable if there was an overlap of one word type between the two data collections, and because of the repetitive nature of language this is a highly unlikely occurrence. Even a very small degree of overlap between the two data collections would reduce our maximum value by a considerable amount. With only five words occurring in both texts, our estimate of the participants' vocabulary size would fall to 2000 words. With 20 words common to both texts, our estimate falls to 500 words. Our narrative description task actually elicited far fewer word types than this – for the advanced group, it generated just over 70 word types for each text, giving a maximum estimate value of about 4900 words. However, the nature of the task meant that it was almost impossible to avoid using some of these words in both texts – *man, boy, stick, dog, throw, water*, as well as the obvious function words. For the advanced learners, about half of the word types found in Text 1 were also found in Text 2, giving a mean Petersen estimate of only 160 word types.

An alternative approach would be to exclude from our counts words that appear more than once in a text, on the grounds that these words are unavoidable components of the narrative, and do not really reflect the vocabulary items available to the participants. This adjustment has the effect of reducing the values of M and N by about 50% – about half the words in a text typically occur only once. However, it also reduces the number of words that appear in both texts. This decreases the divisor in the Petersen formula, and accordingly increases the size of the Petersen estimate. For example, if we have two texts, which each contain 100 words that occur once, and the number of words occurring in both texts is only 10, then the Petersen estimate works out at

$$E = 100 * 100/10 = 10,000/10 = 1000$$

– a figure that looks a lot more plausible than the estimates we reported earlier.

It seems, then, that the choice of task here was more problematic than we realised. The narrative description task did not actually elicit much text, and the constraints of the narrative meant that there was a high probability that words elicited in Text 1 would also be elicited in Text 2. In terms of our animal species analogy, what we have here is a poor trapping device, one that tends to trap the same species twice, but leaves large numbers of other species unaccounted for. Clearly, in future evaluations of this approach, we need to develop a test instrument that elicits longer texts, and is less likely to generate identical word types on both data collection occasions.

It seems to us that 'word traps' of this sort need to take into account a number of factors that were missing from this initial exploratory study. First, the elicitation instrument needs to be aware of the size of the productive vocabulary that we think our participants have at their disposal. That is, if we think that we are dealing with a group of participants whose productive vocabulary is around 5000 words, then we need to have an elicitation instrument that is capable of returning an estimate that is in this general ballpark. Secondly, we also need to take into account the fact that word traps that elicit continuous text will inevitably elicit words that appear in the two separate test events. Let us suppose that we could normally expect about 50% of the word types that appear in Text 1 to appear again in Text 2. In these circumstances, a word trap that elicits about 100 words of running text will typically produce a Petersen estimate of about 200 words – far too few to be a realistic estimate of an advanced participant's productive vocabulary. On the other hand, a word trap that typically elicited more words, with a relatively small number of types that appear in two sequential datasets, might be capable of measuring much larger vocabularies. For example, a task that elicited 200 word types on each test occasion, with an overlap of only 10% of word types appearing in both datasets, would, in principle, be capable of producing reasonable estimates for a productive vocabulary of about 2000 items. A task that elicited 250 words on each test occasion with only a 5% overlap on two test occasions might be capable of producing reasonable estimates for a productive vocabulary of around 5000 words. We think that it might be possible to design a word trap of this sort using the methodology developed by Fitzpatrick and Meara in their Lex30 test, and our guess is that a relatively small test of this sort might be capable of providing reasonable vocabulary size estimates over a wide range of L2 proficiency levels. Meara and Miralpeix's Vocabulary Size Estimator program, for example, suggests that intermediate-level students typically have a productive vocabulary size of about 3500–6000 words. This range could easily be assessed using a well-designed word trap based on a word association methodology instead of the continuous text instrument used in this study.

What the Petersen estimates mean

It would be wrong, however, to give the impression that the Petersen estimates elicited in the present study are completely useless because the figures they generate are clearly not measuring the full extent of the productive vocabulary available to the participants tested here. Our guess is that the estimates may still be providing us with useful information.

First, it is possible that the Petersen estimates are telling us something about the productive vocabulary which is available to participants for this particular task and, if this is correct, then the low level of the estimates might not actually be a serious problem. It would be relatively easy for us to collect data from groups of native speakers (NSs) doing the same task, compute Petersen estimates for them, and then compare the estimates we get for NSs with the estimates our L2 speakers produce. For example, if we find that NSs performing our narrative task typically generate Petersen estimates of, say, 350 words, with a standard deviation of 20 words, then we could report our L2 learner scores as a percentage of this NS score, or as a standardised score based on the NS mean and standard deviation. This looks like the beginnings of a methodology that would allow us to produce objective scores for the vocabulary used by L2 learners in productive tasks. The methodology might also enable us to assess the suitability of specific tasks used in vocabulary testing. For example, if the narrative task discussed in the previous section turns out to generate very low productive vocabulary estimates when it is used with NSs, we might want to conclude that it is not really appropriate as a tool for assessing L2 speakers' productive vocabulary size.

Secondly, it is possible that the Petersen estimates reported in Part 3 may be good enough to act as an ordinal scale, even if they cannot be interpreted as absolute numbers. Clearly, the participants in the advanced group have bigger productive vocabularies than the participants in the intermediate group, and it is possible that the rankings produced by the Petersen estimates might reflect the relative sizes of the participants' vocabularies. It is also possible that there might be a fairly straightforward relationship between each participant's Petersen estimate and their actual productive vocabulary size, if we could measure it. What we need to do here is to compare these results to other estimates of productive vocabulary size, such as the estimates produced by Meara and Miralpeix's Vocabulary Size Estimator or Malvern and Richards' (1997) vocd measure, and see whether there is a close correlation between these sets of measures. This work lies beyond the scope of a short exploratory paper of this sort.

Other detailed points

A number of other minor points are worth discussing here.

First, the significantly higher number of tokens and types produced by the intermediate group on the second test is surprising. Whereas the advanced group produces texts that look very homogeneous from the point of view of the number of word types they contain, the intermediate group seems to behave quite differently in this respect. All but one of the participants in this group generated more word tokens in their second text than in their first text, and all but one participant produced a higher number of word types in Text 2 – in some cases nearly double the number of word types. The advanced participants are much more varied in this respect – about half the participants show an increase in the number of word types from Text 1 to Text 2, while the other half show a reduction. This is an unexpected result which does not have an obvious explanation. We might have expected that performing the same task twice would have reduced the length of the narratives, and so reduced the number of word types contained in the second text, but this does not appear to be the case for the intermediate learners. For tokens, the standard deviation for the learners in Test 1 is much smaller than the other three standard deviations, but again it is difficult to work out what this might mean. For types, we have a very similar pattern of results. There is clearly a need for more work on repeated tasks of this sort if we are to work out whether this pattern of performance is a reliable feature of intermediate-level learners or not, and whether the sort of random variation (and large standard deviations) that we get with the more advanced participants is typical of how participants normally behave.

Secondly, the groups appear to differ in the number of words that appear in both texts, $t = 2.71$, $p < 0.05$, with the advanced group having a much larger number of repeated words than the intermediate group. Again, this is not necessarily what we would have anticipated. We might expect that the number of repeated words in the two groups would have been very similar – basically we might expect that both sets of texts would repeat function words and a small number of unavoidable words required by the narrative, but the degree of repetition found here seems to go beyond this.

Ironically, this tendency has the effect of lowering the Petersen estimates for this group. All other things being equal, the bigger the number of repeated words, the lower the resulting Petersen estimate will be; this makes the significant difference between the groups even more striking than it appears at first sight. Again, what we need here is some further research into how likely it is for word types to reappear in repeated tasks, and how this tendency interacts with vocabulary size.

Thirdly, we need to ask whether the Petersen estimates actually tell us anything that we could not already work out from the raw data presented in Table 1. All the main variables distinguish between the groups: number of tokens in Text 1, $t = 5.50$, $p < 0.001$; number of tokens in Text 2, $t = 2.94$, $p < 0.001$; number of types in Text 1, $t = 5.38$, $p < 0.001$; number of types in Text 2, $t = 3.38$, $p < 0.001$; and Petersen estimate, $t = 5.30$, $p < 0.001$. The pattern of results here is again slightly odd, with the Text 1 scores and the Petersen estimates returning the

Table 4 Correlations (r) between the Petersen estimates and other variables

Participants	Token			Type	
	T1	T2	All	T1	T2
All	0.758	0.671	0.800	0.823	0.861
Intermediate	0.273	0.524	0.477	0.645	0.897
Advanced	0.506	0.476	0.611	0.601	0.726

best values. The values for Text 2 also distinguish the groups, but are not so striking.

Table 4 shows the correlations between the Petersen estimates and the other variables. The data show that the correlations between the raw token counts and the Petersen estimates are generally fairly good, 0.758 for Text 1, 0.671 for Text 2, and rising to 0.800 for the two texts combined. For types the correlations are slightly higher – although given that the Petersen estimates depend very heavily on the type data, this is perhaps not surprising. When we look at the groups separately, we find that the correlations are generally more consistent for the advanced group, with one very striking correlation between types on Text 2 and the Petersen estimates. Again this points to something slightly odd about the way the intermediate learners approach the second story-telling task.

These findings suggest that the Petersen estimates may indeed be tapping into some interesting features of vocabulary use by L2 speakers, but it is not straightforward to work out exactly what these features are without collecting a lot more data.

Conclusion

This paper has looked at the use of Petersen estimates as a way of assessing how much productive vocabulary L2 learners have at their disposal. The data suggest that there might be ways of constructing effective word traps, which can be used to make realistic estimates of productive vocabulary size, and that taken together with other estimates these tools might be able to generate plausible estimates of productive vocabulary size in L2 speakers. Standard essays do not appear to be a good way of collecting the relevant data – it is difficult to collect long essays, which generate large numbers of different words, and unavoidable repetition of function words and key vocabulary items means that the Petersen estimates are a lot smaller than we would expect. Nevertheless, the general approach seems to hold out considerable possibilities, and we think that it might be possible to develop alternative trapping methods based on word association techniques. We will be exploring this methodology in a future paper.

At first sight, it might look as though productive vocabulary does not have much to say about reading in a foreign language. However, a large body of research suggests that a significant component of reading skill is the ability to predict the content of a text, and to anticipate the occurrence of words a text contains. It seems highly likely that there will be some sort of relationship between the predictive vocabulary skills needed for reading and productive vocabulary in general, perhaps even a stronger one than we find between reading and receptive vocabulary size. We hope that the work reported here, despite its very obvious limitations, might turn out to be a small step in the direction of teasing out the nature of this relationship.

References

Corson, D.J. (1983) The Corson measure of passive vocabulary. *Language and Speech* 26 (1), 3–20.
Corson, D.J. (1995) *Using English Words*. Dordrecht: Kluwer Academic.
Heatley, A., Nation, I.S.P. and Coxhead, A. (2002) *Range* [computer software]. See http://www.victoria.ac.nz/lals/about/staff/paul-nation
Laufer, B. (1998) The development of passive and active vocabulary in a second language: Same or different? *Applied Linguistics* 19 (2), 255–271.
Laufer, B. and Nation, I.S.P. (1999) A vocabulary size test of controlled productive ability. *Language Testing* 16 (1), 33–51.
Lincoln, F.C. (1930) Calculating waterfowl abundance on the basis of banding returns. *Current Industrial Reports, US Department of Agriculture* 118, 1–4.
Malvern, D.D. and Richards, B.J. (1997) A new measure of lexical diversity. In A. Ryan and A. Wray (eds) *Evolving Models of Language* (pp. 58–71). Clevedon: Multilingual Matters.
Meara, P. M. and Bell, H. (2001) P_Lex: A simple and effective way of describing the lexical characteristics of short L2 texts. *Prospect* 16 (3), 5–19.
Meara, P. M. and Fitzpatrick, T. (2000) Lex30: An improved method of assessing productive vocabulary in an L2. *System* 28 (1), 19–30.
Meara, P. M. and Miralpeix, I. (2007) *Vocabulary Size Estimator*. Swansea: Lognostics.
Melka Teichroew, F.J. (1982) Receptive versus productive vocabulary: A survey. *Interlanguage Studies Bulletin* 6 (2), 5–33.
Melka Teichroew, F.J. (1989) *Les notions de réception et de production dans le domaine lexicale et sémantique*. Berne: Peter Lang.
Melka, F.J. (1997) Receptive vs. productive aspects of vocabulary. In N. Schmitt and M. McCarthy (eds) *Vocabulary: Description, Acquisition and Pedagogy* (pp. 84–102). Cambridge: Cambridge University Press.
Nation, I.S.P. (1990) *Teaching and Learning Vocabulary*. Rowley, MA: Newbury House.
Petersen, C.G.J. (1896) The yearly immigration of young plaice into the Limfjord from the German Sea. *Report of the Danish Biological Station* 6, 5–84.
Seber, G.A.F. (1982) *The Estimation of Animal Abundance and Related Parameters*. London: Edward Arnold.
Seber, G.A.F. (1986) A review of estimating animal abundance. *Biometrics* 42 (2), 267–292.
Slagter, P. (1979) *Un Nivel Umbral*. Strasburg: Council of Europe.
Zipf, G.K. (1935) *The Psycho-biology of Language*. New York: Houghton-Mifflin.

Reflections on Meara and Olmos Alcoy (2010)

This paper was the first of a series of studies that looked at the capture/recapture methodology as a way of investigating the productive vocabulary of L2 learners. It was not well received at the time when it was published, and a number of people were dismissive of the general approach (e.g. Racine, 2011). Indeed, one anonymous reviewer noted that 'this paper makes so many elementary mistakes that it would take me more time to put them right than the authors spent writing the paper in the first place'. Despite these criticisms, we still feel that the approach has something to recommend it.

A number of people criticised Meara and Olmos Alcoy's paper on the grounds that it is not immediately obvious that the analogy between words and species is a valid one. Meara and Olmos Alcoy explicitly recognise the force of this criticism, which is clearly a valid one. Petersen's work makes a number of assumptions about species that clearly do not hold for words. His model assumes, for example, that the number of animals in the population remains constant across the two testing times – that is, no animals are born or die between the two test events. He also assumes that the two test events are equivalent. Neither of these assumptions holds up completely where words are concerned. Unless your two test events are very close together, then it is very likely that your testees will have forgotten some words and perhaps acquired some new ones as a result of their normal learning processes. It is also not at all clear that two separate tests can be considered 'the same': for example, we know that we get practice effects if students are asked to do perform a task twice in quick succession, and we know that words that always appear in one task will not necessarily appear in a similar but different task. More importantly, however, Petersen's method assumes that all the frogs in a pond are equally likely to get caught. This assumption definitely does *not* hold for words: some words are very likely to appear in any productive context while others are much less likely to appear and, for some contexts, there are many words whose probability of appearing will be close to zero. For instance, if we ask you to describe a picture of a robin on a Christmas tree, then you are almost certain to use the words **the, a, on** and **it** and very likely to use the words **bird, tree** and **red**. The chances of you using words like **crow, flower** and **blue** are tiny, even though they are closely related to other words that you might use.

With hindsight, Meara and Olmos Alcoy's paper made a number of tactical errors. The first error was to ask the experimental subjects to write continuous text. As the paper notes, continuous text has a number of characteristics that cause some problems for the capture/recapture approach. The most important of these characteristics is that continuous text typically contains a large number of high-frequency function words which appear in almost any continuous text. If you have two texts which both contain the same high-frequency words, then the resulting Petersen estimates are very low. The second error was to use a cartoon story as stimulus for the students' writing task. It is almost impossible to complete this task without using words like *man, boy, stick, stone, throw,* and these words will almost always appear in both the first text and the second text. Again, this has the effect of reducing the Petersen estimates that the analysis produces. At the time, the use of this particular cartoon seemed an obvious thing to do. The 'Father and Son' cartoons by E.O. Plauen (1971), from which this story is taken, had been used in a number of data collection projects run by Jeanine Treffers-Daller (e.g. Treffers-Daller *et al.*, n.d.) and we thought that there was a lot to be gained from using a standard data-elicitation task rather than trying to develop a new task whose properties we did not properly understand. The third tactical error was using the same identical writing task in both testing events. At the time, this seemed like an obvious way to proceed. We perhaps interpreted the need for 'equivalent' capture events rather too literally, and should have remembered the old proverb that you cannot fish in the same river twice. Again, this procedure results in very many of the same words appearing in both the first and the second capture events, and this also results in very low Petersen estimates. With tactical errors like this, it is something of a surprise that the results distinguish between the advanced and the intermediate students as clearly as they do.

In spite of these criticisms, we think that the capture/recapture approach is an interesting one. Meara and Olmos Alcoy's analogy between words and frogs is obviously not straightforward, but it is instructive to work out exactly where the analogy breaks down, and how it might be tweaked to provide a better model. The argument that high-frequency words are more likely to be generated in a productive task than low-frequency words looks at first sight like a major obstacle. However, we could solve this problem by designing tasks which make it more likely that low-frequency words will be generated. Or we could just argue that the capture/recapture method is a good way of assessing low-frequency words, but not appropriate for assessing a learner's grasp of high-frequency words. Alternatively, we could design tasks that target words in a particular frequency band, and argue that all the words in a designated frequency band are more or less equally likely to be elicited by these tasks. In this way, the obvious shortcomings of the analogy become positive features that make you think about testing vocabulary in unorthodox ways.

The capture/recapture method only works if the capture method is a sensible one, and this suggests that we need to think quite hard about what would be a sensible way of eliciting words from L2 learners. Most work on productive vocabulary uses essay-writing tasks but, as we have seen, the amount of useful data you get from a task of this sort is quite limited, and there is a good case for looking at other methods of sampling instead. The problem of high-frequency function words can be avoided if you use tasks which do not require your testees to write continuous texts, but require them to generate lists of words instead. A good alternative, which seems to have a lot of potential, is a word association task, where testees are given a list of words and asked to note the first word that comes to mind when they see (or hear) each of these stimulus words. This task does not entirely remove the problems: if you ask someone to associate to FRUIT they are much more likely to say **orange** than **pomegranate**, and they are very unlikely to say **measles**. However, if you use a long list of stimulus words and select your stimulus words carefully, then it is possible to generate a stimulus list which encourages students to generate substantial numbers of unusual response words. Word association tasks also make it easy to collect large numbers of different words from testees in a relatively short space of time, and the data collected typically include only low numbers of words that occur in two separate test events. Both these features tend to produce large Petersen estimates, and make the results more meaningful.

More Research is Needed …

This section contains some ideas that could easily be worked up into small-scale research projects.

- The capture/recapture approach works best if we can elicit very large amounts of data from students. For obvious reasons, this needs to be done efficiently and in a timely manner. Is there a good way of doing this?
- Does the capture/recapture method work with very low level learners?
- How do the Petersen estimates generated by L2 speakers compare with those generated by NSs?
- Can the capture/recapture method distinguish between L2 speakers at several different proficiency levels?
- Can we use the capture/recapture method to assess improvement over, for example, a six-month course?
- What is the relationship between the Petersen estimates and other aspects of vocabulary knowledge?
- Do Petersen estimates correlate with measures of receptive vocabulary size?
- Can we use Petersen estimates as a way of evaluating the effectiveness of particular tasks?
- Is there a way of converting low Petersen estimates of vocabulary size into a more realistic size estimate?

References

Laufer, B. and Nation, I.S.P. (1995) Vocabulary size and use: Lexical richness in L2 written production. *Applied Linguistics* 16 (3), 307–322.

Meara, P.M. and Olmos Alcoy, J.C. (2010) Words as species: An alternative approach to estimating productive vocabulary size. *Reading in a Foreign Language* 22 (1), 222–236.

Petersen, C.G.J. (1896) The yearly immigration of young plaice into the Limfjord from the German Sea. *Report of the Danish Biological Station* 6, 5–84.

Plauen, E.O. (1971) *Vater Und Sohn*. Munich: Max Hueber Verlag.

Racine, J.P. (2011) Feeding, breeding, extinction and river length: Problems with treating words like species. *Reading in a Foreign Language* 23 (2), 235–237.

Treffers-Daller, J. et al. (n.d) *The UWE Corpus of Learner Language and Bilingual Speech*. Bristol: University of the West of England.

Suggestions for further reading

There is a very large amount of research that has looked at capture/recapture models in the context of animal populations. Some of this work is very technical, and probably best avoided unless your mathematics is very advanced. A good, non-technical introduction is:

Manly, B.J.F. and McDonald, L.L. (1996) Sampling wildlife populations. *Chance* 9 (2), 9–19.

Cushing, D.H. (1981) *Fisheries Biology: A Study in Population Dynamics* (2nd edn). Madison, WI: University of Wisconsin Press. [Provides some detailed examples of the use of this approach in fisheries research.]

A more technical analysis is:

Sutherland, W.J. (1996) *Ecological Census Technique: A Handbook*. Cambridge: Cambridge University Press.

Only a small number of research papers have picked up on the general methodology outlined in Meara and Olmos Alcoy's paper. The main sources are listed below.

Olmos Alcoy, J.C. (2013) The Schnabel method: An ecological approach to productive vocabulary size estimation. *International Proceedings of Economic Development and Research* 68 (3), 19–24.

Williams, J., Segalowitz, N. and Leclair, T. (2014) Estimating second language productive vocabulary: A capture-recapture approach. *The Mental Lexicon* 9 (1), 23–47.

Nelson, R. (2015) Issues with the capture-recapture measure of vocabulary size. *The Mental Lexicon* 10 (1), 152–162.

Part 4
Measuring Lexical Access

9 Q_Lex v4.0

Introduction

Q_Lex is an exploratory program that assesses how easy it is for an L2 learner to access a small set of high-frequency words. The program is basically a word recognition task, but it uses an innovative methodology that gets round some of the problems that arise in standard L2 word recognition tasks.

Around the time that the first versions of Q_Lex emerged, most researchers who thought about vocabulary development thought in terms of a single 'continuum' that ranged from passive/receptive vocabulary at one end to active/productive vocabulary at the other. It was never exactly clear how the various stages on this continuum were actually defined, or what caused words to move along the continuum. In spite of this, the metaphor was widely used in the vocabulary research of the 1980s (e.g. Crow, 1986; Melka Teichroew, 1982, 1989). The emphasis in this work was very much concerned with the individual words a learner knew, and where these words fell on the 'continuum', and there was very little interest in describing the larger, global properties of learners' vocabularies, and what these properties enabled learners to do.

However, a few of us were beginning to think about whether it might be possible to go beyond the properties of individual words, and describe learners' lexical competence in terms of a small number of dimensions that were more or less independent of each other. One dimension was obviously going to be vocabulary size, and we thought at the time that we more or less had this dimension sewn up: Paul Nation's Levels Test and Paul Meara's Yes/No tests seemed capable of generating workable measures of how big learners' vocabularies were, and it had been shown that these measures correlated moderately well with other aspects of proficiency. The question that we were interested in at this time was whether vocabularies could also be characterised by other dimensional measures, and if they could, what these additional measures would be. This idea of a multidimensional characterisation of L2 vocabularies became a common currency in vocabulary research in the

1990s, and a number of papers on this theme were delivered at the 1996 AILA Congress. Henriksen's (1999) paper was a particularly important statement of this idea. Although the dimensions that Henriksen outlined were different from the way we were thinking, the general approach was very similar.

Both we and Henriksen thought that multidimensional models of lexical development had the potential to make vocabulary research much more interesting than it appeared to be at the time. As long as you believe that vocabulary acquisition is basically about size, then the types of questions you can ask about the way vocabularies grow and develop are rather limited and, as you would expect, many researchers began to challenge these limitations. In particular, many people criticised what they saw as the 'superficial' aspects of the vocabulary size approach, on the grounds that it merely tested receptive recognition of words, and failed to take account of other ways of knowing a word. This way of looking at things soon settled into an orthodoxy where people made a distinction between **vocabulary breadth** (how many words a learner knows), and **vocabulary depth** (how well these words are known) – largely as a result of some pioneering analyses by Richards (1976) and Nation (1990) and some very influential testing tools developed later by Wesche and Paribakht (1996). Intuitively, this distinction between breadth and depth seems to be an obvious one – partly because *breadth* and *depth* seem like a natural pair. Our view, however, is that breadth and depth are actually fundamentally different concepts. The main difference between them is that breadth is a property of the entire lexicon: a whole vocabulary can have breadth (i.e. we can say how **big** someone's vocabulary is), but individual words do not have breadth. In contrast, individual words can have a depth feature, (i.e. we can say how well someone knows an individual word), but a whole vocabulary cannot be described in this way. We cannot say how **deep** someone's vocabulary is – the idea of depth applies only to individual words. We could, perhaps, in an ideal world, compute a mean depth for a number of items in someone's vocabulary, but it is not clear what this value would mean in practice. And in any case we would need to measure a very large number of words in a very large number of different ways to get a meaningful average depth; the logistical difficulties in the way of doing this are just prohibitive.

However, if we start thinking about characterising lexicons in two or three dimensions rather than a single 'continuum', then we can begin to look for different patterns of development within the spaces that these dimensions define. There is no reason to assume that everybody's lexicon grows in the same way. If vocabularies could be described in terms of a small number of key dimensions, rather than a single 'continuum', then it might be possible to plot developmental vocabulary patterns in L2 learners. Consider, for example, a simple two-dimensional model which encompasses vocabulary size and some measure of lexical accessibility (see Figure 9.1).

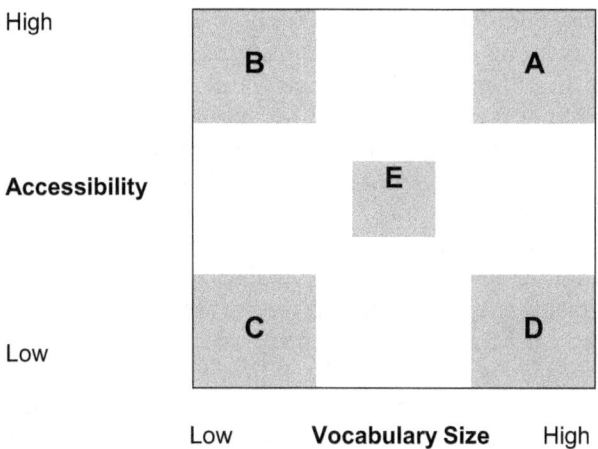

Figure 9.1 How a two-dimensional model might generate questions about the way vocabularies grow

Presumably, L1 speakers have large lexicons in which most of the words are easily accessible; that is, they score highly on the dimensions of size and fluency. It is possible, however, that learners do not develop these competencies to the same extent as L1 speakers do. Some learners, for example, might develop large lexicons where only a small fraction of the words are easily accessible; or we might find that as an L2 lexicon grows it becomes increasingly difficult to access its contents efficiently; or we might find that periods of growth are interspersed with periods of consolidation where a lexicon reorganises itself to take account of the demands that a larger stock of words demands.

These ideas are illustrated in Figure 9.1. Suppose that the axes of the figure represent vocabulary size and some standardised measure of lexical accessibility. Then we can ask questions such as: Do we find learners with large but relatively inaccessible vocabulary (Box D)? Do we find learners with small vocabularies that are highly accessible (Box B), or is a small vocabulary necessarily difficult to access (Box C)? Do all learners eventually get to the promised land of Box A (large, highly accessible vocabulary)? And if not, what prevents that? How do we move a learner from one box to another effectively? Our best guess would be that there are many different possible routes through the space defined by the two dimensions, and this raises all sorts of questions about how much variation we find among learners: Do all the possible routes actually occur, or are some routes impossible? Are some routes successful, while others are not? And so on.

Of course, the questions become much more interesting when we start to think about three-dimensional vocabulary spaces, but let us stick with a simple two-dimensional model for the moment.

Obviously, questions like the ones raised above only make sense if we have proper measures of the relevant dimensions, and this immediately raises the problem that if we decide that we want accessibility to be one of the dimensions of our vocabulary model space, then we need to have a reliable measure that we can plausibly relate to L2 learners' ability to handle words. The Q_Lex methodology developed in this chapter is an attempt to operationalise this idea.

The basic idea behind Q_Lex is that L2 word-processing behaviour is not automatic in the way that it is for L1 speakers. For L1 speakers, and for most tasks, recognising the words the tasks are made up of is not a big deal. The time required for L1 speakers to identify words is, for most practical purposes, instantaneous. For L2 speakers, however, processing words is not instantaneous, and almost any task performed in an L2 takes more time than an equivalent process in a person's first language. This suggests that an important feature of L2 lexical competence is how easy it is to access the necessary words. Q_Lex attempts to operationalise this idea by assessing how good an L2 speaker is at handling a standard list of words.

There are a number of practical difficulties that arise when we try to develop a tool that might measure lexical accessibility. The main decision we need to make is whether we are interested in spoken words or written words. Ideally, we would like to deal with spoken words, since spoken language is generally believed to be the primary form of language. Q_Lex deals exclusively with written words, however. This is principally a pragmatic decision driven by the way testing technology has developed. At the time when we first began to look at lexical access, it was almost impossible to do research on spoken word recognition without very specialised equipment. In the days before MP3 compression, even a small sound file took up around 1 Mb of storage space – a colossal amount of memory at the time, and way beyond the resources of our research budget. On the other hand, written word recognition was much better researched (and is still so today), and the basic differences between L1 word recognition and L2 word recognition were well-established. This seemed to be an argument in favour of designing an accessibility test based on written input.

The standard laboratory test at the time was the Lexical Decision Task. In this method, test takers are shown a string of letters and asked to indicate whether the string is a word or not. So BIRD is a word, but BURD is not, even though the letters make up a sequence which follows the spelling constraints of English. Real words are easier to process than non-words, even for L2 speakers. Unfortunately, one of the basic findings of this research is that the time taken for L2 readers to recognise words was only a fraction of a second longer than the time needed by fluent L1 speakers. These tiny differences are so small that they can only be measured with some difficulty, and this made the standard word recognition method unsuitable for the sort of testing situations that we had in mind. The method developed for Q_Lex side-stepped these difficulties by using a technique which amplifies the differences between L1 readers and L2 readers to the extent that the difference could easily be measured on standard equipment. Instead of presenting words in isolation, Q_Lex presents words hidden in a string of letters, as shown below:

TRRBONAPPLEASHTOVP

The test taker's task is to identify the hidden word in the string. For fluent L1 readers, this is usually a very easy task. The hidden word (here, APPLE) typically stands out very clearly from the background of random letters. For L2 speakers, however, this task is much more difficult: typically it takes a couple of seconds to identify a hidden word, and this difference is easily measurable with standard classroom equipment.

The Q_Lex test consists of a set of 55 test items of this sort – five practice items and 50 scoring items. Each item contains one high-frequency word hidden inside a string of letters. These stimulus items are displayed one at a time on screen for two seconds, and test takers have to identify the word they recognise. For the selected items, fluent L1 readers can usually recognise the hidden word from a two-second exposure. L2 readers find this threshold to be a taxing one. Our research suggests that low-level learners manage to recognise only a small number of the hidden words in two seconds. Q_Lex returns the number of words correctly identified, and our working assumption is that this number can be treated as a measure of accessibility for the whole lexicon.

Obviously, there are a number of untested assumptions here. Our main assumption is that we can devise a standard test based on a relatively small number of words. Ideally, we would like a very large test with hundreds of test items. The much smaller number used here is a compromise that limits the demands made on the test taker. We think that the 50 scoring items used here are sufficient to provide a preliminary assessment of a test taker's performance with a larger vocabulary, but a considerable amount of further work is needed to validate this assumption.

Our second assumption is that it makes sense to test only high-frequency words, rather than to test a spread of words across a wide range of frequency bands. Again, the rationale for this approach is basically pragmatic: testing words across a wide range of frequency bands would mean that our lexical accessibility measure was not independent of vocabulary size, since test takers with small vocabularies would necessarily generate lower scores than test takers with large vocabularies. Limiting the test items to high-frequency words means that our small sample of words actually covers a moderately high proportion of the high-frequency word candidates. It also allows us to use the test with L2 speakers whose proficiency levels vary considerably. All the words in this test should be familiar to learners with a vocabulary size of about 1000 words.

Our third assumption is that a test taker's ability to handle high-frequency words is more or less independent of their ability to handle lower frequency words, or words that have not been well-learned. This assumption is one that is much harder to unravel than the two earlier assumptions, and we will not explore it further here. Ideally, we would want to claim that the number of words test takers correctly identify in the test can be taken as an indication of how easily they can process high-frequency L2 words. Clearly, though, this claim is not a straightforward one. The main problem is that we do not know in detail how scores on Q_Lex are affected by higher levels of overall proficiency in the target language. We know that more advanced learners tend to generate higher scores on Q_Lex than lower level learners do, but we do not know whether this difference corresponds to a gradual improvement with increasing proficiency, or if the test is picking up some sort of threshold effect.

Q_Lex is rather different from tests like V_YesNo, which attempt to sample a learner's vocabulary and estimate its size. Rather, Q_Lex is an attempt to build a standardised test that collects performance data from fluent adult L1 readers on a fixed set of items and compares the performance of L2 learners to the performance of this target group. This makes the data difficult to interpret, and we suspect that considerable further work will be needed before Q_Lex emerges as a reliable test of lexical accessibility. The program offered here is a first step in that direction.

Using Q_Lex

Q_Lex does not require any data preparation before administering the test. However, you will need to check that your internet connection is working reliably and is not subject to long delays.

You will find the Q_Lex program on the Lognostics Tools website, available at: http://www.lognostics.co.uk/tools/Q_Lex4/Q_Lex4.htm.

(1) The Q_Lex opening screen is shown in Figure 9.2.
The program stores any data that are submitted to it in an online database. If you will want to recover your data at some later date, then you should enter a unique ID code into the box on this page. The unique ID code can be any sequence of letters and digits. It is your responsibility to keep a record of any codes that you create. If you are unlikely to need to access the data – for instance, if you are just running a one-off test – then you can leave the ID box in its default state.
(2) Click **Start** when you are ready to begin. Q_Lex moves into its data collection phase, which looks like Figure 9.3. Click **Ready** to start displaying the test items.

Figure 9.2 Q_Lex opening screen

(3) Each test item is displayed in a screen that looks like Figure 9.4. In this display, Q_Lex presents you with a single target word hidden inside a longer string of randomised letters. The test taker's job is to find the hidden word. This display will remain on screen for two seconds. You do not need to take any action during the display.
(4) After two seconds, the data display screen will be replaced by the data capture screen, which looks like Figure 9.5.

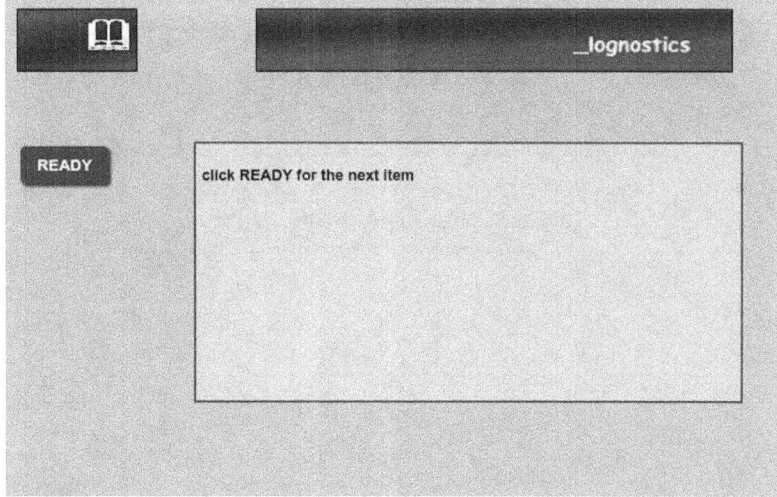

Figure 9.3 Q_Lex initial data collection phase

192 Part 4: Measuring Lexical Access

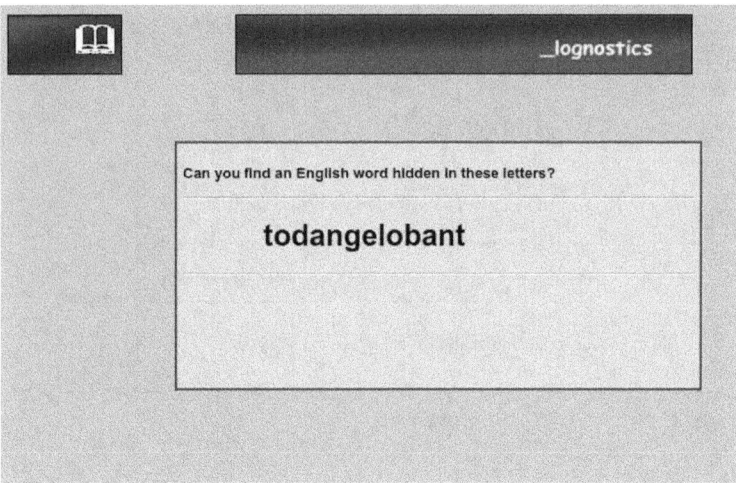

Figure 9.4 Q_Lex: displaying a test item

(5) In the data capture screen we have five buttons, each containing a single word. One of these words is the target word that was hidden in the previous screen. The test taker signals that s/he recognised a target word by clicking the appropriate button, or if s/he has not, by clicking the **Next** button.

There are 55 items in total. The first five items are not scored. They are intended to provide a small number of practice items so that test takers can familiarise themselves with the testing method. This leaves

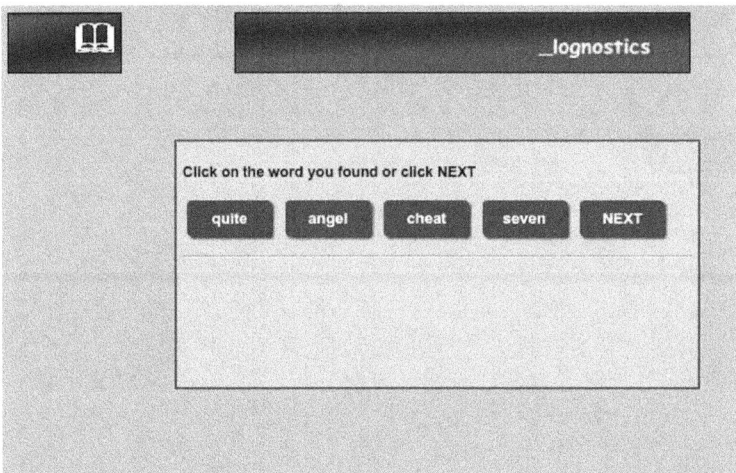

Figure 9.5 Q_Lex data capture screen

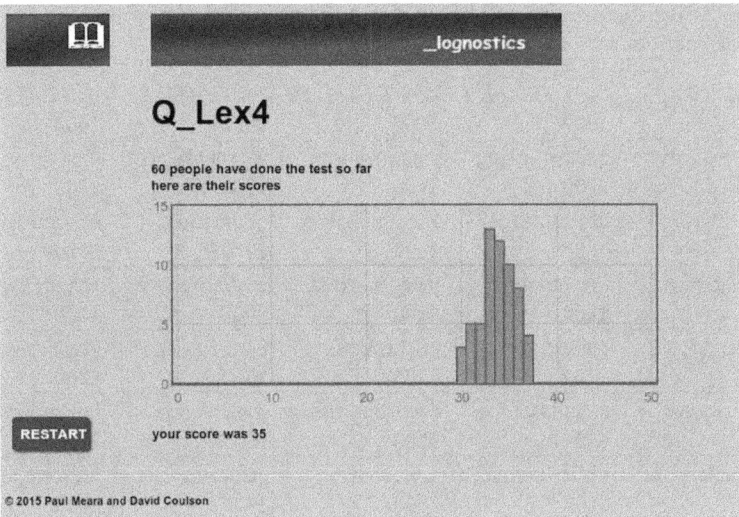

Figure 9.6 Q_Lex report screen

a total of 50 'live' items which are scored. Test takers get one point for each word they correctly identify.

(6) Scores are provided in a report screen that looks like Figure 9.6. The report tells you how many words you correctly identified, and how your score compares with other people who have taken the test.

Q_Lex scores can range between 0 and 50. Native speakers (NSs) typically score above 35 points on this test (normal literate adults usually identify about 40 of the target words). For an L2 learner, anything above 30 is a good score. We do not have any data that relate Q_Lex scores to other aspects of L2 performance.

The technical bits

Q_Lex v4.0 is based on some early work carried out by Brenda Nelson and Riita Hoikkala-Holm at Birkbeck College University of London in the late 1980s. More recently, the methodology was studied by David Coulson in a doctoral study at Swansea University (Coulson, 2010). The items used in v4.0 were extensively evaluated by Coulson. Table 9.1 is a summary of Coulson's data for these items, and shows the upper limit of the time (in msecs) that L1 English speakers required to solve these items. The time reported is two standard deviations above the mean time for each item. Two-thirds of Coulson's test takers correctly identify a word within this time.

Coulson's items each consist of a five-letter English word, hidden in a longer string that consists of randomly selected letters. These strings are

Table 9.1 The items used in Q_Lex v4.0 and the upper limit (mean RT + 2 S.D.) of L1 speakers' performance on these items (msec)

fodguestqborp 2000	tiwtqueenpwnu 1000	bqmwkysensepu 2000	cnrisweetfkhc 1800	obzechecklep 1400
mwpdreamkosy 2000	qddaxbriverpg 2200	sfodgreenuvz 1700	vajzsmokemtsn 1900	umfieldyxshjh 1300
rgqjquickqyup 1300	qtqizagreegek 1800	kahpjguesthpq 1800	hlightepprti 2000	claughirfzidk 2100
dapywncrossda 2100	iupyquietvxft 1200	yjudgecrzksda 2100	wlsfreshyoien 900	xmouthlqybzug 1200
tfkhclerkkfos 2000	tsntesdailysg 1900	arjchestkhfxo 1400	pwezdramapol 1500	yvadultnwqfg 2200
mkosillygczyq 2000	pebuildszfuhe 900	cvvtworrytuem 1900	wmrchildnpxod 900	jnurserjuzrgr 2200
bmksradiocpoz 1700	rlktvhworldvi 1200	azvleundergrl 2000	oclocalbzugxk 1900	jovxzemptyjh 2200
keokucountlew 1200	nrthicklepuqf 1700	eizoagroupwuj 1400	pozjkbreaknuv 1100	mreferwhmajjz 600
lmprizecrzksd 1300	minmtradekgdn 1300	hiefruitfkhcx 1100	yoiextraopwuj 1800	tuemprsleepxe 2200
zqpwnightuemp 1900	sdarguebsttbl 2300	zjyslideuwoyj 1200	cplevelzpaopw 1800	bhappyqgfdedg 1400
pcjeappleeztl 1200	fwttypoundzmd 1200	bzuguardfuihp 1200	vskgrdrivebst 1500	bjzyrelaxttfk 1700

technically known as zero-order approximations to English. Coulson experimented with more complex background string types (first- and second-order approximations to English) but found that the additional complications involved in constructing these masking strings did not greatly affect the recognition of the hidden word. (For a discussion of the properties of different orders of approximation, see Miller & Selfridge, 1950.)

The target words are all high-frequency English words, with the majority taken from the most frequent 1000 words in English. However, they are not a random sample of this frequency band. All the target words are five letters long, and there are about 120 words of this length in the 1K frequency band. However, a large number of the possible candidates contain short letter sequences which are also words in their own right, and this makes them unsuitable as candidate Q_Lex items. TREAT, for example, contains the shorter word EAT, THROW contains ROW, and SKILL contains SKI, KILL and ILL. The 50 scoring items in Q_Lex 4.0 were constructed with a view to avoiding this problem. This means that the target items are roughly a one-in-20 sample from the original 1K vocabulary list, but with very strict constraints on their selection.

Q_Lex 4.0 differs from earlier versions of the program in that it works with a fixed threshold of two seconds for each exposed item. Previous versions used an empirically derived threshold for each item, and this is probably preferable to a fixed threshold, as it provides more information about the test takers' skills. The fixed threshold used here is a compromise driven by the constraints of using an HTML interface.

The test items included in Q_Lex v4.0 are based on work reported in Coulson's PhD thesis. The 55 items are listed in Table 9.1, along with the response times (in msecs) for L1 speakers reported by Coulson.

Cautions

Q_Lex4 has not been widely used in experimental studies of L2 speakers, and this makes it difficult to interpret the results sensibly. On the face of it, we would expect that advanced learners would recognise more target words than less advanced learners do, and there is some evidence to support this belief. However, the test seems to be more sensitive to practice effects than we would really like (e.g. using the same test twice in order to measure 'progress' over a short period of time seems to be a particular problem). There is also a question of face validity with Q_Lex. Q_Lex is clearly tapping in to some features of lexical competence, but it is not at all obvious what these features are, and how they relate to other, more traditional features that researchers usually work with. At the moment, Q_Lex sits uncomfortably on the edge of the lexical research. However, despite these issues, we think that the Q_Lex approach does allow us to investigate some interesting questions about lexical competence, and that is why the test is included in this volume.

Background Reading

> **Meara, P. M. (1986) The *Dígame* Project. In V.J. Cook (ed.) *Experimental Approaches to Second Language Learning* (pp. 101–110). Oxford: Pergamon Press.**
>
> This paper is an informal account of part of a series of experiments on the acquisition of lexis in a second language. It falls into two parts: Part 1 describes the development of a large volunteer subject panel with the help of the BBC; Part 2 details some of the work that we have carried out with the help of this panel.
>
> ## Part 1
>
> Over the last couple of years my students and I have completed a number of experimental studies on the acquisition of vocabulary in a

second language, and on word handling in bilinguals. Some of these studies have already been described elsewhere (cf. Meara, 1982, 1983, 1984a, 1984b). One unsatisfactory aspect of the studies is that they have all used very small numbers of participants – a shortcoming not uncommon in experimental psycholinguistics, but one which is often underplayed where L2 learners are concerned.

NSs tend to behave in a relatively homogeneous fashion in the more common experimental paradigms, and this means that small numbers of participants can produce viable and meaningful results. With NNs, however, performance seems to be much more varied, and this makes it difficult to draw valid conclusions from experiments where only a handful of participants are involved. In the UK it is difficult to get hold of large groups of participants willing to take part in experimental research, and this difficulty is compounded if you work with a 'minority' language, or if your work involves participants visiting a specially equipped laboratory. A combination of both these factors is a recipe for disaster!

The biggest single source of language teaching in the UK is the British Broadcasting Corporation (BBC), whose department of continuing education is responsible for some six hours a week of radio and television courses in a wide range of languages. Audiences for these programmes are very large. The recent BBC Italian series, *Buongiorno Italia*, for instance, was broadcast at peak times on Sundays, and reached an audience of over 250,000. However, this group of language learners has remained largely untapped as a source of research data.

In the spring of 1983 I made a series of approaches to the BBC which culminated in their agreeing to put out a number of short advertisements for me at the start of their beginners' course in Spanish, *Dígame*. These advertisements explained that my team was carrying out a study of vocabulary acquisition, and asked for people following the course who also owned a microcomputer to get in touch with us. The reason for limiting replies to people with a microcomputer was principally because this allowed us to plan a set of studies that were more sophisticated than anything possible using a pencil and paper technology. We were also slightly apprehensive about the number of volunteers who might reply, and this was a convenient, if somewhat arbitrary, way of limiting the numbers to manageable proportions. We predicted that we might get 50 or 60 people for our panel, a significant improvement on the groups of 10 or 15 than we had been using heretofore. In the event, the advertisements produced over 700 volunteers – a figure that far exceeded our expectations and indeed our ability to cope with them.

Our original plan had been to prepare a series of four or five experiments each using 50 subjects or so, and our budgets had been drawn up on the assumption that these estimates were about right. Each volunteer would receive a series of packages containing a cassette tape on which the experiment would be recorded, a datasheet to be returned to us at the end of the experiment, and pre-stamped envelopes to encourage the return of the data. The cost of each package worked out at about 75p, a figure which compared favourably with the going rate of payment (at 1984 rates) for volunteer subjects in the UK. The total budget for this project was a modest £500 which meant that if we sent a letter to all the people we were unable to use in the project we would have used up 25% of the total budget before we even got started. In the end we decided to go ahead with the original programme and not attempt to cater for all the volunteers. One consequence of this decision was a large number of 'unsatisfied customers', and a significant part of our efforts had to be diverted into coping with those who contacted us to find out why they had not been chosen for inclusion.

We were eventually able to run a series of four experiments in a longitudinal study. This study is described in more detail below, but it also raised a number of more general issues which might be of interest to people using a panel of this sort. Our first mailing was sent out to 50 volunteers and produced a return rate of 70%. This is reasonably good, although we think it is actually worse than it might have been, due to a number of unexpected technical problems. The most serious of these was that a significant proportion of the tapes we sent out turned out to be faulty and had to be replaced. This seems to be due to poor quality control by the manufacturer, but it would obviously be a serious problem if you were sending out hundreds of tapes rather than a few tens. We are currently exploring the possibility of having our tapes copied commercially in bulk. This would increase the cost of the operation, but economies to offset this increase could be made relatively easily. For example, instead of posting several tapes to each volunteer, a single tape containing separate experiments could be used. It might be necessary to make it difficult for subjects to gain access to certain parts of the tape before time, but this is a relatively trivial problem. The second technical problem that caused some difficulty was that earlier versions of the microcomputer which we were using were not wholly compatible with the later versions on which the programs had been tested. This meant that a number of volunteers got tapes which loaded but refused to run, and these tapes, too, had to be replaced. We suspect that most of the initial dropout rate was due to these technical causes. The return rate on subsequent mailing was between 80% and 90%, and most of those who failed to reply later explained that they had dropped out because they were unable to keep up with the course.

Towards the end of the course, i.e. six months after the volunteers originally got in touch with us, we attempted to contact another 50 people with a view to running a second set of experiments. This attempt was less successful, however, and only a handful of people responded. Our guess is that this reflects the natural dropout rate on the BBC's language courses, which tends to be high. Large numbers of viewers fail to get beyond the first 10 lessons of a course of this sort. This high dropout rate suggests that a subject panel set up in the way outlined above may have a fairly limited lifespan, although once involved in a project like *Dígame*, people seem more than willing to continue to be involved. It should also be possible to use a panel intensively, and run a series of one-off studies in the early weeks of a course. This strategy is one which will be actively exploring in 1984–1985.

Part 2

This section describes in more detail some of the work that has been carried out as part of the *Dígame* project, and presents an interim report on the main longitudinal study. The work that we initially wanted to carry out with the participants was concerned with their ability to recognise foreign language words. There are many reasons why this is an important line of research, but it is probably not appropriate to discuss them here. Interested readers will find a full discussion in Meara (1984a).

In a conventional laboratory, the obvious way of looking at this issue would be to run a series of experiments involving recognition thresholds. In these experiments, subjects would be seated in front of a display screen, and words would be flashed on a screen for a very short duration. The subjects' task is to say what the word is. If they cannot read the word then it is flashed for a longer period, until eventually an exposure time is reached where they have no difficulty in identifying the word on screen. Typically, L1 words can be recognised by normal adult NSs in exposures of about 600–700 msec.

Unfortunately, it is not possible to run standard experiments of this sort on the equipment that is likely to be available to home computer owners. Home computers linked to a domestic TV set are not sufficiently accurate for work on recognition thresholds. There are two reasons for this. Although the picture on your TV looks as though it is very stable, the picture is actually renewed once every 40 msec as an electron beam sweeps across the screen. This cycle of 40 msec means that it is practically impossible to present something on the screen for less than 40 msec, or to increase an exposure length in steps smaller than 40 msec. In laboratory work on word recognition, it is common to use increments of 2–5 msec. A further technological obstacle is to be found in the way most home micros check their keyboards for input. This again works on a cycle principle: the better machines check their keyboards every 10 msec, whereas others may check every 20 msec. Under these circumstances, it is difficult to measure reaction times very accurately. Most of the standard laboratory paradigms for word recognition are looking for differences in the region of 50 msec or so. A difference of this size is only slightly bigger than the margin of error on a home micro configuration.

Our first task, then, was to develop a word recognition paradigm that was reasonably robust, but produced response times in the region of one to two seconds. After some trial, and lots of error, we eventually developed the method described below.

The word recognition task we used consisted of presenting subjects with a string of letters in a line. This string is 20 letters long, and contains a single word embedded in it. The remaining letters are random, but reflect the likely occurrence of letters in the language being tested. (Technically, they are a first order approximation to the language of the stimulus.) The resulting stimuli looked like this:

weolsulusimpletggiha

Preliminary experiments with this type of display showed that NSs have very little difficulty in identifying the hidden word. In the example above, most NSs recognise SIMPLE immediately. For non-NSs, however, the task seems to be considerably harder, with recognition speeds varying dramatically even for words that cause no difficulty to NSs. The recognition times produced in a series of pilot studies suggested that NSs typically take one or two seconds to recognise a word presented in this way. Learners take considerably longer than this; indeed many learners are unable to recognise even simple words in their L2 when the display is presented for as long as 10 seconds. This pilot work, then, suggested that the reaction times we were getting were easily measurable by the equipment available.

A number of practical problems remained to be solved. If we were relying on people to carry out experiments at home, it was important to ensure that they were not cheating, and this meant that all the data had to be encrypted and ways found of making sure that people did not do the test two or three times. In addition, the actual preparation of the program tapes and the distribution of the materials caused some headaches, and revealed some unexpected incompatibilities between machines. Most of these technical problems were eventually solved, however, and the volunteers selected for the first set of experiments eventually received a series of packages which contained a cassette with a program on it, questionnaires and data sheets for them to fill in, and instructions on how to run the program.

The main study carried out in 1983–1984 was a longitudinal study in which the 'progress' of a set of words was observed. Previous work by Lambert (1955) had suggested that the time speakers require to recognise a word is basically a function of how well they know the language. On the whole bilinguals are able to recognise words in their stronger language faster than they can handle words in their weaker language, Lambert claims. This model seems to me to be intrinsically implausible and it seems much more likely that many frequent words in the L2 can be handled as easily as frequent words in the L1, although obviously the relative amount exposure to each language might also be expected to have an effect.

Lambert's work seems to imply that it is possible to treat learners' vocabularies as two relatively separate wholes. It is not clear why he makes this assumption, however. We already know that there are significant differences to be found among the words of L1 speakers' lexicons. L1 speakers typically react differently to words of different lengths, different frequency, different degrees of spelling regularity, and so on, and it seems likely that similar differences will be found among L2 words. One important variable for an L2 seems to be how recently they learned a particular word. Most L2 speakers of French seem to handle high-frequency French words which they learned in school with a high level of facility. Relatively unfluent speakers of French (e.g. people who did a school French course 15 years previously and had travelled a bit since then) seem to recognise words like *femme* or *fenêtre* or *porte* as quickly as they can recognise the English equivalents. On the other hand, every learner can provide anecdotal evidence about the difficulty of recalling a word they learned only five minutes previously.

One way of approaching these phenomena is to elaborate models in which the acquisition of L2 vocabulary is seen not as an instantaneous occurrence, but as something which progresses slowly over a fairly long period of time. You may be able to recognise a word you have just learned fairly easily, but it is not really an integral part of your personal word stock until you can handle it just as you would handle an L1 word, and this might take many weeks of constant use. Assuming that word recognition tests are a valid way of assessing how well the word is integrated into your personal word stock, models of this sort would predict that the time you needed to recognise an individual word in your L2 would vary systematically as a function of time since learning. Such models fall naturally into three main classes, and these are illustrated in Figure 1. In this diagram, the average time necessary for a speaker to recognise an L1 word is shown by the dotted line. Since these words are reasonably well learned, and recognition time is reasonably stable, this line does not change height.

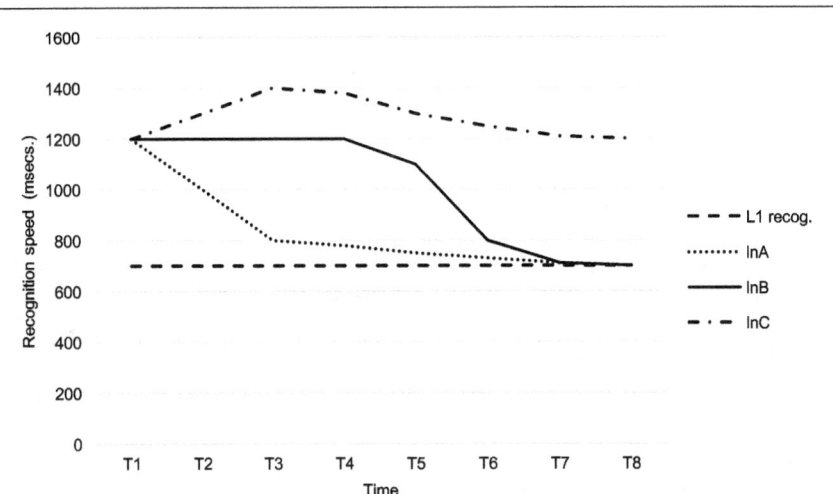

Figure 1 Three possible models for the acquisition of L2 words

The first class of model for describing what happens to L2 words is represented by Line A. This model suggests that word recognition time decreases as a function of time, i.e. the longer ago you learned the word, and assuming the word has not been forgotten since, the more likely you are to handle it like an L1 word. This type of model raises two interesting questions. First, is it the case that L2 words asymptote out at the same level as L1 words, as is implied in the diagram? Lambert's work seems to imply that this is not the case, and that L2 words always remain at a higher level on the graph than L1 words, unless the two languages are properly balanced. The second question that this model raises is how long does it take for an L2 word to reach asymptote? At the moment we have no way of predicting whether the timescale for this change covers a few hours or several months.

The second class of model for describing what happens to L2 words is represented by Line B. This model suggests that newly acquired words in the L2 are essentially stable, and that the time required to recognise them does not actually change a lot. At some stage, however, a catastrophic change occurs, and the word suddenly crosses some threshold which causes it to be treated like an L1 word. Again, this model raises a number of subsidiary questions: what sort of experience might cause the catastrophe, and whether the catastrophe affects only individual words, or if it is part of a major restructuring of whole areas of the L2 word stock.

The third class of model for describing what happens to L2 words is represented by Line C. This model suggests that words in the L2 may initially become harder to recognise as time passes. This may seem implausible at first glance, but it seems more likely if one considers that the learners are typically exposed to large numbers of new words. It is relatively easy to recognise one member of a small set of items, but increasing the size of the set often makes recognition of individual members harder. In this case, it may become harder to recognise L2 words if the total L2 vocabulary increases too fast.

The obvious way to distinguish between the models is to run a longitudinal study in which a set of words learned early in a course is observed at intervals. Each model makes a different prediction. Model B corresponds with a null hypothesis, in which there is no change in recognition time, but recognition time should consistently exceed recognition time for L1 words. Model A and Model C both predict that recognition times will change over time. Model A predicts that recognition times will decrease, while Model C predicts that recognition times will increase over time.

A series of experimental studies designed to test the claims was carried out using 24 words taught in the first five lessons of *Dígame*. All 24 words tested were six letters long. The frequency was not controlled in any way. There were two reasons for omitting controlling for frequency. The principal reason was that standard frequency counts do not well reflect the use of individual items in a beginners' course. The second reason was that the only feasible alternative measure of frequency – the actual occurrence of items on the course – could not take account of individual variation in the use of the materials. Recognition times were obtained using the paradigm outlined above. Four experiments were carried out, but this interim report covers only the first three experiments of the series.

In Experiment 1, each subject was tested on the 24 Spanish words and 24 English words of the same length and similar frequency. The experimental session was preceded by a lengthy practice session. Each subject's results were displayed at the end of the session in an easily comprehensible graphic form, and the actual results were then displayed on screen for the subject to copy onto the results sheet. These results were encrypted so as to avoid cheating.

The three subsequent experiments took basically the same form, except that Spanish words were used in place of the English ones. In these experiments, words learned later on the course were compared with the original 24 words learned in Lessons 1–5.

Results

The results of this set of experiments proved to be more difficult to analyse than had been expected (Figure 2). The initial pilot work suggested that the experimental paradigm produced results with a fairly

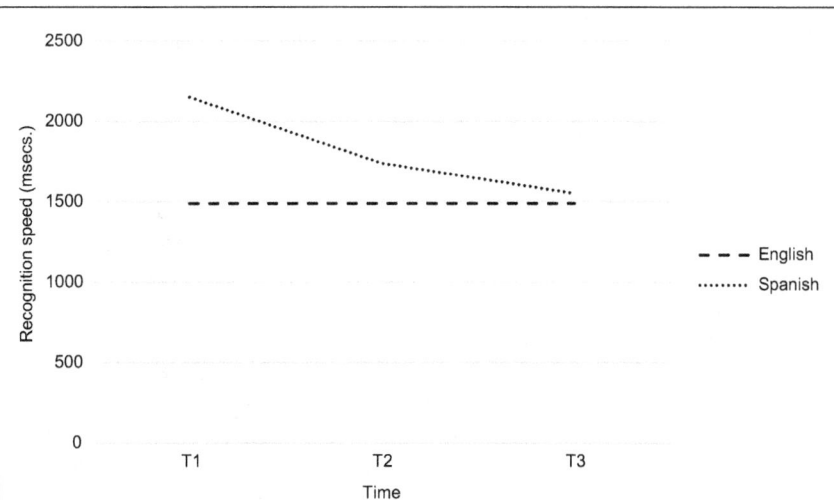

Figure 2 Mean median recognition times (msec) for words in Spanish over a period of 12 weeks

small standard deviation and fairly small individual differences. This was certainly not the case with the results recorded here, however, where very large individual differences were found, together with large differences between individual words. A close examination of the detailed results suggests that there was something like bi-modal distribution in the data. Almost all the responses to English words took less than four seconds, but responses to Spanish words, while generally in the upper part of this range, showed a large proportion of very slow responses. In order to reduce the very large variances, we adopted a cut-off point of four seconds for the data reported in this analysis. This is not an entirely satisfactory procedure, because it has a greater effect on the Spanish words than on the English words. It also has the effect of reducing the difference between the two types of words, and thus making the Spanish words seem more like English words than they really were.

Nevertheless, it seemed fairly clear that when subjects took a very long time to recognise a word, whatever they were doing was something quite different from the apparently instantaneous recognition that seems to occur with L1 words. For the purposes of analysis, then, scores of more than four seconds were treated as errors.

Table 1 shows the mean median identification time for words in English and Spanish. Figures for the Spanish words were collected in weeks 7, 12 and 17 of the 20-lesson course. The same data are also displayed in Figure 2.

Table 1 Mean median recognition times for words in English and Spanish (in seconds)

English	Spanish T1	Spanish T2	Spanish T3
1.47	2.15	1.74	1.55

There is a significant difference within the Spanish words [$F(2,29) = 14.9$, $p < 0.001$]. This indicates that recognition times for Spanish words decrease with time. Closer analysis suggests that most of the variance on this dimension can be accounted for in terms of the difference between Test 1 and the other two tests (2 and 3). Scores on Spanish(1) are significantly higher than those of Spanish(2) and Spanish(3), but the latter two scores do not differ significantly.

On the face of it, the results seemed to fit most closely the prediction made by Model A. That is, it looks as though new words in a foreign language start off by being recognised very slowly, but over a period time they are handled with greater facility. This facilitation period seems to take about 10 weeks, but by the end of this time the L2 words are handled with the sort of facility one would normally expect of L1 words.

Two other considerations suggest that this interpretation is somewhat of an oversimplification, however. In the first place, it should be borne in mind that the scores used in this analysis treat any score over four seconds as an error. Such errors were not included in the analysis, and as a result the figures presented in Table 1 represented only those words which are responded to in a way which is broadly comparable with L1 words. In fact, a large quantity of data is excluded on this criterion. The mean number of slow responses in each of the four tests is shown in Table 2. This table also shows errors of other kinds.

These figures for errors and slow responses show that a large proportion of the L2 responses were not included in the analysis reported here. The proportion of discounted responses declined with time until by the third test it is not very different from what one would expect of English words. To some extent, therefore, these figures confirm the analysis of the main results. There is a large difference between L2 and L1 words at the first test, but this difference gets smaller over the testing period.

A more important problem is to be found in the detailed responses to individual words. The discussion so far has suggested that all L2

Table 2 Mean number of responses over four seconds and errors

	English	Spanish T1	Spanish T2	Spanish T3
Slow	2.0	4.5	3.5	1.3
Error	1.1	3.5	2.2	1.5

words start off by being recognised very slowly, and gradually come to be handled in a more L1-like way. Again a more detailed analysis of the results for individual words suggests that this conclusion is rather wide of the mark. From the data available so far, it appears as though almost all subjects produced faster recognition times for almost all words on the second test compared with the first. Recognition times on the second and third tests seem to vary in an unpredictable way, within certain loosely defined limits. The most likely interpretation of these figures is that the words start off by being recognised fairly slowly, but soon begin to behave like L1 words. On this interpretation, the relatively smooth curve which appears in Figure 2 may actually be an artefact in which a series of discontinuous jumps has been smoothed out by averaging. Certainly, most of the action seems to have taken place between the first two tests, but the data available do not allow us to specify what the nature of this 'action' is.

In terms of the three models we discussed earlier, either Model A or Model B seems plausible. The process by which individual words move from relatively slow recognition times to reasonably faster ones could be a gradual process (Model A) or a sudden one (Model B). In either case, it looks as though the whole process is completed within 5–10 weeks. The data currently available do not allow us to distinguish between these guesses. It should be possible, though, to establish which is the correct description by sampling recognition speeds at closer intervals than was possible here.

In addition to these reservations, which arise directly out of the work reported, another serious reservation surfaces from the second series of experiments carried out with the same participants. These experiments monitored the way learners reacted to words that they met later on in the course, and our main aim was to examine whether new words are easier to handle as your vocabulary grows, whether all new words go through the same sort of processing as we found for the words tested in the first set of experiments, or whether learning new words actually gets harder as your L2 vocabulary increases.

The most striking thing to come out of our preliminary analyses of this data is that there is a huge increase in the number of errors and failures to recognise words as the course progresses. Some words are handled relatively easily – i.e. they are recognised in much the same way as the new words in the early lessons of the course. Presumably, these words, like their earlier counterparts, are absorbed fairly quickly, although this claim is only a hunch at this stage and needs to be properly tested. A very high proportion of words fail to be recognised in the four seconds available – indeed, many of the test words fail to be recognised at all, even when the time available was extended to 10 seconds. This finding suggests that the generalisations outlined above may apply only in the very early stages of learning a language.

There are two possible explanations for this high failure rate. First, it is possible that the words introduced were peculiar in some way, and that this demotivated the students and inhibited their learning. For example, it is possible that the frequency characteristics of the words introduced in the later lessons showed a bias towards less frequent (and less useful) words. This sort of explanation would suggest that how words are chosen for learners and how they are presented should be considered the main factors in determining the growth of vocabulary in L2. An alternative explanation might be to suggest that the vocabulary presented in this course exceeds the number of words that learners of this kind can handle. In this case, we would be dealing with some sort of intrinsic limitation in L2 learners, rather than with an accidental effect of presentation or word choice. Maybe, for instance, learners can only handle 200 new words in a month, even under ideal conditions. Exceeding this limit would then produce an apparent failure rate of the sort we noted here. Again, given the data available at present, it is not possible to distinguish between these two explanations. It should be obvious, however, that the methods reported in this paper could be used to sort out which type of explanation is best.

Conclusion

This paper has presented an interim report on a project where the acquisition of Spanish words by English learners was studied. The first part of the report outlined how the project used the new possibilities raised by widespread ownership of microcomputers, and discussed a new word recognition technique which was developed around this technology. The second part of the paper discussed the interim results of one part of the study. The results suggest that in the early stages of learning, at least, word recognition times decrease gradually with experience of using the word. There was, however, some evidence to suggest that this may be an oversimplification. There are very large differences between individual learners and individual words, both of which will require further investigation.

The main point to emerge from this report is that investigations of word recognition in L2 can provide interesting insights into the nature of vocabulary acquisition. A simple technique like the one discussed here is ideal for use with a highly motivated and willing group of subjects, such as adults following BBC courses, and raises the possibility of looking at vocabulary acquisition in a completely new light. We hope soon to be in a position to extend this project considerably and we intend to run a series of very large studies of vocabulary acquisition in a range of different languages in the near future.

Notes

The author would like to thank Maddalena Fagandini of the BBC for her help in making the project described in this paper possible.

References

Lambert, W.E. (1955) Measurement of linguistic dominance of bilinguals. *Journal of Abnormal and Social Psychology* 50 (2), 197–200.
Meara, P.M. (1982) Word associations in a foreign language. *Nottingham Linguistic Circular* 11 (2), 29–38.
Meara, P.M. (1983) *Vocabulary in a Second Language*. London: CILT.
Meara, P.M. (1984a) Word recognition in foreign languages. In A.K. Pugh and J.M. Ulijn (eds) *Reading for Professional Purposes* (pp. 97–105). London: Heinemann Educational Books.
Meara, P.M. (1984b) The study of lexis in interlanguage. In A. Davies, C. Criper and A. Howatt (eds) *Interlanguage* (pp. 225–235). Edinburgh: Edinburgh University Press.

Reflections on Meara (1986)

This paper is reproduced here mainly for its historical interest. Back in the late 1980s, it was generally assumed by most researchers that vocabulary acquisition was a non-problem. Some learners might have learned words more efficiently than others, perhaps, but the basic process of acquiring L2 words was generally believed to be straightforward. Most SLA researchers were not equipped with the research tools necessary to formulate good research questions about the partial learning of words, and even if they had been that way inclined, most people would have looked at the development of semantics, rather than the development of word recognition in L2 learners.

It is difficult for modern-day researchers to realise just how difficult it was to carry out even simple experimental studies of vocabulary at the time this work was undertaken. There was no tradition of empirical work of this sort in applied linguistics at the time, and few departments had any kind of equipment of the sort that was routinely used by psychologists. Our early work on word recognition by L2 speakers was carried out using a *tachistoscope*. This was a large cube with a viewing port on one side and small slits on the other sides. The slits were designed to hold cards on which stimulus words or pictures had been placed. An ingenious arrangement of lamps and half-silvered mirrors made it possible to display a stimulus for a fraction of a second, and this allowed an experimenter to measure the time a test taker needed to recognise individual stimuli. The process was incredibly laborious: each stimulus word had to be carefully loaded by hand. You could only work with one test taker at a time, and each result had to be recorded by hand. Testing even a small number of stimulus words could take a very long time indeed. At the time, we thought we were lucky. The earliest work on L2 word recognition (Cattell, 1886) displayed words using a guillotine-like mechanism (see Figure 9.7). The falling guillotine revealed the target word as it fell, and started a highly accurate clockwork timer, which was stopped when the guillotine fell into a small bath of mercury at the foot of the display. The entire system had to be recalibrated after every item. Cattell's apparatus looks crude by modern standards, but it was really at the cutting edge of late 19th-century technology, and produced results that were astonishingly accurate, even by modern-day standards.

The arrival of microcomputers in the 1980s changed things dramatically, but it took some time for these changes to work through into research practice. My own department had one computer, a BBC model B. It had 32K of memory and no external storage. Floppy disk drives were available, but they were prohibitively expensive. Instead, programs were stored on ordinary cassette tapes, and we loaded them onto the computer by playing them through a cassette player. Even a short program took three or four minutes to load, and the loading process itself was error-prone and unreliable.

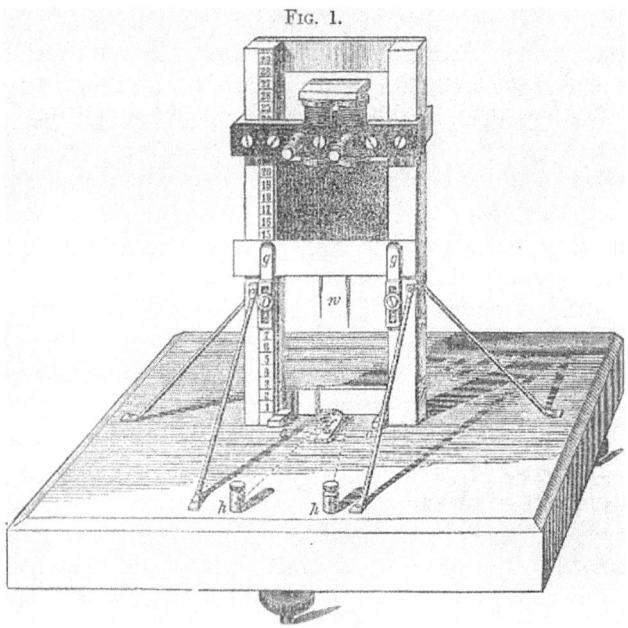

Figure 9.7 Cattell's word recognition apparatus

Looking back, the idea of involving large numbers of adult learners in an experimental study of this sort was actually quite revolutionary. Nowadays, of course, it would be possible to run studies of this sort very easily by distributing programs over the internet, and collecting and processing the data automatically. Back in 1985, the internet was primitive and not widely available outside the major research institutions.

In the event, the *Dígame* project was surprisingly successful, and allowed us to carry out a promising evaluation of what eventually became the Q_Lex methodology. The mechanics of sending out cassettes by post and collecting the data that were phoned in to our answerphone each week turned out to be an organisational nightmare, and it would have been difficult to scale up to much larger numbers.

The paper itself might have been more successful if I had been properly clued up about how to build on this early experimental work, and if I had felt more confident about taking the work to a wider audience. In the event, I took it to only one very small conference, where no-one showed much interest, and the promised further development described in the paper never took place because of organisational changes in the university where I was working at the time, and a change of personnel at the BBC. With hindsight – and there are lessons here for budding researchers! – it was also a big mistake to give the paper an obscure and non-transparent title, and to publish it in a little-known volume of conference papers. If I had given it a title like *Learning to recognise words in a second language*, it would probably have had a bigger impact. And, of course, I should also have sent a copy to Wallace Lambert, whose early work looking at the behaviour of bilingual French/English speakers in Montreal had inspired this study.

Despite its striking lack of impact – at the time of writing, Google Scholar lists only two citations, one in 2000 and one in 2003 – I still feel that the paper asks some interesting questions about the way words are learned in a second language. The general assumption at the time was that learning words was a straightforward, simple process that did not require any elucidation. Lambert's work had hinted that things might be more complicated than that, but his work owed much more to experimental psychology than to linguistics, and it was not widely known outside the circles of social psychology. Obviously, with hindsight, words in an L2 are not learned instantaneously, and it would have been interesting to develop some formal models which explored how acquisition really worked. The Q_Lex methodology offers an interesting way of doing this.

More Research is Needed ...

This section contains some ideas that could easily be worked up into small-scale research projects.

- How stable are the scores generated by Q_Lex?
- What is the effect of using different lengths of masking strings?
- How does the length of the hidden words affect the time it takes to recognise them?
- What is the effect of using masking strings that reflect the frequency of letters in English words? Does this make words harder to recognise? If so, are beginners more affected by this change than more advanced learners?
- Do Q_Lex scores correlate with other aspects of lexical competence?
- Do Q_Lex scores vary with the test taker's vocabulary size? If so, why? Is this relationship linear? Does this relationship hold for both L1 and L2 speakers?
- Q_Lex thresholds are fixed at two seconds. Is there any advantage in having a variable threshold instead? Can we determine the exposure time that a test taker needs in order to recognise about half of the hidden words? Would this measure be a better measure than the mean number of words recognised with a two-second exposure time?
- There is some evidence that word recognition is affected by font, and that cursive fonts are better processed by the brain's right hemisphere, while more square fonts are better processed by the left hemisphere. What happens if we ask test takers to recognise hidden words printed in unusual fonts? Can we build an index of lexical accessibility on this basis?
- Q_Lex only tests high-frequency words, mainly because this means that the test can be used with a wide range of learner abilities. How do Q_Lex scores vary with the frequency of the hidden words?

References

Cattell, J.M. (1886) The time taken up by cerebral operations. *Mind* 11, 220–242.
Coulson, D. (2010) Q_Lex: A quick test of visual recognition for learners of English. PhD thesis, Swansea University.
Crow, J.T. (1986) Receptive vocabulary acquisition for reading comprehension. *Modern Language Journal* 70 (3), 242–250.
Henriksen, B. (1999) Three dimensions of vocabulary development. *Studies in Second Language Acquisition* 21 (2), 303–317.
Meara, P.M. (1986) The *Dígame* Project. In V.J. Cook (ed.) *Experimental Approaches to Second Language Learning* (pp. 101–110). Oxford: Pergamon Press.
Melka Teichroew, F.J. (1982) Receptive versus productive vocabulary: A survey. *Interlanguage Studies Bulletin* 6 (2), 5–33.
Melka Teichroew, F.J. (1989) *Les notions de réception et de production dans le domaine lexicale et sémantique*. Bern: Peter Lang.
Miller, G.A. and Selfridge, J.A. (1950) Verbal context and the recall of meaningful material. *American Journal of Psychology* 63 (2), 176–185.
Nation, I.S.P. (1990) *Teaching and Learning Vocabulary*. Rowley, MA: Newbury House.
Richards, J.C. (1976) The role of vocabulary teaching. *TESOL Quarterly* 10 (1), 77–89.
Wesche, M.B. and Paribakht, T.S. (1996) Assessing vocabulary knowledge: Depth vs. breadth. *Canadian Modern Language Review* 53 (1), 13–40.

Suggestions for further reading

Chapnik Smith, M. (1997) How do bilinguals access lexical information? In A.M.B. de Groot and J.F. Kroll (eds) *Tutorials in Bilingualism: Psycholinguistic Perspectives* (pp. 145–168). Mahwah, NJ: Lawrence Erlbaum.

Harrington, M. (2006) The lexical decision task as a measure of L2 proficiency. *EuroSLA Yearbook* 6, 47–68.

Hulstijn, J.H., van Gelderen, A. and Schoonen, R. (2009) Automatization in second language acquisition: What does the coefficient of variation tell us? *Applied Psycholinguistics* 30 (4), 555–582.

Jiang, N. (2012) *Conducting Reaction Time Research in Second Language Studies*. New York: Routledge.

Miralpeix, I. and Meara, P.M. (2014) The written word. In J.L. Milton and T. Fitzpatrick (eds) *Dimensions of Vocabulary Knowledge* (pp. 30–44). Basingstoke: Palgrave Macmillan.

Segalowitz, N., Watson, V. and Segalowitz, S. (1995) Vocabulary skill: Single-case assessment of automaticity of word recognition in a timed lexical decision task. *Second Language Research* 11 (2), 121–136.

Part 5

Assessing Aptitude for L2 Vocabulary Learning

10 LLAMA_B v2.0

Introduction

LLAMA_B is one of a suite of programs dealing with language aptitude. It deals specifically with vocabulary acquisition – learning names for things. The programs were developed as part of a research training programme for Masters students at Swansea University. The main motivation behind the programs was not in fact to develop a language aptitude test, but rather to provide a research environment in which students could naturally develop a critical attitude towards the data collection tools that they were using. In our experience, this critical attitude towards tools was rather rare in the students. Most of them would happily download a program from the web, and use it uncritically in their own dissertation work, even when it was obvious to us that the tool was of dubious origins, not at all reliable, or just completely inappropriate. So we gave the students the LLAMA tests, and instructed them to find out if they were any good. There were four tests in all, somewhat unimaginatively called LLAMA_B, LLAMA_D, LLAMA_E and LLAMA_F.

Each program was loosely based on one of the parts of Carroll and Sapon's Modern Language Aptitude Test (Carroll & Sapon, 1959): LLAMA_D was a sound recognition task that owed something to the work of Elizabeth Service (e.g. Service, 1992; Service & Kohonen, 1995); LLAMA_E was a sound–symbol correspondence task that tested test takers' ability to associate familiar sounds with unfamiliar symbols; LLAMA_F was an innovative test that exposed users to an invented language, and asked them to work out what its grammatical features were; LLAMA_B covered vocabulary acquisition skills. This feature of language aptitude was considered to be very important by Carroll and Sapon, contributing a significant amount of variance to overall language-learning performance. LLAMA_B was similar in content to the vocabulary learning section of MLAT, but it used a more modern interface. Carroll and Sapon had asked their testees to learn a small set of unfamiliar L2 words, but their format merely presented the test takers with a list of English and Kurdish word pairs. We felt that this was an unattractive and demotivating format, which encouraged a rather rigid approach to vocabulary acquisition. LLAMA_B was designed with a more attractive interface, and it used pictures rather than words as stimuli. The pictures were chosen so that it was not obvious what the pictures showed, and this made the task rather more fluid and more challenging than Carroll and Sapon's list-learning task. This format had the additional advantage that it allowed the test takers a lot of freedom in how they approached the task, and did not force them to follow a predetermined learning method.

Using LLAMA_B

You will find LLAMA_B on the Lognostics Tools website, available at: http://www.lognostics.co.uk/tools/LLAMA_B/LLAMA_B.htm.

(1) The LLAMA_B opening page looks like Figure 10.1.
(2) When you click the **Start** button, LLAMA_B takes you to a display page which contains 20 pictures. Each picture is an unusual object. You can find out the name of the object by moving your mouse over it. The display page looks like Figure 10.2.

The program allows you two minutes to study this material and to learn the names of the 20 objects. You can do this in any way you like.

At the end of two minutes, the pictures will disappear. Click the **Continue** button to go on to the LLAMA_B testing phase.
(3) The testing screen looks very similar to the learning screen, but the objects have been moved around. The program presents you with each

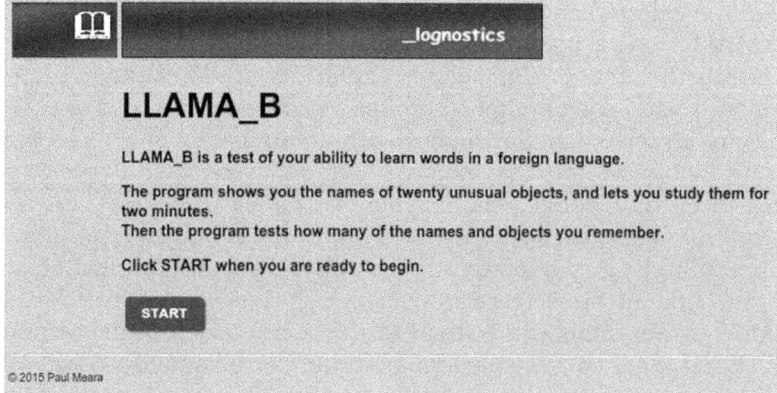

Figure 10.1 LLAMA_B opening screen

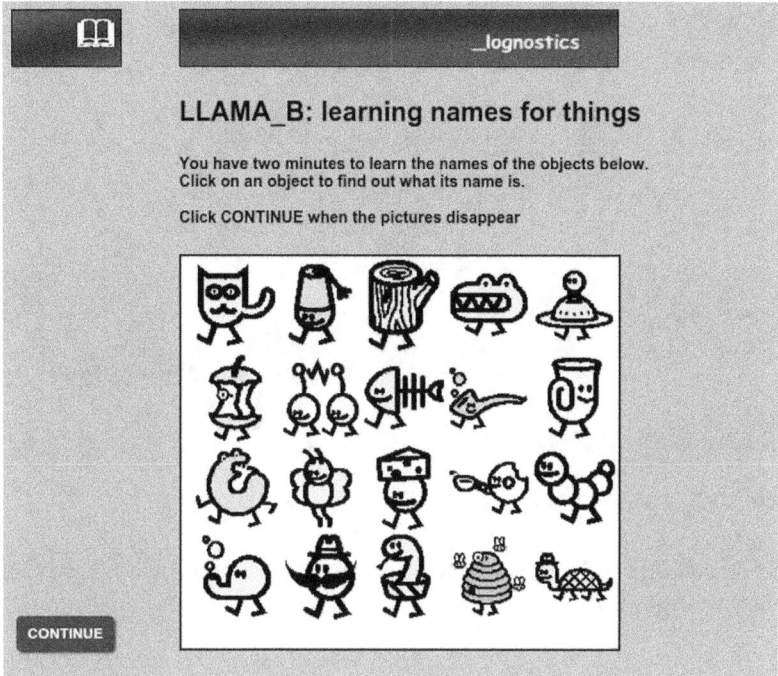

Figure 10.2 LLAMA_B display page

of the 20 object names in turn, and for each name asks you to click on the picture of the relevant object.

This part of the program is not timed. When you have completed all 20 naming tasks, the program will automatically transfer you to the LLAMA_B report page.

(4) The report page is shown in Figure 10.3. LLAMA_B keeps a record of all the scores people get on the test, and prints out a graph showing how these scores are distributed. This means that the program will build up over a time a fairly comprehensive picture of what 'normal' performance on the test is like. This is a significant improvement on the impressionistic reporting that was incorporated into the early versions of the test.

LLAMA_B also reports your own score on the test. This figure ranges from 0 to 20. Random guessing should produce a score of 1.

The technical bits

The illustrations used in the LLAMA_B test are part of the Microsoft clip-art collection. The names of the objects are names for naturally

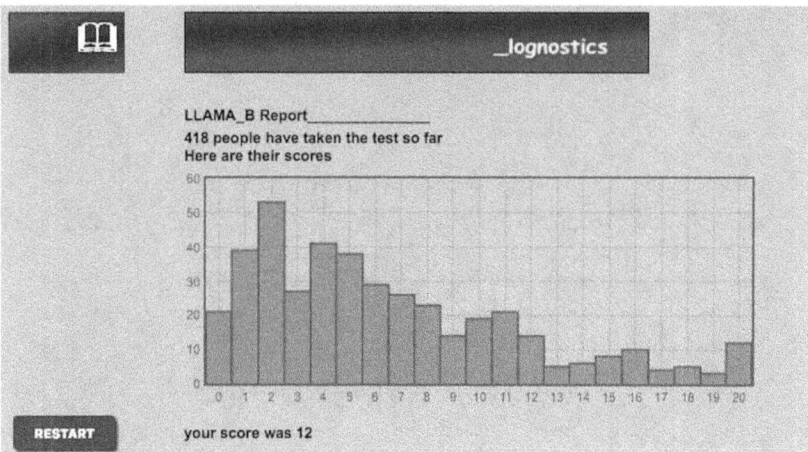

Figure 10.3 LLAMA_B report page

occurring plants and animals in Mixtec, an Oto-Manguean language spoken in Central America.

Background Reading

> **Rogers, V. A brief evaluation of the LLAMA_B Test. (Report written for this book).**
>
> The LLAMA tests (Meara, 2005) were developed as a suite of research training tools aimed at students doing small-scale research projects. The LLAMA suite is loosely based on the work of Carroll and Sapon (1959), but it differs from that early work in taking advantage of the possibilities offered by computers to collect and analyse data. The LLAMA tests were not originally intended as standard language aptitude tests, although a surprisingly large number of people have used them in this way. The intention behind developing these tests was to provide a space where final year undergraduate students and Masters-level students doing small-scale independent research could develop their research skills by thinking critically about the strengths and weaknesses of the research tools that they adopt for this work. Surprisingly, perhaps, the tests have been used by a number of researchers in high-stakes contexts that are not training exercises. Given that the LLAMA tests have never been properly validated, this is something of a problem, and particularly so as some of these users appear not to have heeded the

warnings in the LLAMA manual about the tentative, exploratory nature of the tests, and the need for the results they generate to be treated with appropriate caution.

One unanticipated side-effect of people using the LLAMA tests outside the context they were intended for is that the student projects evaluating the LLAMA tests have become considerably more significant than is normally the case for projects of this sort. For this reason, we are summarising in this paper a set of undergraduate projects carried out in 2013 and 2014. The work reported was developed by Rachel Aspinall, Thomas Barnett-Leigh, Clare Curry, Emma Davie, Louise Fallon, Tom Goss, Emily Keey and Rosa Thomas in their final year projects. The work reported here is concerned with the LLAMA_B test. We hope that this work will be of interest to users of the LLAMA_B test.

LLAMA_B is the LLAMA equivalent of MLAT's Paired Associate Learning Task, and deals with test takers' ability to learn new L2 words; that is, LLAMA_B attempts to assess how good a testee is at learning new vocabulary. It does this by presenting test takers with pictures of 20 unusual objects and the names for these objects in an unfamiliar language. The test takers have two minutes to work with this material, and to study the new vocabulary in any way they want to. After two minutes, the program enters a test phase, where each of the new words is presented one at a time, and the test taker has to identify the object that it refers to.

The students were asked to work with this test and to rigorously evaluate it. Between the two year groups, data from over 400 participants have been gathered for this test. Each student group project may collect data from only 20 or 30 subjects. However, because we teach the students how to properly archive their data, it is possible for us to interrogate the data in ways that the students did not envisage at the time it was collected. And this means that the LLAMA evaluation projects become increasingly interesting as the database increases in size.

The types of questions the students typically ask when they are left to themselves include:

(1) Are the LLAMA tests language neutral?
(2) Does previous instructed language-learning experience influence LLAMA scores?
(3) Is there an effect of age or gender on LLAMA test scores?
(4) Does a person's general education level influence their LLAMA scores?
(5) Do LLAMA scores change if we vary the time allowed for learning the names?

These questions will be addressed in this report. The first four questions are related to individual variables and their possible effect on the test scores. As you will see below, some of the 404 test takers did not provide all the necessary personal information for them to be included in several analyses we wanted to perform (e.g. on the role of the L1, age, etc.) and therefore had to be excluded from particular analyses. The exact numbers of participants involved in the analyses for each of our research questions are specified in each section. The last research question examines a test condition (the study time allowed to learn the words). We investigated this point with some additional participants who were given more or less time in the first phase of the test to learn the vocabulary that would be tested.

Exploring the data

The effects of L1 background

One of the design features of the LLAMA_B test is that it uses picture stimuli and non-English words. This feature was a deliberate improvement on the vocabulary learning task in MLAT which used pairs of words in English and Kurdish. Obviously, the original MLAT tests assumed that the test takers would be L1 English speakers. Later on, a large number of MLAT variants were developed in order to cope with test takers whose L1 was not English (e.g. Stansfield *et al.*, 2005; Suárez & Muñoz, 2011). For LLAMA_B translations should not be necessary, as the material is essentially language neutral. However, students naturally tend to ask whether the LLAMA tests really are language-neutral in the way they are intended to be. This question was first examined by the 2013 student group, and then re-examined in more detail by the 2014 group. Collapsing all the data together, a large number of participants have taken this test, and this has allowed us to look at the performance of several different L1 testee groups. These data are summarised in Table 1.

Table 1 Mean scores on the LLAMA_B test by L1 background

L1 group	N	Mean	S.D.
English	260	8.48	4.28
Chinese	69	10.78	5.41
Arabic	34	10.91	4.73
Other Roman alphabet languages	28	9.04	3.62
Total	391		

A one-way ANOVA showed an overall effect of language background [$F(3, 387) = 6.669, p < 0.001$]. A post hoc Games–Howell analysis assuming unequal variances found a statistically significant difference between the L1 English speakers and the Chinese and Arabic speakers, with the latter two groups outperforming the L1 English group ($p < 0.05$).

Clearly, there *is* an effect of L1 background on the way test takers perform on the LLAMA_B test. However, we think it probable that the effect found here is actually something rather different. We suspect that the most likely explanation of this unexpected result is that the L1 English speakers were mostly monolingual subjects with little or no foreign language learning experience, whereas the L1 Chinese and Arabic speakers were all following English language courses outside of their countries, and were to some extent pre-selected as good language learners. An obvious follow-up study here would be to identify a group of L1 English speakers with extensive language-learning experience, and compare this group with other L1 speakers with limited experience of learning foreign languages.

Generally speaking, there is considerable variation within the groups on this test – the standard deviations are about 50% of the mean score for all the groups. Another obvious follow-up study would be to examine whether test takers who score high on the LLAMA_B test tend to have larger L1 vocabularies than test takers with lower scores on the LLAMA_B test.

The effects of previous language-learning experience

The results reported in the previous section suggest that language experience might be a factor which impacts on the LLAMA_B scores. We can address this question by interrogating our data in terms of the test takers' language-learning background. Specifically, the data allowed us to identify three groups of test takers who differed in this respect: 222 of the test takers were learning a second language; 51 considered themselves to be bilingual from childhood; and 130 were monolingual English speakers. We therefore re-analysed the LLAMA_B data in these terms, and the results are shown in Table 2.

Table 2 Mean scores on the LLAMA_B test by language-learning experience

Language experience	N	Mean	S.D.
L2 learners	222	10.27	4.76
Monolinguals	130	7.84	4.09
Bilinguals	51	7.27	3.97
Total	403		

A one-way ANOVA again showed an overall significant group effect $[F(2, 400) = 17.209, p < 0.001]$. A post hoc Games–Howell test assuming unequal variances found statistically significant differences between the L2 learner group and the other two groups ($p < 0.05$), with the L2 learner group outperforming both of the other groups. This finding is not entirely surprising: the obvious explanation of the result is that second language learners will generally have had to learn new vocabulary explicitly, and will have developed their own strategies for doing this. Monolinguals, and childhood bilinguals, on the other hand, will have developed their vocabularies through implicit learning, rather than explicit learning, and may not have developed more formal vocabulary acquisition strategies.

The effects of age

The LLAMA tests were not originally intended for use with young children, but some of the work on language aptitude has been using the tests with young adolescent language learners. This raises the question of whether the tests are age sensitive. Alongside our older testees, we tested 50 10–11 year-olds, and the scores of these learners were compared with the scores of several groups of older learners. Results are reported in Table 3.

Table 3 Mean scores on the LLAMA_B test by age

Age range in years	N	Mean	S.D.
10–11	50	6.76	3.21
15–21	148	9.19	4.65
22–29	124	10.03	4.92
30–45	42	9.24	4.81
Above 45	31	8.35	3.96
Total	395		

The results show that the young learner group has the lowest mean score of all the age groups. When a one-way ANOVA was conducted, significant differences were found between groups $[F(4, 390) = 4.832, p < 0.001]$. More specifically, the Games–Howell post hoc test revealed that the young learners performed significantly worse than all the other groups, except for the 'above 45' group. That is, this young group performs significantly more poorly than adolescents and young adults, but the difference in mean scores with the oldest group does not reach significance. The performance of the three groups comprising test takers aged 15+ is consistent and there are no significant differences between these groups. It should be noted, though, that all the standard deviations are again relatively large (about 50% of the mean group score), and this indicates that there are substantial within-group differences in this test.

The results confirm our view that the LLAMA_B tests should be treated with caution when used with children. The results may also suggest that aptitude changes with age, with general cognitive ability being a defining factor in young children, but less so in older subjects. In addition, although the oldest group ('above 45') is the least numerous ($N = 31$), the findings could also indicate a variation in aptitude beyond 45, as the mean for this group does not significantly differ from that of the youngest group (10–11). However, there is not a significant difference between the mean of the oldest group and that of adolescents and younger adults, so further research on these age ranges is required to throw light on this issue.

The effects of gender

Grañena (2013) investigated whether gender had an effect on LLAMA test scores. She failed to find any gender effect in a study with 186 participants. This finding was replicated in our own data with an even larger participant group ($N = 404$). These results are reported in Table 4. An independent-samples t-test did not show any significant differences in the scores due to gender [$t(402) = 0.328, p = 0.743$].

Table 4 Mean scores on the LLAMA_B test by gender

Gender of participants	N	Mean	S.D.
Male	186	9.19	4.42
Female	218	9.04	4.81
Total	404		

The effects of educational level

A number of previous studies have suggested that social class or educational levels might affect language aptitude (e.g. Skehan, 1989) and our data also allow us to investigate this question. The descriptive results are presented in Table 5.

Table 5 Mean scores on the LLAMA_B test by educational level

Highest qualifications obtained	N	Mean	S.D.
No qualifications or GCSE	74	6.88	3.38
A-level equivalent	178	9.36	4.68
University graduate and/or postgraduate	152	9.90	4.77
Total	404		

Note: In the UK, GCSE examinations are usually taken at age 16; A-level examinations are usually taken at age 18. The legal school leaving age is 16. The first test-taker group therefore consists of people who have completed compulsory education in the UK. About 50% of the population go on to take university degrees.

A one-way ANOVA found an overall significant effect of educational level [$F(2, 401) = 11.668$, $p < 0.001$]. A post hoc Games–Howell test indicated that there were statistically significant differences between the *No qualifications or GCSE* group and the other two groups (*A-level* and *university graduate/postgraduate* groups), with the lowest qualification group performing significantly worse than the other two. There were no other significant differences in the data.

This would suggest that a low educational level is related to poor language aptitude. It should also be noted that the wording of the question asked to the test takers was 'What is the highest qualification you have already achieved?'. Therefore, current undergraduate students should have indicated that their highest qualification is an A-level or equivalent. We suspect that some of the participants did not read the question properly, and answered with the qualification that they were currently studying for. This means that the data in the graduate group may be unreliable, as some of the 152 participants could actually belong to the 'A-level equivalent' group. However, significant differences were found between the 'below A-level' group and the 'A-level equivalent and beyond' participants.

Individual variables as predictors of aptitude

The variables explored in the previous sections may probably affect the aptitude scores to different extents. We carried out a multiple linear regression analysis ($N = 381$) to assess the possible contribution of the test takers' individual variables (predictor variables) to the LLAMA_B scores (dependent variable). Our data did not violate the assumptions of normality, linearity and multicollinearity, but in some cases homogeneity of variance was not met. For this reason, we used bootstrap regression.

The analysis showed that our five variables (i.e. L1, previous experience with learning languages, age range, gender and educational level) accounted for 10.3% of the variance in the scores. Only two factors made a significant contribution to the model ($p < 0.05$): previous experience in learning foreign languages (ß-coefficient = 1.590, S.E. = 0.310, $p = 0.001$) and educational level (ß-coefficient = 0.826, S.E. = 0.340, $p = 0.016$).

These results suggest that the LLAMA_B test is measuring something independent of these factors. Future research will need to examine other factors (e.g. IQ, working memory or other cognitive abilities), which might be able to account for more of the variance in the scores.

The mechanics of the LLAMA_B test

Finally, we also examined the length of time allowed to learn the 20 words in the LLAMA_B test. We collected data from 96 participants, equally divided into three groups, matched for age, gender and educational level. One group took the test with the default two minutes learning time. A second group took the tests with a reduced learning time of one minute. The third group took the test with an increased learning time of three minutes. The results of this study are shown in Table 6.

Table 6 The effect of study time on the LLAMA_B test scores

Study time available	N	Mean	S.D.
Short (1 minute)	30	6.70	2.64
Default (2 minutes)	33	10.06	4.90
Long (3 minutes)	33	10.79	4.56
Total	96		

It can be seen that test takers perform worse when they are allowed less time to complete the task, and slightly better when they are allowed more time. An ANOVA was performed to compare the results in the three conditions and it showed a significant study time effect $[F(2, 93) = 8.370, p < 0.001]$. Post hoc Tukey tests indicated that this effect was due to the lower scores in the short study time condition, as this group was significantly different from the other two. The difference between the two longer times was not significant. We interpret this to mean that the default of two minutes study time is optimal, since shortening the time available for study produces significantly worse results, while increasing the time does not provide any significant gains.

References

Carroll, J.B. and Sapon, S.M. (1959) *Modern Language Aptitude Test (MLAT)*. San Antonio, TX: Psychological Corporation.

Grañena, G. (2013) Individual differences in sequence learning ability and SLA in early childhood and adulthood. *Language Learning* 63 (4), 665–703.

Meara, P.M. (2005) *LLAMA Language Aptitude Tests: The Manual*. Swansea: Lognostics.

Skehan, P. (1989, 2014) *Individual Differences in Second Language Learning* (2nd edn). New York: Routledge.

Stansfield, C.W., Reed, D.J. and Velasco, A.M. (2005) *Prueba de aptitud para lenguas extranjeras – versión de primaria (MLAT-ES)*. Rockville, MD: Second Language Testing.

Suárez, M. and Muñoz, C. (2011) Aptitude, age and cognitive development: The MLAT-E in Spanish and Catalan. *EuroSLA Yearbook* 11, 5–29.

Reflections on Rogers

For some years now, we have used the LLAMA language aptitude tests (Meara, 2005) with our final year undergraduates at Swansea University, and with our Masters-level students. These students are required to undertake a small piece of empirical work and submit it in the form of a dissertation which counts towards their final degree classification. The undergraduate students find dissertation work extremely hard, and for this reason we have been developing group projects where the students are put into small teams and given specific projects to work on. This seems to us to be a realistic way of working with inexperienced students, in that it more closely resembles the sort of problem that they might have to deal with in future employment. Not everyone in real life has the luxury of being able to pursue a topic of their own choice, and there are obvious benefits to be had from working as part of a team rather than struggling alone. The approach also has the significant advantage that it makes the students spend time and effort on evaluating the tools they are asked to use rather than encouraging them to develop new tools from scratch.

The LLAMA tests were devised as an umbrella project which could provide a useful framework for small projects of this sort. Our overall philosophy here is that it makes a lot of sense for groups of final year students to work together on projects which are all linked together by a single overarching theme. This way of working naturally provides spaces where students can evaluate their different approaches to the questions they are researching, and to the data they collect. Over a number of years, this approach leads to a number of linked studies, which can be exploited by the students in later work. This set of reports make up a small literature set which is generally more accessible to students in a way that standard journal articles usually are not.

Despite its simplicity, LLAMA_B has turned out to be one of the most robust of the LLAMA tests. The test produces scores ranging from 0 to 20, and the task we gave the students was to establish whether these scores were measuring useful traits in language learners. This task is a lot trickier than it looks at first sight. The test generates a reasonable range of scores in the target population, i.e. it produces a good range of scores, with little evidence of a ceiling effect, but it is not easy to establish whether these scores are related to actual language-learning performance. In practice, the main difficulty that the students ran up against was finding a good measure of language-learning performance that could be used as a criterion to evaluate the LLAMA_B test. This problem caused the students to reflect seriously on the nature of language testing, and by extension to question the way the university evaluated their own competence in the languages they were studying as part of their degree courses. The problem also raised a whole series of discussions about the nature of language aptitude, what it meant to say that vocabulary acquisition skills contributed X% to overall language-learning performance, how you might set about quantifying this contribution, or what information you needed to classify someone as 'a good language learner'. As a training instrument, LLAMA_B was very effective.

However, there remain some internal test issues that need to be addressed. LLAMA_B is basically about learning nouns, and it is not obvious that results for this part of speech also apply to verbs and adjectives. The physical properties of the words to be learned also seem to be important. The words in LLAMA_B are all short and relatively easy to remember, and we might expect very different results if we used words which were structurally or semantically more complex (cf. Laufer, 1997). More important, perhaps, is the fact that LLAMA_B asks test takers to learn only 20 words. It is not at all obvious that a 20-word test provides very much information about learners' ability to learn the much larger numbers of words required for fluent L2 performance. Nor is it obvious that a 20-word test is really capable of discriminating between test takers in a meaningful way. At the moment, all we can say is that most test takers appear to score about 40% on the test – i.e. they manage to associate about eight of the words with the correct picture, but there is considerable variation around this figure. A significant number of test takers score very badly on the test, but on further examination these low scores can mostly be ascribed to learning strategies that do not match the test format very well, rather than poor vocabulary learning ability. A very few test takers score very highly on the test. This suggests that the LLAMA_B test might be good at identifying very poor learners and exceptionally good ones, but might perform less well with learners whose scores are only middling. Some of these technical issues are highlighted in the More Research is Needed section that follows.

Much to our surprise, a lot of people have used the LLAMA tests in serious research on language aptitude. At the time of writing, Google Scholar lists several hundred papers which have cited work based on the LLAMA tests – although only a few of these studies include a reference to the LLAMA Manual, where our reservations about the robustness of the tests and the limited nature of the data they generate are explicitly documented. It is obvious to us that some of this work uses the LLAMA programs in inappropriate contexts, and some of the work makes claims about language aptitude which are very difficult to justify given the tentative nature of the testing tools. This high level of interest reinforced our view that there is a real need for properly documented research tools for vocabulary researchers, and convinced us to include this revised version of LLAMA_B in this volume. We hope to revise the remaining LLAMA tests in the near future.

More Research is Needed ...

This section contains some ideas that could easily be worked up into small-scale research projects.

- Are scores on the LLAMA_B test affected by the instructions given to test takers?
- Does LLAMA_B discriminate between good language learners and weaker learners?
- What strategies do test takers use when they are tested on LLAMA_B? Are some strategies more effective than others?
- This version of LLAMA_B presents you with a word and asks you to identify the associated picture. Would you get the same results if you gave test takers a picture and asked them to identify its name from a list of words?
- How well would LLAMA_B work if it used spoken input rather than written words to name the pictures? Do people differ in their ability to learn spoken and written words?
- Are scores on LLAMA_B affected by test takers' short-term memory span?
- Apart from the obvious learner variables discussed in Rogers' report, what other personality variables and individual differences might you expect to influence the LLAMA_B scores?
- Can you train students to perform well on a LLAMA_B type of test?
- LLAMA_B uses real words from an unfamiliar language. Does it matter that the words to be learned are very different from English nonsense words? (There is a very large literature on how people learn sets of nonsense words paired with real English words. How much of this literature is relevant to L2 vocabulary learning?)
- How do LLAMA_B scores relate to learners' self-assessment of their ability to learn vocabulary?

References

Carroll, J.B. and Sapon, S.M. (1959) *Modern Language Aptitude Test (MLAT)*. San Antonio, TX: Psychological Corporation.

Laufer, B. (1997) What's in a word that makes it hard or easy? Intralexical factors affecting the difficulty of vocabulary acquisition. In N. Schmitt and M. McCarthy (eds) *Vocabulary: Description, Acquisition and Pedagogy* (pp. 140–155). Cambridge: Cambridge University Press.

Meara, P.M. (2005) *LLAMA Language Aptitude Tests: The Manual*. Swansea: Lognostics.

Service, E. (1992) Phonology, working memory and foreign language learning. *Quarterly Journal of Experimental Psychology* 45a, 21–50.

Service, E. and Kohonen, V. (1995) Is the relation between phonological memory and foreign language learning accounted for by vocabulary acquisition? *Applied Psycholinguistics* 16 (2), 155–172.

Further reading

Dahlen, K. and Caldwell-Harris, C. (2013) Rehearsal and aptitude in foreign language vocabulary learning. *Modern Language Journal* 97 (4), 902–916.

Grañena, G. (2013) Cognitive aptitudes for second language learning and the LLAMA Language Aptitude test. In G. Grañena and M. Long (eds) *Sensitive Periods, Language Aptitude, and L2 Attainment* (pp. 105–130). Amsterdam: John Benjamins.

Parry, T. and Stansfield, C.W. (eds) (1990) *Language Aptitude Reconsidered*. Englewood Cliffs, NJ: Prentice Hall.

Qais, A. How to pass the MLAT. See http://www.suitqaisdiaries.com/how-to-pass-the-mlat/.

Robinson, P. (2005) Aptitude and second language acquisition. *Annual Review of Applied Linguistics* 25, 46–73.

Stansfield, C.W. and Reed, D.J. (2004) The story behind the Modern Language Aptitude Test: An interview with John B. Carroll (1916–2003). *Language Assessment Quarterly* 1 (1), 43–56.

Part 6
Modelling Vocabulary Growth

11 Mezzofanti v1.0

Introduction

The program described in this chapter is rather different from the programs we have seen so far. In the previous chapters we were working either with programs that processed data, or with programs that collected data. In this chapter, the program generates data. This is an important difference.

The program is named after Cardinal Giuseppe Mezzofanti (1774–1849). Mezzofanti was Professor of Arabic at the University of Bologna, and subsequently Custodian-in-Chief of the Vatican Library. He had a reputation for being able to speak a very large number of languages, including Hebrew, Arabic, Aramaic, Coptic, Armenian, Persian, Turkish, Albanian, Ancient Greek, Modern Greek, Latin, Italian, Spanish, Portuguese, French, German, Swedish, Danish, Dutch, English, Illyrian, Russian, Czech, Hungarian and Chinese (cf. Russell, 1863, for a biography written shortly after Mezzofanti's death).

Cases like his have led modern scholars to ask whether there might be an upper limit on the number of languages a single person can learn. This issue is discussed in Erard (2013). **Mezzofanti,** the program, was developed as a way of investigating the way different languages might interact with each other in a simplified learning environment.

Mezzofanti is a simulator program. It sets up a very simple model of how the acquisition of vocabulary might work. The model used here relies on a small number of **parameters** which can take different values. We plug these parameters into the model, run it, and see what kind of outputs the model generates for various combinations of values. Playing with models of this sort can be a useful way of generating ideas for future research projects, partly because models force you to be very specific about the assumptions you are making, and how different assumptions interact with one another. This way of approaching research is not very common in vocabulary research, and it sometimes generates controversy.

The model that Mezzofanti is based on comes from a little-known paper by Klaus Riegel (1968). Riegel argued that a first approximation to modelling vocabulary acquisition was to assume that it was governed by three basic factors: the number of words available in the learning environment; the rate at which the words are taken up by learners; and the amount of time learners spend learning the language. He argued that these factors could be modelled with a general formula that is commonly used to describe situations involving growth. The formula looks like this:

$$V = A*(1 - \exp^{-mt}) \tag{1}$$

where V = current vocabulary size
A = the size of the vocabulary available in the environment
m = the rate at which words are encountered by a learner
t = the length of time spent in the environment.

Formulae of this sort are not usual in vocabulary research, so it is worth spending some time getting your head around what this particular formula does before going any further. The difficult bit is **exp^{-mt}**. All you need to understand here is that this expression generates a set of numbers that vary between 0 and 1.

For example, $\exp^0 = 1$; $\exp^{-1} = 0.358$; $\exp^{-2} = 0.135$; $\exp^{-4} = 0.183$. In general terms, $\exp^{-x}$ gets closer to 0 as x gets bigger. This means that the expression in brackets $(1 - \exp^{-mt})$, also varies between 0 and 1, but $1 - \exp^{-mt}$ gets closer to 1 as the $-mt$ bit gets bigger. If we assume that m is a constant, and t stands for the amount of time you spend in the environment, then $(1 - \exp^{-mt})$ is a fraction that gets closer to 1 as you spend more time in the environment. If you multiply A (the size of the available vocabulary) by this fraction, it tells you how many words you would expect someone to have encountered by time t. This number increases as t gets bigger. In ordinary language this says: the more time you spend in an environment, the more words you encounter, but you never encounter all the words available for learning.

Despite its simplicity, this seems like a good approximation to what happens in real life. Mezzofanti allows you to experiment with these basic parameters, and work out how vocabulary acquisition varies when you change the parameters. Mezzofanti also allows you to explore what happens when a person learns two languages, either in early childhood or later as an adult.

Using Mezzofanti

You will find Mezzofanti on the Lognostics Tools website, available at: http://www.lognostics.co.uk/tools/Mezzofanti/Mezzofanti.htm.

Mezzofanti does not require you to do any advance data preparation. However, you should be familiar with the parameters below.

The parameters that appear in the basic equation are:

A   the number of words available in the vocabulary the learner is exposed to
m   a factor that describes the richness of the lexical environment
t   the length of time available for learning

More advanced models that deal with bilingual inputs also use two additional parameters:

p   the proportion of time available for the main language
o   the delay in starting the L2

Mezzofanti lets you experiment with these parameters and explore how they affect the way vocabulary development takes place.

(1) The Mezzofanti opening screen is shown in Figure 11.1.
(2) Click **Start** to begin the program. The initial Mezzofanti workspace is shown in Figure 11.2.
(3) You can work with a single language, or with two languages simultaneously. Each language is associated with four parameters.
    - *Parameter A* is the number of words available in the environment being modelled. Conventionally, this figure is set to 20,000. This means that there are about 20,000 words available in the environment for the model to acquire. This figure is a simplification which needs to be explored. If you are working with multilingual models, then you might want to change this parameter to a lower figure: e.g. if you are modelling the way an adult learner acquires an L2 in

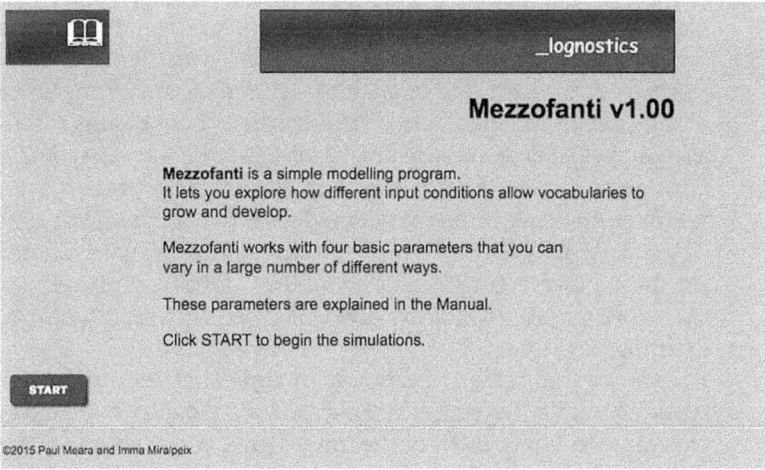

Figure 11.1 Mezzofanti opening screen

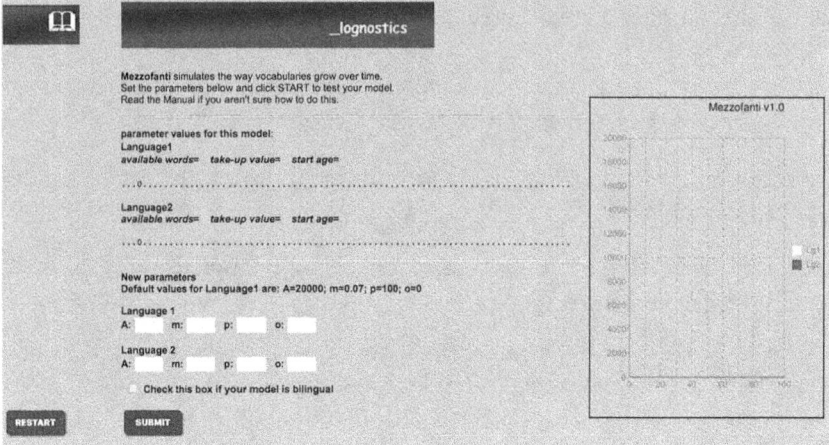

Figure 11.2 Initial Mezzofanti workspace

evening classes, you might want to set the A parameter at around 2000–3000 words.
- *Parameter m* is an environmental richness factor which determines how good the model is at picking up words in the environment. Conventionally, this factor is set to 0.07. This value means that under normal conditions the model acquires a vocabulary of around 10,000 words by age 10: this figure seems to correspond roughly to what happens in real life. Riegel is careful to say that his model is *not* a psycholinguistic model of how learners acquire words. However, we think that there are some advantages to interpreting this parameter as a characteristic of learners, rather than as a characteristic of the environment they operate in. It makes some sense to interpret *m* as an index of how well a learner notices words in the environment, rather than as a characteristic of the environment that is independent of the learner. This change of focus allows you to explore different types of learners by varying the *m* parameter. To model a precocious learner who notices a lot of words in the environment, we might set the *m* parameter to 0.09. To model a slow learner who is not linguistically aware, we might set the *m* parameter to a value about 0.05. This feature is especially useful if you are modelling an L2 learner with poor vocabulary learning skills.
- *Parameter p* indicates the amount of time that the model spends working with a language. If your model is a monolingual model, set this value to 100 (= 100% of the time). If you are modelling bilingual cases, then you will need to vary this value appropriately. For instance, if you are modelling a bilingual child learning two

languages simultaneously, then you might set parameter *p* for Language 1 to 50 (= 50% of the time) and parameter *p* for Language 2 to 50 (= the other 50% of the time). If you are modelling an adult learner acquiring Chinese in an evening class for a few hours a week, then you might set parameter *p* to a much lower value.
- *Parameter o* indicates the age at which the model starts to acquire the language. For Language 1 this figure will normally be 0. Other values might be appropriate for L2 learners – e.g. if you are modelling an adult L2 learner who starts learning Chinese at age 30, then set parameter *o* for Language 2 to 30. For simplicity, parameter *o* should be divisible by five.

(4) When you have finished setting your parameters, click the **Submit** button. Mezzofanti generates a graph which shows you how many words your model would be expected to acquire given its initial parameter settings.

(5) Figure 11.3 shows an example of the way Mezzofanti reports.

In this report, Mezzofanti shows vocabulary growth for a single individual learning two languages. For both languages, parameter *A* is set to 20,000 and parameter *m* is set to 0.07. The start age for Language 2 is 10 years, and the proportion of time spent in an L2 environment is 60%. This reduces the time available for Language 1 to 40% once the learner reaches 10 years. These settings are shown in the top left-hand sector of the report page.

The graph on the right-hand side of the report page shows vocabulary uptake in the two languages (Lg1 and Lg2). In the report screen of the program, the yellow line represents Language 1, the blue line Language 2 (clear line and dark line in the screenshot, Figure 11.3). Language 1 follows

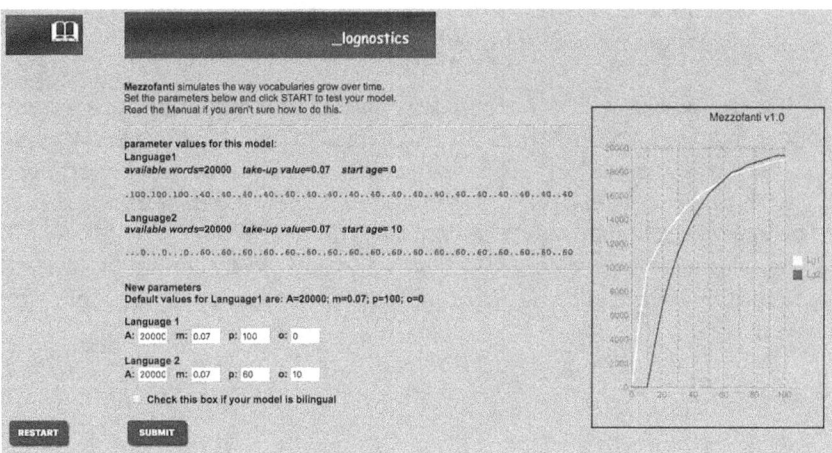

Figure 11.3 Mezzofanti report page

a normal trajectory up to age 10, continuing to rise after that, but at a slower rate than we would expect in a monolingual learner. Language 2 rises sharply from age 10, and continues to grow at a faster rate than Language 1. The two languages are roughly in balance from around age 60.

(6) Simulations are only as good as the assumptions that are built into them. A significant number of simplifications are built into Mezzofanti, and you need to be aware of their implications, as they seriously affect the way that the model works.

   (a) Mezzofanti assumes that the amount of vocabulary available is a constant and does not vary with time. This assumption is an obvious simplification. In real life, young children are exposed to a limited vocabulary. Adolescents in formal schooling are exposed to a lot more vocabulary. Ideally we would like to allow our A parameter to vary so that it reflects changes of this sort, but for simplicity we do not allow this.

   (b) Mezzofanti's second simplifying assumption concerns the m parameter. Again, for simplicity, the model treats m as a fixed parameter which remains constant throughout life. Ideally what we would like is a parameter that reflects young children's limited ability to notice words in their linguistic environment. One way to do this would be to model early vocabulary acquisition as a separate process, and start the model at five years of age rather than 0 years. Mezzofanti also assumes that the m parameter remains constant into old age. Ideally, we might want to allow this parameter to get smaller with age.

   (c) The third assumption that is built into the program is that words are not generally subject to attrition. This is probably a reasonable assumption, at least for L1 learners who are not in advanced years. Attrition seems to be quite high for L2 learners, especially when their vocabularies are small.

For the purposes of an exploratory model, these assumptions are not critical, but you need to think how changes in these assumptions might affect the way the model works, how you can simulate them by experimenting with the parameter combinations, and what new parameters might need to be included in a more advanced model.

Some questions which will allow you to explore the effects of these assumptions are included in the More Research is Needed … section of this chapter.

The technical bits

Two of the default values that Mezzofanti uses may need some explanation.

- *Parameter A* – the number of words available in the environment – is normally set at 20,000 words. This value reflects current conservative estimates of the number of words people know in a language. The program allows you to set this parameter to a larger figure, but the report page will only show data up to 20,000 words.
- *Parameter m* – the lexical environment factor – is normally set to 0.07. This value means that about half the available vocabulary has been encountered by the time the model reaches 10 years and there are few opportunities for learning new words after age 60.

Background Reading

> **Meara, P.M. (2001) The mathematics of vocabularies. In M. Gill, A. Johnson, L. Koski, R. Sell and B. Wårvik (eds)** *Language, Learning, Literature: Studies Presented to Håkan Ringbom* **(pp. 151–166). Åbo: Åbo Akademi.**
>
> This paper is a very exploratory piece about the mathematics of vocabularies, intended to provoke discussion rather than to provide answers. Like many British linguists, my own mathematical education is fairly rudimentary, and over the many years that I have been working on vocabulary acquisition I have increasingly found this to be a problem. In other areas of applied linguistics it is still possible to work with informal models – indeed, a great deal of British applied linguistics is work of this sort. However, when it comes to working on vocabularies the limitations of informal models make themselves apparent very quickly.
>
> The main problem with vocabularies is that they are big: even by the most conservative estimates of vocabulary size in monolinguals, we must be dealing with 15,000 or more items in the average person's lexicon and it is, frankly, difficult to see how we can talk sensibly about something as large as this without using some sort of mathematical simplification. Most people get round this problem by treating the lexicon as if it were a simple, monolithic whole, happily ignoring the fact that words have remarkably different properties and that different parts of the lexicon behave in remarkably different ways. This can sometimes lead to wild generalisations about 'the lexicon', often based on very limited data. Most of us would be able to think of a dozen or so papers where very strong claims about lexicons have been developed on the back of experimental evidence involving a mere handful of different lexical items. When it comes to bilingual lexicons, we are dealing with larger and even more complex systems, and you would expect people to

be more cautious about the generalisations they make. In fact, here too, we have claims made about 'the bilingual lexicon' based on very small amounts of data. Stroop tests (for example, Kiyak, 1982) make up a surprisingly large fraction of all the studies on bilingual lexical storage, and yet they employ an experimental method which uses at most a dozen words from a particularly specialised part of the lexicon. It is difficult to see how data from studies of this sort can be generalised in a meaningful way.

This paper is principally concerned with a very specific problem in lexical studies – the question of how vocabularies grow, and how we can describe this growth. Growth is a phenomenon which has attracted a lot of attention in other disciplines, and models for most types of growth and decay are available. The growth of populations, the growth of economies, the spread of disease among a population, and so on, all have analogues in the area of the lexicon and, in principle, it ought to be possible to apply these models to the way people's vocabularies grow and decline throughout their lives. As far as I am aware, however, this very basic property of lexicons has not been modelled seriously. There are, of course, a number of unwritten assumptions about vocabulary growth in the research literature, although it is often difficult to disentangle just what these assumptions are because of difficulties in measuring vocabulary size anyway. In general, we all accept that growth in monolinguals begins very slowly and increases throughout childhood. After that, vocabularies increase in a more-or-less linear fashion at a rate of about 1000 words per year, perhaps with spurts around the ages of seven and 14. This growth seems to tail off in adulthood, and vocabulary may even decline in old age. Where bilinguals are concerned, the general assumption seems to be: that learning a second language does not seriously impair your first language in any way; that learning vocabulary in childhood is probably easier than learning as an adult; and that the more languages you learn, the easier it seems to be to acquire vocabulary in further languages. However, the price you pay for this is that you forget them more easily; once learned, a second language vocabulary can quickly regenerate under the right conditions. I do not think that many people would quarrel with these statements, although there might be some quibbles with the detailed figures. In fact, it is very difficult to find anywhere that they are made as explicit as I have done here. They represent a set of commonly held views that we all take for granted, and which do not seem to be in need of an explanation.

Important as these assumptions are, there is very little work which examines them in any depth, and the only serious example of modelling in this area that I know is an article published by Klaus Riegel in 1968.

This article, a wide-ranging, almost rambling piece, published shortly before Riegel's early death, deals with several different aspects of bilingual performance, with special reference to the lexicon. I first came across Riegel's work shortly after it was published, and it impressed me a lot – mainly because it seemed to talk about mathematical models of the bilingual lexicon that were extraordinarily simple, and yet far more comprehensive than anything else that was available. At the time, my own rather limited mathematics made it difficult for me to take Riegel's model any further than his original sketch did, although one could not help realising that this was an important new direction for research. Surprisingly, Riegel's paper seems not to have generated any interest among linguists. When I searched the standard databases in preparation for this paper, I was able to locate only a handful of people citing this work. This handful was mostly restricted to Riegel's immediate friends and colleagues working in the field of transactional analysis, and publishing in the journal *Human Development*. As far as I am aware, no one has seriously taken up Riegel's ideas about the mathematics of lexical growth, and the way the growth patterns in two languages interact in bilinguals.

Riegel's ideas in this respect are basically very simple and they can be summarised very quickly. Riegel's initial assumption is that people are exposed to the total lexicon of a language in a way that can be described in terms of a few simple parameters: the total number of words in a language (A), the current size of their vocabulary (N), and a factor (m) which describes the richness of the linguistic environment, or the rate at which new words are experienced. This suggests that the rate at which you encounter new words in a vocabulary will gradually slow down over time: the more words you know, the fewer words there are left for you to learn. A plot of cumulative exposure to words against time will show a rising curve that gradually levels off.

Growth patterns of this sort can be described by simple exponential equations like the one shown in Equation (2):

$$dN/dt = m(A - N) \qquad (2)$$

where $N = A(1 - \exp(-mt))$.

This equation states that the change in N over time gradually decreases as N gets larger, and that this slowing in the rate depends on the value of m. Setting $m = 0.07$, for instance, and measuring time in years, produces a curve implying that normal monolingual speakers would have been exposed to about half the vocabulary of their L1 by the age of 10, just over three-quarters by age 20, and 90% of their vocabulary by age 33. Readers may recognise the mathematics here: it is the same sort of argument that is sometimes used in lexico-statistics to describe the accumulation of lexical types in long texts. Setting m at other values makes the slope of the graph steeper or shallower, but does not change its basic shape or affect the other arguments that depend on it.

Riegel goes on to show how the basic equations can be adapted to cover some simple bilingual situations. In particular, he shows that introducing a second language into a linguistic environment changes the patterns of exposure that people experience. Depending on how old you are when you begin a new language, and depending on how much time you devote to it, Riegel's model is able to predict how the two languages will interact.

Riegel distinguishes between two different types of bilingual environment. The first of these is an 'independent' condition, in which a proportion of the total language input occurs exclusively and consistently in a second language. He suggests that this condition occurs when a learner takes regular classes in the L2, but the model covers a whole range of cases, including the extreme one where a complete change of language occurs – for instance the case of children who leave their native country and never speak their native language again. Riegel's second condition, which he calls 'confounded', occurs when two languages are randomly encountered in the environment. Riegel suggests that two similar sets of equations describe the way in which these two conditions affect the type of linguistic exposure that a bilingual experiences. The confounded condition is the more complex of the two, so we will leave it out of account here. In the independent condition, Equation (2) describes what happens up to the point when the second language is introduced. After that point – call it t1 – Riegel suggests that two equations are required, one for each language. Suppose that input in Language A is reduced to a proportion p, and that the second language B is introduced at proportion q where $q = 1 - p$, then exposure to the two languages can be described by Equations (3) and (4), respectively.

For Language A:

$$N = (A*1 - \exp(-mp(t1/p + t - t1))) \qquad (3)$$

for Language B:

$$N = (B*1 - \exp(-mq(t - t1))) \qquad (4)$$

These abstract formulae will make more sense if you look at Figure 1, which shows how these equations perform with some reasonable

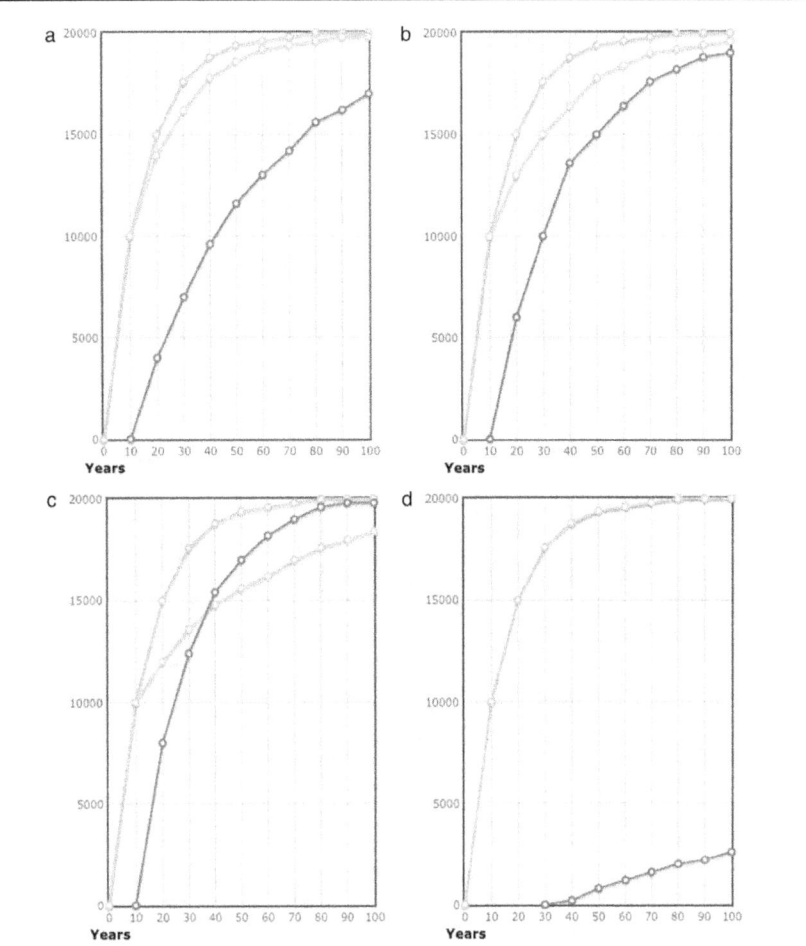

Figure 1 Examples of bilingual environments with different values for the parameters p, q and t. Y axes: Cumulative exposure to language. Notes: Left-to-right and top-to-bottom:
Figure 1(a) ($t1 = 10$; $m = 0.07$; $p = 0.7$; $q = 0.3$)
Figure 1(b) ($t1 = 10$; $m = 0.07$; $p = 0.5$; $q = 0.5$)
Figure 1(c) ($t1 = 10$; $m = 0.07$; $p = 0.3$; $q = 0.7$)
Figure 1(d) ($t1 = 30$; $m = 0.07$; $p = 0.97$; $q = 0.03$)

assumptions about p, q and $t1$. Models (a)–(c) in Figure 1 are taken from Riegel's paper. In these graphs, $t1$ is assumed to be 10 years, and the proportion of L2 input is varied from 0.3 to 0.7. Riegel notes that, in all three cases, substantial exposure occurs in the L2, with only a very slight loss in the L1 relative to the monolingual condition. Even in Riegel's extreme case, where the L2 receives 70% of the total exposure after age

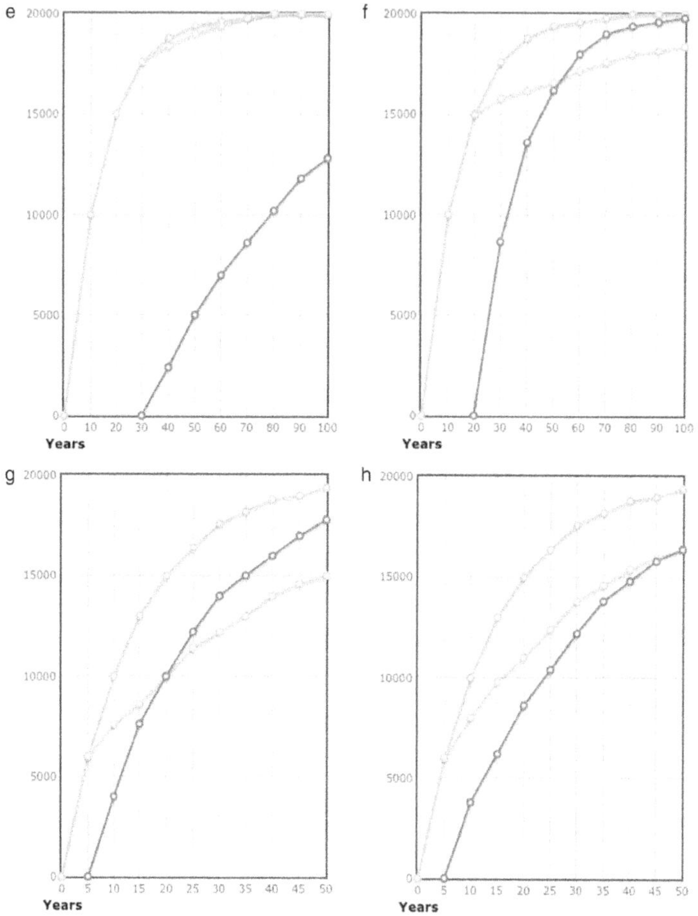

Figure 1 (*Continued*) Examples of bilingual environments with different values for the parameters *p*, *q* and *t*. Y axes: Cumulative exposure to language. Notes: Left-to-right and top-to-bottom:
Figure 1(e) (*t1* = 30; *m* = 0.07; *p* = 0.79; *q* = 0.21)
Figure 1(f) (*t1* = 20; *m* = 0.07; *p* = 0.2; *q* = 0.8)
Figure 1(g) (*t1* = 5; *m* = 0.33; *p* = 0.3; *q* = 0.67)
Figure 1(h) (*t1* = 5; *m* = 0.07; *p* = 0.45; *q* = 0.55).

10 and the L1 only 30%, it still takes a very long time for the cumulative exposure to L2 to exceed the cumulative total for L1.

It is important to stress here that the curves in Figure 1 do not represent vocabulary growth directly. Riegel's model is a model of the linguistic environment in which learners find themselves, and it is explicitly not a psycholinguistic model. Later on in this paper, we will look at some ways in which the model can be adapted in the direction of a psycholinguistic model. For the moment, however, let us introduce a couple of benchmarks that will make the discussion slightly more concrete. It is obviously not the case that language proficiency varies directly with exposure to vocabulary, but we can reasonably establish some plausible achievement levels based on what we know about L1 speakers' ability to perform in their L1. An obvious benchmark of this sort seems to be the sort of competence level achieved by a five-year-old child. A second useful benchmark is the level of competence achieved by a young adult, a person aged 15, say. We do not need to put actual numbers to the vocabularies at these benchmark levels: we can simply say that the level reached as a result of five years' exposure to the language produces a certain level of competence, call it C5, while further exposure up to age 15 results in a higher level of competence, which we can call C15. In Figure 1 models (a)–(c), these levels seem to correspond roughly to exposure to 0.25 and 0.6 of the vocabulary, respectively. All three of Riegel's illustrative cases reach the benchmarks, although it may take a considerable time to achieve this.

Not all possible cases have this happy outcome, however, and some other plausible cases are shown in Figure 1 models (d)–(h), a set of more interesting cases not discussed in Riegel's paper, but implicit in his model. Figure 1, models (d) and (e) represent the classic case of a person who takes up a second language late in life and spends a strictly limited amount of time working on it or in it. Case (d) – the three hours a week learner – fails to get anywhere near our first competence level, C5: the cumulative exposure at this level of input is just not enough for this level to be achieved. The two hours a day learner shown in Figure 1 model (e) does considerably better. Figure 1 model (f) represents a more extreme case, a young adult aged 20, who settles in a new country and spends four-fifths of their time exposed to the L2. In this case, both benchmarks are easily reached. In due course, cumulative exposure to the L2, and presumably linguistic competence, overtakes exposure to the L1. Figure 1 models (g) and (h) show two cases of child bilingualism, where a child is brought up monolingually until the age of five, but subsequently goes to a school where the language of instruction is an L2. These two graphs show the effects of relatively small differences in the amount of L2 exposure in this situation.

As we noted earlier, it is important to stress that Riegel's model is a model of how people are exposed to the vocabularies of their L1 and L2, and not a model of how they acquire these vocabularies. Nevertheless, even working at this simplistic level, one or two points come out very strongly. The first point concerns the lasting impact of the L1 in any bilingual situation where the L2 is introduced after the L1. Even when the L2 is introduced quite early on, and when it receives greater exposure than the L1, cumulative exposure to the L2 lags behind cumulative exposure to the L1 for a very long time. The second point is that the greatest difference between the L1 bilingual condition and the monolingual condition is a longer term difference, rather than shorter term one. For instance, in Figure 1 model (b), the greatest difference between the monolingual condition and the L1 bilingual condition occurs around $t = 40$. After that point, the differences decline and eventually disappear.

It goes without saying that Riegel's model is a grossly oversimplified and idealised picture of the way real people become acquainted with their language. It assumes, for example, that the language people are exposed to does not vary with their age – all the words are available all the time; it assumes that the languages being learned are stable, and do not themselves vary over time, and so on. Taking these simplifications into account, however, it is clear that Riegel's model throws some interesting light on the assumptions that we listed earlier. In particular, Riegel's model suggests an explanation as to why learning a second language does not appear to affect your first language: the answer is that it does, but only in the medium term, and only in the marginal areas of the lexicon. If exposure is the principal determinant of uptake, then only the very rarest of words will be affected by learning a second language. It follows, of course, that we would not expect to find great differences in the vocabularies of monolingual children and bilinguals with only a few years of exposure to their L2 – although this is precisely the stage where most people have attempted to look for differences of this sort. Even bilingual children with equal exposure to both languages from birth show very little deviation from the monolingual pattern over most of their school years on this model. A further prediction that we can derive from Riegel's model is that the richness of the linguistic environment is the crucial factor that determines vocabulary growth. Very small changes in the parameter m make very large differences in the rate at which new words are met, and these differences are particularly important in the early stages of learning a language. A lexically rich environment can make up for a relatively small amount of exposure time. At the same time, the effects of a lexically poor environment can be compensated for in the long run, as long as the exposure to the linguistic environment is not too restricted. Combining a limited proportion of exposure time with a deliberately limited exposure rate – the pattern that we normally find for adults learning a language on their own and using textbooks with limited vocabularies – does not look like a regime that will generate a high success rate in the long term.

How important is it that Riegel's model deals with lexical environments, rather than with vocabulary acquisition per se? On the face of it, this simplification is a very important one, but on closer consideration it might be less so. The crucial insight in Riegel's model is that it attempts to describe the learning environment in terms of a few simple parameters, and we can adapt this idea to make the model more plausible from a psychological point of view. The main problem with the model as it stands is that it implies that vocabulary growth is fastest at birth, and declines steadily after that. This is obviously false. Very young children do not have any vocabulary worth talking about, and vocabulary growth remains small until age two or three. However, we can make the model behave more plausibly by including a single extra parameter in the model, one that varies with age and is particularly sensitive to very small ages. Let us call this parameter a take-up factor, and let us assume that in very young children the take-up factor is very small, and that it reaches a maximum around 18 years. At first sight, you might expect that introducing a factor of this sort would have a very dramatic effect on total vocabulary size. In practice, this is not the case. Introducing a factor of this kind does not actually make a great deal of difference to the way Riegel's model works, except in the very early stages. Imagine, for example, a take-up factor that starts off very small, reaches 60% by age 10, eventually levels off at, say, 80% at age 20, and after that does not vary very much. In effect, a take-up factor of this sort slows growth at the very early stages of language acquisition, but once the asymptotic level is reached all it does is impose a maximum level on the proportion of the vocabulary in the environment that is acquired. You can see this in Figure 2, where the data plotted in Figure 1 – the first two models (a)–(b) and the last two (g)–(h) – have this additional take-up factor imposed upon them. The similarities between the two sets of curves will be apparent. Growth in the early stages of acquisition is slower than in Figure 1, and the final level of achievement is limited by the value of the take-up factor. Since the take-up rate is affected mainly by age, and the L2 is introduced when the take-up rate is already high, the acquisition of L2 words is relatively fast, and the large differences between L1 and L2 recorded in Figure 1 are considerably reduced. The take-up factor also affects the size of vocabulary associated with our benchmark levels, C5 and C15, but perhaps not as markedly as we might have expected. If we plot out the early stages of these curves in more detail, there are some differences in the way the L1 and the L2 develop, but these differences have few obvious long-term effects. The main difference seems to be that take-up in an L2 acquired in adulthood will not be constrained in the same way as acquisition of an L1 in early childhood. The take-up

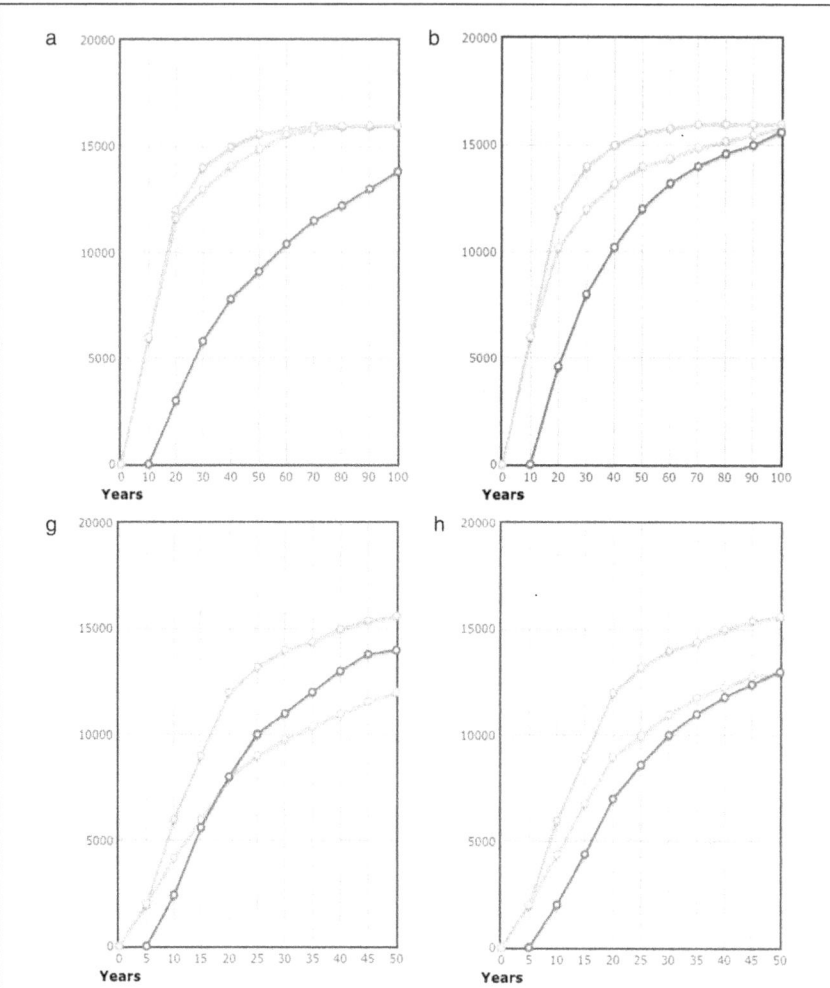

Figure 2 Examples of Riegel's model, with the addition of an uptake parameter. Y axes: Cumulative exposure to language. Notes: Left-to-right and top-to-bottom:
Figure 2(a) ($t1 = 10$; $m = 0.07$; $p = 0.7$; $q = 0.3$)
Figure 2(b) ($t1 = 10$; $m = 0.07$; $p = 0.5$; $q = 0.5$)
Figure 2(g) ($t1 = 5$; $m = 0.33$; $p = 0.3$; $q = 0.67$)
Figure 1(h) ($t1 = 5$; $m = 0.07$; $p = 0.45$; $q = 0.55$).

factor is one that we might expect to vary a lot between individuals – an obvious candidate for a study of individual differences among second language learners.

There is in fact some evidence that our ability to pick up words from the environment might be a stable trait, and that it strongly affects our ability to learn second languages (Gathercole *et al.*, 1997; Skehan, 1993). This suggests that, despite its simplicity and despite the reservations that Riegel is at pains to make, the model may actually be more powerful than it looks. Furthermore, it is easy to see how the model might be developed to include other factors which it currently does not. At the moment, for example, the model assumes that the number of words in the linguistic environment is constant: it would be very easy to model a changing linguistic environment that included the sudden increase of vocabulary that children encounter when they go to school, or the massively large vocabularies that come into play in higher education environments. It would also be easy to introduce an attrition factor into the model, with very low levels of exposure resulting in an overall loss of the underexposed language.

The general point to be made here is that simple mathematical models can be surprisingly powerful, and given the fact that large lexicons are difficult to explore in an experimental context, there might be much to be gained from using models of this type in the study of vocabulary. Models of this sort can sometimes suggest fruitful areas of research that do not become apparent on their own – as we have seen here with the idea of take-up rate. Furthermore, there is no reason why models of this sort should be limited to the realms of theory. We now have a number of very large scale studies of young children learning two languages in reasonably well-understood environments (e.g. Verhallen & Schoonen, 1993), and it ought to be possible for us to use these data to evaluate models like Riegel's and to work out approximate values for the parameters his model uses. This would obviously be a significant step forward, opening up new and important fields of research.

Phenomena like growth and decay are well-studied in other disciplines, particularly biology (cf. Thompson, 1917/1961), and in these fields simple models like the one I have outlined here have proved to be surprisingly productive. Despite its power, the mathematics that underlies these models is not difficult, so why is it that no work building on Riegel's model has been undertaken since the publication of this paper 25 years ago? The answer seems to be that simple mathematical modelling of this sort does not normally form part of the usual range of training provided to applied linguists. My personal view is that this is a serious problem: it puts applied linguistics at a serious disadvantage relative to other social sciences, by severely limiting the types of questions we can ask and the kinds of solutions we can propose to those questions. In the long run, we are going to have to address this issue, and make sure that formal modelling, if only at an elementary level, becomes part of the training of at least some young applied linguists, in much the same way as it has always been part of the training given to psychologists. As far as vocabulary is concerned, if we do not do this, then we will end up working with superficial models that greatly oversimplify the nature of vocabularies, but at the same time manage to miss out on the important general properties that vocabularies share with other large systems that grow, decay and reorganise themselves over time.

References

Gathercole, S.E., Hitch, G.J., Service, E. and Martin, A.J. (1997) Phonological short-term memory and new word learning in children. *Developmental Psychology* 33, 966–979.

Kiyak, H.A. (1982) Interlingual interference in naming colour words. *Journal of Cross-Cultural Psychology* 13 (1), 125–135.

Riegel, K. (1968) Some theoretical considerations of bilingual development. *Psychological Bulletin* 70 (6), 647–670.

Skehan, P. (1993) Foreign language learning ability: Cognitive or linguistic? *Thames Valley University Working Papers in English Language Teaching* 2, 151–191.

Thompson, D'A.W. (1917/1961) *On Growth and Form*. Cambridge: Cambridge University Press. Abridged edn. 1961.

Verhallen, M. and Schoonen, R. (1993) Lexical knowledge of monolingual and bilingual children. *Applied Linguistics* 14 (4), 344–363.

Reflections on Meara (2001)

Riegel's 1968 paper has always struck me as one of the great underrated papers in vocabulary acquisition research. It is still cited only rarely – a mere 30 citations at the time of writing, and only a handful of these in papers published after 2008. I still think that the main reason people do not interact with Riegel's work is that most research students in applied linguistics have very little in the way of mathematical training, and they are seriously put off by the idea of working with formal models. This is something that we are going to have to address if we want to make any serious progress in vocabulary research. At the moment, most of the papers published in vocabulary research are focused on a very small set of problem types – what sort of strategies people use to learn vocabulary, the effectiveness of different types of treatments, assessing vocabulary size, the relationship between vocabulary breadth and vocabulary depth, etc. There is actually very little research that pushes the field in new directions.

One of the reasons for this is that applied linguists typically do not use models in their research. Models are useful because they allow you to explore different aspects that would be very difficult to study using more normal research methods. For example, it would be logistically very difficult to study vocabulary growth in an individual learner over a period of, say, 50 years. With a model, however, we can easily examine this type of question, and by working with different parameter sets we can quickly home in on the important factors that are likely to influence vocabulary growth. In this way, modelling research suggests things that it might be worth investigating in more detail. A number of interesting features emerge in this paper.

The first feature is the importance of the amount of vocabulary available in the lexical environment. The reason this feature is important is that current language teaching practice puts a heavy premium on restricted environments, and not overburdening learners with a large vocabulary. The Mezzofanti model suggests that limiting the vocabulary targets we provide to students will have serious long-term effects on their L2 language ability. A typical language syllabus works to a target of about 2000 words over four or five years. If you plug these figures into the Mezzofanti parameters, you quickly notice that the resulting graphs are very different from the more normal growth patterns that we get with larger vocabulary environments.

The second feature that emerges from the Mezzofanti simulations is that start age and proportion of time spent on an L2 interact in interesting ways. This is particularly obvious when we model immersion environments, or learning situations where a second language gets much larger exposure than an existing first language. Learning two languages simultaneously seems to produce very different outcomes from starting to learn an L2 at age five, at least as far as vocabulary size is concerned. However, it is rare to see arguments about the age factor in the L2 using models to evaluate some of the policies that are in place in schools. In Wales, for instance, all primary schools include some Welsh classes. Let us be generous, and say that this exposure amounts to 5% of a child's total language exposure, and let us be equally generous and say that the language environment contains about 5000 words (it probably contains a much smaller number than this). Plug these figures into the Mezzofanti model, and we find that the children's expected attainment levels after 10 years of schooling barely registers on the graph. Certainly, it is nowhere near the C5 competence level that is described in the paper. The model also suggests that bringing down the age of onset in EFL learning does not actually provide substantial benefits for vocabulary size in the long term, unless the amount of exposure to the foreign language is considerable (in line, for instance, with the results in Muñoz, 2006, among others).

The third feature that emerges from the Mezzofantil simulations is the importance of the *m* parameter. In the paper, it was accepted that *m* is a measure of the richness of the lexical environment, and not a psycholinguistic feature that characterises individual learners (Riegel's argument). However, the interpretation of *m* might be different: there is actually a very strong case for suggesting that *m* is indeed a psycholinguistic trait, and that it corresponds to something like the ability of an individual learner to notice new words in the environment. Good learners, who notice words all the time and interact with them, would have higher m-values than learners who are not interested in words, and do not notice them when they occur.

Treating m as a psycholinguistic variable opens up a number of new avenues of research for vocabulary. We could ask, for instance, how much variation there is among learners as far as m is concerned. Are there some learners with very high values for m, as well as some with very low values? What is an 'average' value for m? We could also ask whether m is really a fixed value parameter, or one which changes with age. If m is variable, then we need to think about the ways in which it might vary – for example, does learning a new language increase the value of m? Is this perhaps why it seems to become easier to acquire a new language the more languages you already know? Can we train m? Can m become negative in old age? What effect does this have on the words we already know?

Questions of this sort are very different from other ordinary run-of-the-mill research questions that appear in research journals. If you find questions like this intriguing, then you will find it well worth while to get some proper training in writing computer programs that will allow you to explore them further. Mezzofanti is a very simple simulator, but it would be a relatively easy programming task to extend its capabilities.

More Research is Needed ...

This section contains some ideas that could easily be worked up into small-scale research projects.

Doing simulation work is very different from collecting data in the normal way of research, and the questions in this section reflect this. Basically, the way you work with a model like Mezzofanti is to run the model with different combinations of parameter values, and see if you can make sense of the data that the model generates. It is fairly easy to find cases where the data do not fit what we know about real language learners. In these cases, we need to think why the model is failing. Sometimes we might be able to resolve the failure by allowing one or more of our fixed parameters to vary – for example, you might want to argue that the value of parameter A starts off very small, and gets larger as the model grows older. Sometimes, we might feel that it is necessary to add a new parameter – for example, Mezzofanti does not allow for vocabulary loss, and it would make a big difference to the outcomes if attrition were factored in as an additional parameter. Adding parameters is usually considered to be something to be avoided in model-building work, unless it is absolutely necessary. The simpler your model, the better. If you do need to factor in a new parameter, then you need to work out exactly how it operates, and build this new feature into the mathematics.

Here are some questions that you could ask of Mezzofanti 1.0.

- What happens if the model is operating in a very restricted lexical environment? (Change the A parameter to a very low value).
- How flexible is the m parameter? (Try raising and lowering the value of m. What values of m produce unrealistic outputs?)
- What is the effect of L2 immersion? (Try raising the value of the p parameter for Language B to 90% or higher).
- How does early L2 immersion compare with later L2 immersion? (Set Language A to start at age five, and Language B to start at age 10).
- Under what conditions of bilingual acquisition does Language B come to dominate Language A? Is it reasonable to expect bilingual migrant children to reach the vocabulary levels of their monolingual peers?
- How could you model a case of bilingual acquisition where one parent speaks one language and the other parent speaks the other language?
- How could you use Mezzofanti to explore the idea that learning one foreign language makes it easier for you to learn another language?
- Suppose you want an L2 learner to acquire a vocabulary of 5000 words. What conditions do you need to make this a plausible aim?
- Suppose that parameter m starts to decline in value from age 40. What effects would this have on the model?
- Do the results suggest that 'learning a foreign language in old age keeps your brain alive'?
- How could you model vocabulary uptake in a language which shares lots of cognates with your L1, and a language in which there are very few cognates?
- What is the total vocabulary size at age 10 of a child who learns two languages from birth? How does this figure compare with the vocabulary size of a monolingual child?
- How could you model the acquisition of three or more languages?
- Is there an upper limit to the number of languages a person can learn?
- Are intensive courses for adult language learners a good idea?

References

Erard, M. (2013) *Mezzofanti's Gift: The Search for the World's Most Extraordinary Language Learners*. London: Duckworth Overlook.

Meara, P.M. (2001) The mathematics of vocabularies. In M. Gill, A. Johnson, L. Koski, R. Sell and B. Wårvik (eds) *Language, Learning, Literature: Studies Presented to Håkan Ringbom* (pp. 151–166). Åbo: Åbo Akademi.

Muñoz, C. (ed.) (2006) *Age and the Rate of Foreign Language Learning*. Clevedon: Multilingual Matters.

Riegel, K. (1968) Some theoretical considerations of bilingual development. *Psychological Bulletin* 70 (6), 647–670.

Russell, C.W. (1863) *The Life of Cardinal Mezzofanti: With an Introductory Memoir of Eminent Linguists, Ancient and Modern*. London: Longman.

Suggestions for further reading

De Houwer, A., Bornstein, M.H. and Putnick, D.L. (2014) A bilingual-monolingual comparison of young children's vocabulary size: Evidence from comprehension and production. *Applied Psycholinguistics* 35 (6), 1189–1211.

Grosjean, F. (1989) Neurolinguists, beware! The bilingual is not two monolinguals in one person. *Brain and Language* 36 (1), 3–15.

Krashen, S. and Kiss, N. (1996) Notes on a polyglot: Kato Lomb. *System* 24 (2), 207–210.

Li, P. (2013) Computational modeling of bilingualism: How can models tell us more about the bilingual mind? *Bilingualism: Language and Cognition* 16 (2), 241–245.

Meara, P.M., Lightbown, P.M. and Halter, R. (1997) Classrooms as lexical environments. *Language Teaching Research* 1 (1), 28–47.

Envoi

The programs discussed in this book were designed to encourage novice researchers to explore issues in L2 vocabulary acquisition in ways that are uncommon in applied linguistics research. Some of the tools – particularly the ones in the early chapters – are simple text analysis tools, and using these programs should be fairly straightforward and problem free. Some of the other programs – particularly the programs in Part 3 – push the boundaries of current research a bit. They provide ways of analysing data that are not widely used in current research, and for this reason they need to be treated with considerable caution. We hope that you will find that the programs allow you to ask interesting questions about L2 vocabulary acquisition and vocabulary use.

The programs are freely available. You do not need permission to use them in your own research projects. However, you do need to bear in mind that most of the programs in this collection are 'work in progress', and we value your comments and suggestions for improvement. If the programs work for you, then tell your friends; if they do not work for you, please tell *us*, so that we can fix them. We would also be glad to receive copies of any work you produce that uses these tools: student projects are not routinely included in the VARGA database (http://www.lognostics.co.uk/varga/), so we will be adding a new page on the Lognostics site where you can discuss issues that these testing tools raise, and tell other people about the work you are doing.

One of the themes that runs through this book is the importance of critically evaluating the tools you use in your research. It is very easy to collect data using tools of the sort described in this book, especially when the data are scored automatically and reported in a convincing way. When the tools you use look good, run smoothly and generate plausible datasets, it is very easy to be seduced into believing that the answers they give you are meaningful and true. However, it is very important not to let yourself get seduced in this way. We have stressed throughout this text that the programs are exploratory and tentative. We have tried to develop tools that will work in most situations, but inevitably there are special circumstances that we will not have anticipated, or situations where the programs generate data that are nonsense. You need to be alive to this possibility. Maybe the tests are just too hard for your test takers; perhaps the texts your students generate are very different from the type of texts we expected when we designed the programs; perhaps your test takers are approaching the tasks in ways that we simply did not envisage? Factors like this will invalidate any data you collect, so it is important that you get into the habit of asking critical questions about the way the programs work and the data they generate. Do not just take the outputs at face value.

You also need to develop a critical approach to the assumptions that underpin the programs, and question whether they are assumptions that you can accept. For example, the capture/recapture approach developed in Chapter 8 is based on the assumption that there is a good analogy between counting word types in a text and counting frogs in a pond. In both cases we are trying to count things that we cannot see – words that do not get used in a text, and frogs that do not get caught in a trap. However, analogies of this sort usually break down if you push them hard enough – frogs have a limited life span, but words do not; frogs breed, but words do not; tadpoles eat each other, but words do not; frogs are strongly affected by the environment, but words probably are not – and so on. Considerations such as these strongly affect the usefulness of the programs, and limit their applicability. In addition, some of the programs make assumptions which are not overtly discussed – for example, the programs in Chapters 7 and 8 both assume that *productive vocabulary* is a feature of an L2 learner's competence that it is relatively stable and therefore can be usefully measured. Is this really the case? And what would be the implications for our understanding of L2 lexical competence if it turned out that productive vocabulary was not stable, or if it was heavily dependent on external factors such as mood or task engagement? You need to get into the habit of critically evaluating whether the assumptions – both overt and hidden – that the programs use are the best ones we can call on, and what implications they have for how you interpret the data.

The second theme that runs through this book is the importance of bringing to your research ideas that are not common currency in applied linguistics. A lot of the programs described here depend on some basic mathematics, and illustrate how important it is for linguists to be familiar with things that go beyond high school maths. We also think that it is important for applied linguists to read science in other areas, and steal the research methods that have been developed for other research fields. We have already seen how the V_Capture program is based on research on animal diversity. But once you get into a topic like this, it soon becomes clear that there is massive amount of research using different types of capture/recapture models, and some of these more sophisticated models may be much more effective analogies for vocabulary counting than the simple model we have introduced here. Suddenly what looks like an odd off-the-wall idea changes into a whole research programme. Similar comments might be made about V_YesNo (originally based on research aimed at tracking Russian submarines in the North Atlantic), Mezzofanti (based on some simple mathematical models about change and growth in plants) or V_Size (based on the Power Law, a ranked distribution not just found in language but in other physical and biological phenomena such as the size of earthquakes or social network connectivity). The point here is that reading and thinking about research in areas other than applied linguistics is perhaps more likely to lead you to an interesting research idea than reading extensively in the standard sources. Spending time in your university library browsing journals that have nothing to do with linguistics is always a good idea.

A third theme that runs through this book is that any serious researcher needs to develop programming skills. Most postgraduate research training programmes in applied linguistics will include a module or two on how to use standard programming tools such as word processors, spreadsheets, presentation tools and basic statistical analyses. Some of the programs described in this book could have been implemented using these tools, so, for example, it would have been possible, but rather laborious, to implement the program in Chapter 2 (D_Tools) in this way. The other programs cannot be easily handled using standard tools. What this means is that if you rely on standard tools, then your research is strongly limited by what the standard tools can do, and if you really want to ask a different type of question you may be prevented from following it up because the standard tools do not allow you to do so. Even the programs described in this book are limiting in some important ways. V_YesNo, for instance, assumes that you want to test vocabulary size in English, so if you are interested in testing the vocabulary size of learners of Spanish then it is of no use to you. You could employ a friendly programmer who might be able to adapt V_YesNo for you so that you could test a set of Spanish words. However, this sort of solution is usually a costly one, and if your programmer moves away to a new job or falls out with you, then you may be stuck with a program that you want to change but cannot.

The long-term solution to this problem is to pick up some basic programming skills as part of your basic research training. The programs in this book are all short – mostly they are about 100 lines long, but most of this is handling the layout and onscreen presentation. Most of the real work is done by just a few lines of code that could easily be explained in just a few minutes. Nevertheless, we hope you will agree that they provide a useful set of real research tools, a rich resource that allows you to explore some important issues in L2 vocabulary acquisition.

The programs in this book are basically written in HTML. This is a language that allows you to design web-pages and display them in a browser (Firefox, Chrome, Safari, etc.). HTML is very easy to learn and seriously repays any time that you invest in learning it. HTML programs will run on stand-alone computers, and this may be all that you need if you are running small-scale studies in a local environment. In the programs presented in this book, HTML is used to display instructions, to display test items, to collect basic information from test takers and to display the results of the program's analysis.

The more complex analyses are carried out using a language called PERL, which works behind the scenes. Like HTML, PERL is free software, but you need to have a PERL interpreter on your computer to make it work. PERL comes bundled with some computer operating systems, so if you are using a Linux operating system, for example, you should find that PERL is already installed on your computer. PERL is more complex than HTML. It is a very powerful language, and it is particularly easy to process texts in PERL. To give you an idea of just how powerful PERL is, a really short program – about 500 bytes long – can read a large text and generate concordance lines for every word the text contains. This power makes PERL an ideal language for doing simple statistical analysis on word counts, or manipulating linguistic data. PERL is harder to learn than HTML, but again learning to write simple PERL programs will hugely increase your potential as a researcher.

The graphs and diagrams that appear in programs were produced using jQuery. jQuery is definitely *not* an easy option and you will probably need professional help to get it to work for you.

The bibliography at the end of this chapter contains some books that you can use to teach yourself how to write simple programs, and we strongly urge you to invest some time in learning this skill. Do not be put off by the '... *for Dummies*' titles. These are well-written textbooks that will guide you through all the basic steps you need to follow to get your programs up and running. The book by Elizabeth Castro is particularly useful if you know a little about programming already and want to write interactive programs that store data for future analysis.

If you want to write programs that collect data over the web, rather than on stand-alone machines, you may find it useful to contact Lognostics (the address is on the website: http://www.lognostics.co.uk/). We can upload suitable programs to the Lognostics site, and let you run them online provided that your programs meet some security and safeguarding criteria. You may also find the Lognostics Small Research Grant scheme of interest. Follow the links on the website.

In short, we hope that the programs in this book will open up for you a world which goes beyond the sometimes very limited horizons of traditional mainstream vocabulary research projects.

The Small Print

The programs in this book are freely available, in exchange for critical evaluations of how they work. You can freely use any data that they generate. It would be nice if you let us know that you are using the programs so that we can judge the impact they have. And we welcome any feedback on how well (or badly) the programs work. All the programs are updated from time to time. More serious errors will be corrected as soon as possible; however, we can only fix these problems if you let us know about them. Updates and revisions are usually advertised on the Lognostics Facebook page, and if you become a Lognostics friend then you will be automatically notified of any updates that may affect you. This page will also tell you if we are experiencing technical difficulties with the site.

All the programs described in this book are exploratory tools in the process of development. The authors do not accept any liability for damage that may be caused by running these programs on your own equipment, or for issues arising from the use of the programs in inappropriate situations. Specifically, the programs should **not** be used in high-stakes situations where the outcomes are critically dependent on the data they generate.

Some of the programs collect data which we intend to use in further revisions of the site. This applies to V_YesNo, Q_Lex and LLAMA_B. The data saved by these programs are anonymised, so we will not know who provided it. By using these programs you are agreeing to allow us to store the data you provide and to use them to improve the tests. These programs ask the user to provide a unique ID code. If your user IDs are sufficiently distinctive, then it is possible for us to recover the data, and we can do this for you if the data are needed for research purposes. There are some notes on the Lognostics ToolBox page which explain how you can extract your own data.

Paul Meara
Imma Miralpeix
2016

Further reading

Castro, E. (2001) *PERL and CGI for the World Wide Web* (2nd edn). Berkeley, CA: Peachpit Press.
Hoffman, P. (2003) *Perl for Dummies* (4th edn). New York: Wiley Publishing.
Tittel, E. (2013) *Beginning HTML5 and CSS3 for Dummies*. Hoboken, NJ: John Wiley.

Author Index

*Please note this index does not include the authors cited in the 'Background Readings' of the book.

Admiraal, W. 132
Al-Hazemi, H. 130, 132
Alderson, J.C. 115, 132
Anderson, R. 113, 128, 132
Anthony, L. 13, 17
August, D. 16

Baker, M.D. 83
Bauer, L. 48, 64
Beeckmans, R. 119, 132
Beglar, D. 114, 132
Bell, H. 13, 16, 48, 62, 65
Blackwell, A.A. 109
Bornstein, M.H. 254
Broeder, P. 21, 42
Bull, W.E. 17

Caldwell-Harris, C. 229
Cameron, L. 133
Carey, M. 133
Carlo, M.S. 16
Carroll, J.B. 215–216, 228–229
Carroll, S.E. 17
Cattell, J.M. 208, 210
Chapnik Smith, M. 211
Chipere, N. 42, 155
Chung, C.K. 110
Clapham, C. 133
Cobb, T. 14, 17
Collins, L. 12, 16, 151, 154–155
Coulson, D. 193–195, 210
Coxhead, A. 17
Crossley, S.A. 43
Crow, J.T. 185, 210
Crystal, D. 153, 154
Cushing, D.H. 181

Dahlen, K. 229
Daller, H. 16, 22, 41–43, 65, 155

Davidson, D.J. 12, 16
De Houwer, A. 254
Dressler, C. 13, 16
Dufranne, M. 132
Durán, P. 42, 155

Echeverría, M.S. 108–109
Edwards, R. 12, 16, 151, 154–155
Egghe, L. 155
Ellegård, A. 134, 154
Erard, M. 233, 253
Extra, G. 42
Eyckmans, J. 115, 132

Fairbanks, H. 21, 42
Farringdon, J.M. 83
Farringdon, M.G. 83
Ferreira, R. 108–109
Ferrer i Cancho, R. 153, 155
Fitzpatrick, T. 13, 16, 65, 108–109, 133, 211
Foster, D. 83
Foster, P. 43
Freebody, P. 113, 128, 132
Fukś, H. 153, 155

Gardner, D. 153, 155
Gesa, F. 150–153, 155
Gonzales, E.A. 152, 155
Gougenheim, G. 13, 16
Graňena, G. 229
Grosjean, F. 254
Gullberg, M. 16

Haastrup, K. 109
Häcker, M. 12, 16
Hall, C.J. 13, 16
Halter, R. 16, 254
Hamilton-Smith, N. 83

Harlech-Jones, B. 17
Harrington, M. 133, 211
Heatley, A. 13–14, 17
Henmon, V.A.C. 113, 132
Henriksen, B. 109, 186, 210
Herdan, G. 134, 155
Higgins, J. 113, 132
Horst, M. 17
Huhta, A. 115, 132
Huibregtse, I. 119, 132
Hulstijn, J.H. 110, 211
Hunt, A. 114, 132
Hwang, K. 17

In'nami, Y. 43
Indefrey, P. 16
Ishikawa, S. 63–64, 137, 155

Jacobs, G. 83
Janssens, V. 132
Jarvis, S. 16, 41–43, 155
Jiang, N. 211
Jiménez Catalán, R.M. 12–13, 16, 108–109
Job, R. 16
Johnson, C.L. 17
Jones, G. 113, 115, 119, 128–129, 132

Kaneda, M. 64, 155
Kanter, I. 153, 155
Kelly, C. 21, 43
Kessler, D.A. 153, 155
Kiss, N. 254
Kohonen, V. 215, 228
Koizumi, R. 43
Kormos, J. 43
Krashen, S. 254
Kuczaj, S.A. 110

Laufer, B. 43–44, 64–65, 134, 151, 154–155, 157, 180, 227–228
Leclair, T. 181
Leech, G. 63, 65, 110
Li, P. 254
Lightbown, P. 16, 254
Lotto, L. 16

MacWhinney, B. 21, 42
Malvern, D. 21–23, 25, 39–40, 42–44, 65, 80, 134, 151, 155
Mancebo, R. 12, 16
Manly, B.J.F. 181
McCarthy, P.M. 41–43

McDonald, L.L. 181
McNamara, D.S. 43
McNamara, T. 154–155
Meara, P.M. 13, 16, 41–42, 48, 62, 65, 79, 81, 83, 108–109, 113, 115, 119, 128–129, 132–133, 156, 178–179, 181, 185, 207, 210–211, 226, 228, 250, 253–254
Melka Teichroew, F. 185, 210
Michaelson, S. 83
Michéa, R. 16
Miller, G.A. 194, 210
Miller, J.F. 21, 42
Milton, J. 42, 65, 119, 133, 211
Miralpeix, I. 25, 39, 41, 43, 63, 65, 84, 107, 109, 151, 155, 211
Mochida, A. 133
Mochizuki, M. 64, 155
Moreno Espinosa, S. 65
Morgan, C. 10–13
Morris, S. 13, 16
Morton, A.Q. 83
Mulder, K. 110
Muñoz, C. 43, 251, 253
Murata, M. 64, 155

Nation, I.S.P. 12, 16–17, 44, 48, 63–65, 114, 133–134, 154–155, 157, 180, 185–186, 210
Nelson, R. 181
Ninio, A. 153, 155

O'Loughlin, R. 12, 16
Ojeda, J. 13, 16
Oller, J.W. 114, 133
Olmos Alcoy, J.C. 156, 178–179, 181

Pang, F. 62–63, 65
Paribakht, T.S. 133, 186, 210
Parry, T. 229
Pennebaker, J.W. 83, 110
Phipps, C. 153, 155
Plauen, E.O. 179, 181
Putnick, D.L. 254

Qais, A. 229
Qian, J. 62–63, 65

Racine, J.P. 178, 181
Rayson, P. 65, 110
Read, J. 40–41, 43, 63, 65
Ready, D. 133

Reed, D.J. 229
Richards, B. 21–23, 25, 40, 42–44, 65, 151, 155
Richards, J.C. 17, 186, 210
Ridgeway, D.W. 110
Ridley, D.R. 152–153, 155
Riegel, K. 233, 236, 250–251, 253
Rivenc, P. 16
Robinson, P. 229
Rockwell, G. 17
Rodgers, C. 83
Rodgers, M. 17
Rogers, V. 226, 228
Russell, C.W. 233, 253
Ryden, E.R. 113, 133

Salsbury, T. 43
Sapon, S.M. 215–216, 228
Sauvageot, A. 16
Schmitt, D. 133
Schmitt, N. 114, 133, 228
Scholfield, P. 128, 133
Schoonen, R. 211
Scott, M. 13, 17
Segalowitz, N. 181, 211
Segalowitz, S. 211
Service, E. 215, 228
Shillaw, J. 130, 133
Shimizu, S. 64, 155
Sinclair, S. 13, 17
Skehan, P. 62–63, 65
Slatcher, R.B. 110
Smith, J.A. 21, 43
Snow, C.E. 16
Stansfield, C.W. 229

Stone, L.D. 110
Strömqvist, S. 42
Stubbe, R. 133
Sugimori, N. 64, 155
Sutherland, W.J. 181

Tavakoli, P. 43
Taylor, J.R. 17
Tono, Y. 64, 155
Tonzar, C. 13, 16
Treffers-Daller, J. 42–43, 65, 179, 181
Tzima, F.E. 84, 107, 109

Uemura, T. 64, 155

Van de Velde, H. 132
van Hout, R. 42
Vermeer, A. 22, 41, 43
Voionmaa, K. 42

Waters, E. 110
Watson, V. 211
Webb, S. 17
Wesche, M.B. 128, 133, 186, 210
West, M. 63, 65
White, C.E. 16
Williams, J. 181
Wilson, A. 65, 110

Yu, G. 43

Zipf, G.K. 11–12, 16, 134–135, 138, 151–155

Subject Index

Aptitude 42, 215, 218, 222–229

British National Corpus (BNC) List 63, 92–93, 110, 137, 141–143, 150, 152–153

Capture/Recapture 156, 161, 165, 178–181, 256
CHILDES 21, 25, 42, 143, 150
Cognate 13, 16–17, 62–63, 91–92, 94, 105, 130, 253
Coverage 12–15, 100
Curve fitting 22–23, 25, 27, 36–38, 43, 55, 61–62, 152

D 21–22, 25, 27, 29–37, 39–44, 49, 63, 89
D_Tools 21, 23–25, 29, 38, 257
Dimensions (of lexical competence) 94, 104, 108–109, 150, 185–188, 210–211

Eurocentres Vocabulary Size Test (EVST) 113–115, 118–19, 129, 132–133

Fluency 43, 62, 65, 106, 187
Frequency band 81, 95, 99–101, 108, 123–124, 129, 140–146, 151–152, 179, 189, 194
Frequency list 3, 14, 60, 88–94, 96–97, 103–104, 110, 134, 137, 142–144, 146, 148, 151

General Service List (GSL) 63, 65
Genetic Algorithm 78, 81
Guiraud's Index 26, 39–41, 49, 90–91

Hapax 49, 97–98, 102, 107–108

JACET word list 63–64, 137, 142–143, 145–146, 148–149, 152, 155

Lambda 48, 54–56, 58, 61, 63–64, 90–91
Lexical accessibility 186–190, 210
Lexical density 26–27, 36, 39, 41–42, 88–90
Lexical diversity 27, 37–39, 41–44, 49, 61, 63, 65, 106, 149, 155, 177
Lexical Frequency Profile (LFP) 14, 16, 44, 50–52, 55, 57–60, 63–64, 91–92, 99, 103, 106, 108–109, 134–135, 140–141, 150, 154, 157
See also Vocabulary Profile
Lexical growth 89, 241
See also Vocabulary growth
Lexical organisation 104, 108
Lexical originality 84, 88–95, 97, 100, 103–105, 107–109
Lexical richness 21–22, 26–27, 30, 34, 37–39, 41–43, 49, 50, 60–61, 64–65, 88, 105–106, 134, 140, 149, 155, 163, 180, 235–236, 241, 246, 251
Lexical signatures 66–67, 69–72, 74, 75–84, 90–91, 106
Lexical sophistication 41–42, 44, 63, 88–93, 103, 105, 140
Lexical variation 36, 49, 88–91
Llama_B 215–228, 259
Logarithmic transformation 87, 138
Lognostics 3, 6, 23, 38, 45, 67, 69, 84, 106, 116, 132–133, 135, 150, 157, 177, 190, 216, 225, 228, 234, 255, 258–259

Mezzofanti 233–238, 251–253, 257
Modelling 16, 42, 65, 105–106, 133, 155, 233, 235–237, 240, 249, 251

P_Lex 38, 44–48, 53–65, 90–92, 106, 177
Parameter 22, 62, 153, 163, 177, 233–239, 241, 243–244, 246–249, 251–253
Petersen estimate 158–160, 170–176, 179–180
Poisson distribution 54, 61
Productive vocabulary 26, 34–37, 44, 55, 59, 79, 80, 109–110, 131, 134–135, 138–144, 146–147, 149–150, 154–156, 160–164, 166, 171, 173–174, 176–179, 181, 185, 210, 256
   Controlled 29, 32–34, 141, 154
   Free 28–29, 34, 141
Productive Levels Test 162
Programming 252, 257–258

Q_Lex 185, 188–195, 209–210, 259

Receptive vocabulary 37, 82, 110, 131–133, 139–140, 149–150, 154, 161–162, 177, 180, 185, 210
Recognition
   Formal 126
   Passive 115, 126
   Receptive 186
   Thresholds 198
   Time 199–206
   Vocabulary 123
   Word 185, 188, 198–201, 206–208, 210–211
Reliability 29, 78, 120

SigSorter 66–70
Simulation 155, 238, 251, 252

Target word 66–67, 69–71, 73, 78, 113–114, 116, 164, 179, 191–195, 208
Tasks 28–30, 33–35, 37, 40, 59, 62–63, 65, 72–73, 103, 107, 142, 147–149, 152, 156, 160, 169, 170–171, 174–175, 179–180, 185, 188, 217, 256
Textbook 10–12, 16–17, 90, 246
Type-Token ratio (TTR) 15, 21–23, 25–27, 30–37, 39–41, 43, 49–50, 89, 134

V_Capture 154, 156–158, 256
V_LexSig 66–69
V_Lists 3, 5–7, 11, 13, 17, 80, 96, 106
V_Size 12, 134–139, 141–154, 163, 257
V_Unique 79, 84–87, 107–108, 154
V_Words 3–6, 11, 13, 17, 96, 106, 143–144, 150, 158
V_YesNo 113, 116–121, 131, 154, 190, 257, 259
   V_YesNo_Rdr 132
Validity 43, 59–60, 109, 153, 161, 171, 195
VARGA 255
VocabProfile 29, 39, 141, 150
Vocabulary breadth 186, 210, 250
Vocabulary depth 186, 210, 250
Vocabulary growth 15, 237, 240, 244, 246–247, 250–251
   See also Lexical growth
Vocabulary Levels Test (VLT) 56–59, 114–115, 133, 141, 161–162, 185
Vocabulary profile 90, 106–107, 161, 163
   See also Lexical Frequency Profile
Vocabulary size 38–39, 42–43, 53, 61, 64–65, 80, 104, 106, 108, 113, 121–122, 126–127, 129–133, 135–136, 138–141, 143, 147, 149–150, 154–156, 160–164, 166, 172–177, 180–181, 185–187, 189, 210, 234, 239–240, 247, 250–251, 253–254, 257
   Estimate 120, 135, 141–144, 146–147, 151–152, 161–173
VOCD 21–22, 25, 42, 127, 134, 151, 174

Word association 13, 16, 108, 140, 162, 173, 176, 180, 207
Word list 3, 5–7, 11, 14, 17, 50–51, 53, 59, 61, 63, 66–67, 69–71, 73, 91–92, 142, 144, 151–152, 157

Yes/No vocabulary test 113–116, 119, 128–133, 185

Zipf's Law 11–12, 16, 134–135, 142, 152–155

For Product Safety Concerns and Information please contact our EU Authorised Representative:

Easy Access System Europe

Mustamäe tee 50

10621 Tallinn

Estonia

gpsr.requests@easproject.com

www.ingramcontent.com/pod-product-compliance
Lightning Source LLC
Chambersburg PA
CBHW070557300426
44113CB00010B/1285